PASSAGES: KEY MOMENTS IN HISTORY

The Greco-Persian Wars

A Short History with Documents

PASSAGES: KEY MOMENTS IN HISTORY

The Greco-Persian Wars

A Short History with Documents

Erik Jensen

Hackett Publishing Company, Inc.
Indianapolis/Cambridge

Copyright © 2021 by Hackett Publishing Company, Inc.

All rights reserved
Printed in the United States of America

24 23 22 21   1 2 3 4 5 6 7

For further information, please address
    Hackett Publishing Company, Inc.
    P.O. Box 44937
    Indianapolis, Indiana 46244-0937

    www.hackettpublishing.com

Cover design by Rick Todhunter
Interior design by Laura Clark
Maps by Beehive Mapping
Composition by Aptara, Inc.

Library of Congress Control Number: 2020943576

ISBN-13: 978-1-62466-955-2 (cloth)
ISBN-13: 978-1-62466-954-5 (pbk.)

The paper used in this publication meets the minimum requirements of American National Standard for Information Sciences—Permanence of Paper for Printed Library Materials, ANSI Z39.48–1984.

∞

CONTENTS

Acknowledgments x
Abbreviations xi
Chronology xii
Glossary xv
Maps xix

Introduction 1
About the Sources 34

Documents

Section 1: Organization of the Persian Empire 45
   1.1 Darius' inscription from Susa (DSe) 45
   1.2 Darius' account of the empire (DPe 1–2) 46
   1.3 The Demotic Chronicle: Restoring the laws of Egypt (BN 215, C 6–16) 47
   1.4 Native rulers in Cilicia and Cyprus (Xenophon, *The Education of Cyrus* 7.4.1–2) 48
   1.5 A royal woman requisitions wine and sheep (PF 1795; Fort. 6754) 48
   1.6 Estate workers receive their pay (PF 1028; PF 876; PF 847; PF 1226; PF-NN 358) 49
   1.7 Royal women's property (Plato, *Alcibiades 1* 123b–c; Herodotus, *Histories* 2.98; Xenophon, *Anabasis* 1.4.9) 51
   1.8 Non-Persian workers in Persia (PF 1049; PF 873) 52

Section 2: Persian ideology 53
   2.1 Darius' second inscription from Naqsh-e Rustam (DNb 1–10) 53
   2.2 Xerxes' *daiva* inscription (XPh) 54
   2.3 The king's relationship to Ahura Mazda (DSk) 56
   2.4 Maintaining the religions of non-Persian peoples (PF 339; PF 759) 56
   2.5 Stamped brick of Cyrus as patron of Babylonian temples 57

2.6 Jews in the Babylonian Captivity
(2 Chronicles 36:15–20) 58
2.7 Persian kings support rebuilding in Jerusalem
(Ezra 1:1–7, 6:1–5) 59
2.8 Inscription from the temple at Hibis 60
2.9 Letter to Gadatas (SIG 13 no. 22) 61
2.10 The king receives gifts (Plutarch, *Life of Artaxerxes* 4.4–5.1) 62
2.11 The Persian king rewards a loyal Jew (Esther 6:1–11) 63
2.12 Artaxerxes rewards a Greek friend (Plutarch, *Life of Artaxerxes* 22.5–6) 64
2.13 "Custom is king" (Herodotus, *Histories* 3.38) 65

Section 3: Cyrus' conquests 66
3.1 The Nabonidus Chronicle (BM 35382, column 3, lines 12b–22) 66
3.2 The Cyrus Cylinder (BM 90920) 67
3.3 The fate of Croesus (Bacchylides, *Epinikian Odes* 3.24–59) 70

Section 4: Greek relations with Egypt 73
4.1 Psammetichus recruits Greek and Carian mercenaries (Diodorus of Sicily, *Library of History* 1.66–67) 73
4.2 Foundation of Naucratis (Herodotus, *Histories* 2.178–179) 74
4.3 Graffiti by Greek mercenary soldiers in Egypt (SEG 16.863) 75

Section 5: Egypt under Persian rule 76
5.1 Autobiographical inscription of Udjahorresne (VM 158) 76
5.2 Seal of Cambyses as Pharaoh of Egypt 79
5.3 Epitaph and sarcophagus inscription for the Apis bull 80
5.4 Murder of the Apis bull (Herodotus, *Histories* 3.27–29) 81
5.5 The Demotic Chronicle: Cambyses' reorganization of Egyptian temples (BN 215, D 1–14) 82

5.6	Statue inscription proclaiming Darius Pharaoh of Egypt (DSab)	84
Section 6: The rise of Darius		85
6.1	Bardiya, heir of Cambyses (Xenophon, *The Education of Cyrus* 8.7.11–12; Ctesias, FGrH 688 F 9.8)	85
6.2	Bardiya as king in Babylon	86
6.3	The overthrow of Bardiya (DB 10–15)	87
6.4	Inscriptions of Ariaramnes and Arsames (AmH; AsH)	88
6.5	Rebellions against Darius (DB 52–54)	89
6.6	Darius' foundation charter from Susa (DSf 3–4)	90
6.7	Darius' military victories (DB 71–76)	91
Section 7: Greek relations with Persia		93
7.1	Athens seeks an alliance with Persia (Herodotus, *Histories* 5.73)	93
7.2	Hippias plans his return to Athens with Persian help (Herodotus, *Histories* 5.96)	94
7.3	Demaratus goes over to Darius (Herodotus, *Histories* 6.70)	94
7.4	Argos makes an alliance with Persia (Herodotus, *Histories* 7.150–151)	95
7.5	Greek stone-cutters at Persepolis (Pugliese Carratelli I 1–3)	96
7.6	A Greek-speaking administrator at Persepolis (PF-NN 1771)	97
7.7	Ionian women receive childbirth rations at Persepolis (PF 1224)	97
7.8	Friendship and its complications (Xenophon, *Hellenica* 4.1.31–39)	97
Section 8: The Ionian Revolt, 499–493 BCE		100
8.1	Herodotus' narrative of the revolt (Herodotus, *Histories* 5.97–124)	100
8.2	Ration authorization for Datis (PF-NN 1809)	109
8.3	The Lindos Chronicle (IG XII, Lindos II, 2, D.1.4–47)	110

8.4	The sack of Miletus (Herodotus, *Histories* 6.18–20)	111
8.5	A peaceful settlement with the Ionians (Herodotus, *Histories* 6.42–43; Diodorus of Sicily, *Library of History* 10.25 F 4)	112

Section 9: Darius' Aegean campaigns, 492–490 BCE — 115
- 9.1 Diplomatic initiatives (Herodotus, *Histories* 6.48–49) — 115
- 9.2 The Aegean campaign and the battle of Marathon (Herodotus, *Histories* 6.94–117) — 116

Section 10: Xerxes' Aegean campaign, 480–479 BCE — 127
- 10.1 The accession of Xerxes (XPf) — 127
- 10.2 Revolt in Babylon (Ctesias, FGrH 688 F 13.25–26) — 127
- 10.3 Persian preparations (Herodotus, *Histories* 7.20–25, 36) — 129
- 10.4 List of Greeks who gave earth and water to Xerxes (Herodotus, *Histories* 7.131–132) — 132
- 10.5 The story of the Persian and Spartan heralds (Herodotus, *Histories* 7.133–134, 136–137) — 133
- 10.6 The battle of Thermopylae (Herodotus, *Histories* 7.210–225) — 134
- 10.7 The battle of Cape Artemisium (Herodotus, *Histories* 8.6–21) — 140
- 10.8 A message to Xerxes (Herodotus, *Histories* 8.75–76) — 146
- 10.9 The battle of Salamis (Herodotus, *Histories* 8.83–97) — 147
- 10.10 An eyewitness account of Salamis (Aeschylus, *The Persians* 353–471) — 153
- 10.11 Diplomatic outreach to Athens (Herodotus, *Histories* 8.136, 140–144) — 157
- 10.12 Maneuvers and skirmishing at Plataea (Herodotus, *Histories* 9.19–25, 38–40) — 160
- 10.13 The battle of Plataea (Herodotus, *Histories* 9.49–63) — 163

Section 11: The Persian response to the wars in Greece — 169
- 11.1 A Persian version of the wars in the Aegean (Herodotus, *Histories* 8.102; Dio Chrysostom, *Discourses* 11.148–149) — 169
- 11.2 Greek booty distributed in Persia (Plutarch, *Parallel Lives*, "Themistocles" 31.1; Arrian, *Anabasis* 7.19.2) — 170

11.3	Reorganization in Anatolia (Herodotus, *Histories* 9.107; Xenophon, *Hellenica* 3.1.6)	171

Section 12: A troublesome frontier, 478–451 BCE — 173

12.1	Greek leaders collaborating with Persia (Thucydides, *History* 1.128–129, 135–138; Plutarch, *Parallel Lives*, "Themistocles" 21.5)	173
12.2	The formation of the Delian League (Thucydides, *History* 1.96)	176
12.3	Greek victory at Eurymedon (Diodorus of Sicily, *Library of History* 11.60–61)	177
12.4	Revolt in Egypt (Thucydides, *History* 1.104, 109–110)	179
12.5	An Athenian expedition in Cyprus (Thucydides, *History* 1.112)	180

Section 13: Diplomacy and stability, 450–387 BCE — 181

13.1	The "Peace of Callias" (Diodorus of Sicily, *Library of History* 12.4)	181
13.2	Pericles honors the peace with Persia (Plutarch, *Parallel Lives*, "Pericles" 20.2)	182
13.3	Athens at war with Samos (Plutarch, *Parallel Lives*, "Pericles" 25)	182
13.4	Unproductive negotiations (Thucydides, *History* 4.50)	183
13.5	A treaty between Persia and Sparta (Thucydides, *History* 8.17–18; TAM I, 44, b64–c9)	184
13.6	Cyrus the Younger's revolt (Xenophon, *Anabasis* 1.1.3–11)	186
13.7	Diplomatic complications (Xenophon, *Hellenica* 4.8.24)	188
13.8	A Persian arbitration between Greek cities (SIG 13 no. 134)	188
13.9	The King's Peace (Xenophon, *Hellenica* 5.1.25, 29–31)	189

Select Bibliography — *191*
Index — *199*

ACKNOWLEDGMENTS

Many people have contributed to making this history and source collection possible. First of all, credit must go to Rick Todhunter, who first approached me with the idea. I am grateful to him, to Elana Rosenthal, and the whole team at Hackett, whose hard work has brought this book into being. I am also grateful to Guy Ridge for providing the translations from Akkadian, and to my friend and fellow historian Marita von Weissenberg who brought us together.

My wife, Eppu Jensen, contributed immeasurably to the success of this project by providing a critical first reading of my text and translations. Her input has made the result better than I could have achieved alone.

And my final thanks must go to my undergraduate classics professor, Sam Siegel, under whose guidance I first learned to appreciate the wisdom and whimsy of Herodotus. *Gratias ago, O magister.*

ABBREVIATIONS

AmH	Inscription of Ariaramnes from Hamdan
AsH	Inscription of Arsamnes from Hamdan
BM	Collections of the British Museum, London
BN	Collections of the Bibliothèque Nationale, Paris
DB	Inscriptions of Darius from Bisitun Rock
DN	Inscriptions of Darius from Naqsh-e Rustam
DP	Inscriptions of Darius from Persepolis
DS	Inscriptions of Darius from Susa
F	Fragment
FGrH	Jacoby, *Fragmente der griechischen Historiker*
Fort.	Persepolis Fortification Texts (Cameron collated)
IG	*Inscriptiones Graecae*
PF	Persepolis Fortification Texts (Hallock published)
PF-NN	Persepolis Fortification Texts (Hallock manuscript)
SEG	*Supplementum Epigraphicum Graecum*
SIG	*Sylloge Inscriptionum Graecarum*
TAM	*Tituli Asiae Minoris*
VM	Collections of the Vatican Museum
XP	Inscriptions of Xerxes from Persepolis

CHRONOLOGY

All dates are BCE

670	Assyrian Empire invades and conquers Egypt
664	Psammetichus I takes power in Egypt, leads a rebellion in Egypt against the Assyrian Empire and founds the Twenty-Sixth Dynasty
c. 625	Greek mercenaries in Egypt settle at a location that would become Naucratis
625–609	Wars between the Assyrian Empire on one side and an alliance of Medes and Babylonians on the other, ending with the destruction of the Assyrian Empire
592	Psammetichus II of Egypt campaigns in Kush with Greek mercenaries
c. 570	The city of Naucratis formally established as a Greek enclave in Egypt
c. 560	The kingdom of Lydia conquers many of the Ionian Greek cities
c. 559	Cyrus II comes to power in Persia
c. 550	Cyrus begins the conquest of what would become the Achaemenid Persian Empire
546	Cyrus conquers Lydia
530	Cyrus dies, succeeded by Cambyses II
525	Cambyses invades and conquers Egypt
522	Cambyses dies, succeeded by Bardiya; Bardiya killed in a coup led by Darius, who becomes Darius I
513	Darius campaigns against the Scythians
510	Hippias, tyrant of Athens, forced out of power and flees the city
499–493	Ionian Revolt

492	A Persian expedition against mainland Greece fails when the fleet carrying it is wrecked off the Athos peninsula
490	A Persian expedition against Naxos, Eretria, and Athens ends with the battle of Marathon
486	Darius dies, succeeded by Xerxes I
484	Revolt in Babylon
480	Xerxes' expedition against mainland Greece; the battles of Thermopylae, Artemisium, and Salamis
479	Battles of Plataea and Mycale, end of Xerxes' Greek expedition
478	Pausanias accused of conspiring with Xerxes, dies before he can be brought to trial
472 or 471	Themistocles ostracized from Athens
470s	Delian League founded and begins operations against Persian possessions in Anatolia and the eastern Mediterranean
466	Battle of the Eurymedon River
465	Xerxes killed, succeeded by Artaxerxes I; during the struggle for succession in Persia, a rebellion begins in Egypt led by Inarus
450s	Egyptian and Athenian forces defeated in Egypt, Inarus' rebellion ends with Persian reconquest
450	"Peace of Callias," détente between Persia and Athens
431–404	Peloponnesian War between Athens and Sparta
414	Persians begin an alliance with Sparta through Tissaphernes
c. 410	Amyrtaeus begins revolt against Persia in Egypt
401	Cyrus the Younger attempts coup against Artaxerxes II with Greek mercenary army, defeated at Cunaxa
396–395	Spartan invasion of Persian-held territories in Anatolia
395–387	Corinthian War, between Sparta on one side and a Persian-backed alliance of Athens, Corinth, Thebes, and Argos on the other
387	The King's Peace/Peace of Antalcidas

Achaemenid kings of Persia

Cyrus II	c. 559–530
Cambyses II	530–522
Bardiya	522
Darius I	522–486
Xerxes I	486–465
Artaxerxes I	465–424
Xerxes II	424–423
Darius II	423–404
Artaxerxes II	404–359
Artaxerxes III	358–338
Artaxerxes IV	338–336
Darius III	336–330

Saite (Twenty-Sixth Dynasty) kings of Egypt

Psammetichus I	664–610
Necho II	610–595
Psammetichus II	595–589
Apries	589–570
Amasis	570–526
Psammetichus III	526–525

GLOSSARY

Achaemenid dynasty: The ruling dynasty of the Persian Empire. Although the term does not appear in any sources before Darius I, it is conventionally used to refer to earlier kings beginning with Cyrus II.

Aeacids: Descendants of the Greek mythic hero Aeacus, including the Trojan War heroes Achilles and Greater Ajax.

Ahura Mazda: The god of the Persian kings.

Alcmaeonids: One of the prominent noble families in Athens.

arashshara: A female supervisor in charge of the other laborers on a Persian estate.

archon: One of the magistrates elected or allotted to govern a Greek city.

aristeion: An award for exceptional bravery or effectiveness in combat often given by Greek armies after a battle.

Bacis: The name of several legendary Greek seers to whom a number of oracular predictions were attributed.

cleruch: An Athenian settler on land seized from another city after an Athenian victory in war.

cubit: A unit of measure based on the length of a man's forearm from elbow to fingertip. The exact length varied in different cultures and times, but it was generally around half a meter.

daiva: A divine being in Persian tradition, at least in some cases an evil spirit or false god.

daric: A gold coin minted by the Persian kings, approximately the value of a month's pay for a soldier.

drachma: A Greek silver coin roughly equivalent to a day's wage for a skilled laborer.

dukshish: Though conventionally translated as "princess," refers to any female member of the Persian royal family.

Elamites: One of the peoples of the Persian Empire, who lived in the mountains of southwestern Iran where they had previously ruled an independent kingdom.

Esagil: The temple of Marduk, the principal god of Babylon in the period of these texts.

esparto: A grass-like plant native to Spain and North Africa used for its tough fibers.

hoplite: A heavily armored Greek soldier equipped with a spear and a broad round shield.

House of Life: A term for the collective activity of learned priests in Egypt whose skills included medicine, study of the gods and their rituals, and the management of temples.

Humban: The Elamite sky god.

Immortals: A core unit of the Persian army, made up of 10,000 professional soldiers. Called "Immortals" because the unit was immediately brought back up to 10,000 after any casualties.

***lan*:** A religious ceremony celebrated in Persia, possibly associated with Humban.

Leto: A Greek goddess, the mother of the sun god Apollo and the moon goddess Artemis.

Levites: A Jewish tribe whose members traditionally performed certain religious and administrative duties.

magus (plural magi): A Median priest.

Medes: One of the peoples of the Persian Empire, who shared much culture and history with the Persians and in earlier times had ruled a state of their own in western Iran.

Mesuti-Re: The Egyptian name that Cambyses used as his formal name as king of Egypt.

Mithra: A Persian god associated with light and truth.

Montu: An Egyptian warrior god associated with the city of Letopolis.

Neith: An Egyptian goddess worshiped especially in Sais and revered by the Twenty-Sixth Dynasty kings.

Nine Bows: A traditional term for the foreign enemies of Egypt.

Nisaean horse: A special breed of horse from Central Asia with exceptional strength and endurance.

nome: An administrative region of Egypt.

Osiris-Hemag: A specific local version of the Egyptian god Osiris worshiped in Sais.

ostracism: A procedure by which an individual could be exiled from Athens for a period of ten years.

Pan: A Greek god of the wilderness.

parasang: A Persian unit of length whose precise measure is hard to define. It was apparently based not on actual distance but on the length of time it would take an army to march over terrain, so that a parasang of flat, dry road might be much longer than one of wet or hilly ground. In general, it seems to have ranged between four and six kilometers.

Perseids: Descendants of the Greek mythic hero Perseus.

Perses: A legendary ancestor of the Persians invented by the Greeks.

phalanx: A fighting unit of heavy infantry, such as Greek hoplites, arranged in a densely packed formation of ranks and files.

phyle (plural phylae): A "tribe," or administrative unit of Athenian citizens.

polemarch: An Athenian magistrate chosen by lot to handle certain military affairs. The polemarch's exact powers and duties changed over time and are not always clear.

polis (plural poleis): A Greek city-state, an independent political entity consisting of one city and its surrounding lands.

proxenos: An official friend of a Greek city among a foreign people.

Pythia: The title of the chief priestess of Apollo at Delphi, who induced an altered state of consciousness during which the Greeks believed that Apollo spoke directly to humans through her.

***rnp*-priest:** A religious and administrative position connected with the management of the western delta region of Egypt under the Saite kings.

satrap: The governor of a province, or satrapy, of the Persian Empire.

satrapy: A province of the Persian Empire.

Spartiate: A citizen of Sparta. "Spartan" may apply to non-citizen residents in Sparta; "Spartiate" specifies citizenship.

***stadion* (plural *stadia*):** A Greek unit of length. There was no consistent standard for the length of a *stadion*, which could vary from around 160 to around 190 meters.

stela: A stone monument often carved with text or images.

***strategoi* (singular *strategos*):** A board of ten generals elected annually by the citizens of Athens.

talent: A unit of weight whose exact value varied from place to place. The Attic talent, widely used in the Aegean region, weighed approximately twenty-six kilograms. Also a unit of monetary value based on the value of a talent's weight of silver, conventionally equivalent to 6,000 drachmas.

Tanaoxares: The name Xenophon uses for Bardiya.

Tanyoxarkes: The name Ctesias uses for Bardiya.

Tintir: A Sumerian name for Babylon or Babylonia.

trophy: A rough wooden model adorned with armor captured from the defeated forces set up by the victor on the battlefield.

Wadjet: An Egyptian goddess associated with the union of Upper and Lower Egypt.

White Fortress *or* White Wall: An ancient fortress in Memphis possibly dating back to the earliest years of the Egyptian Old Kingdom.

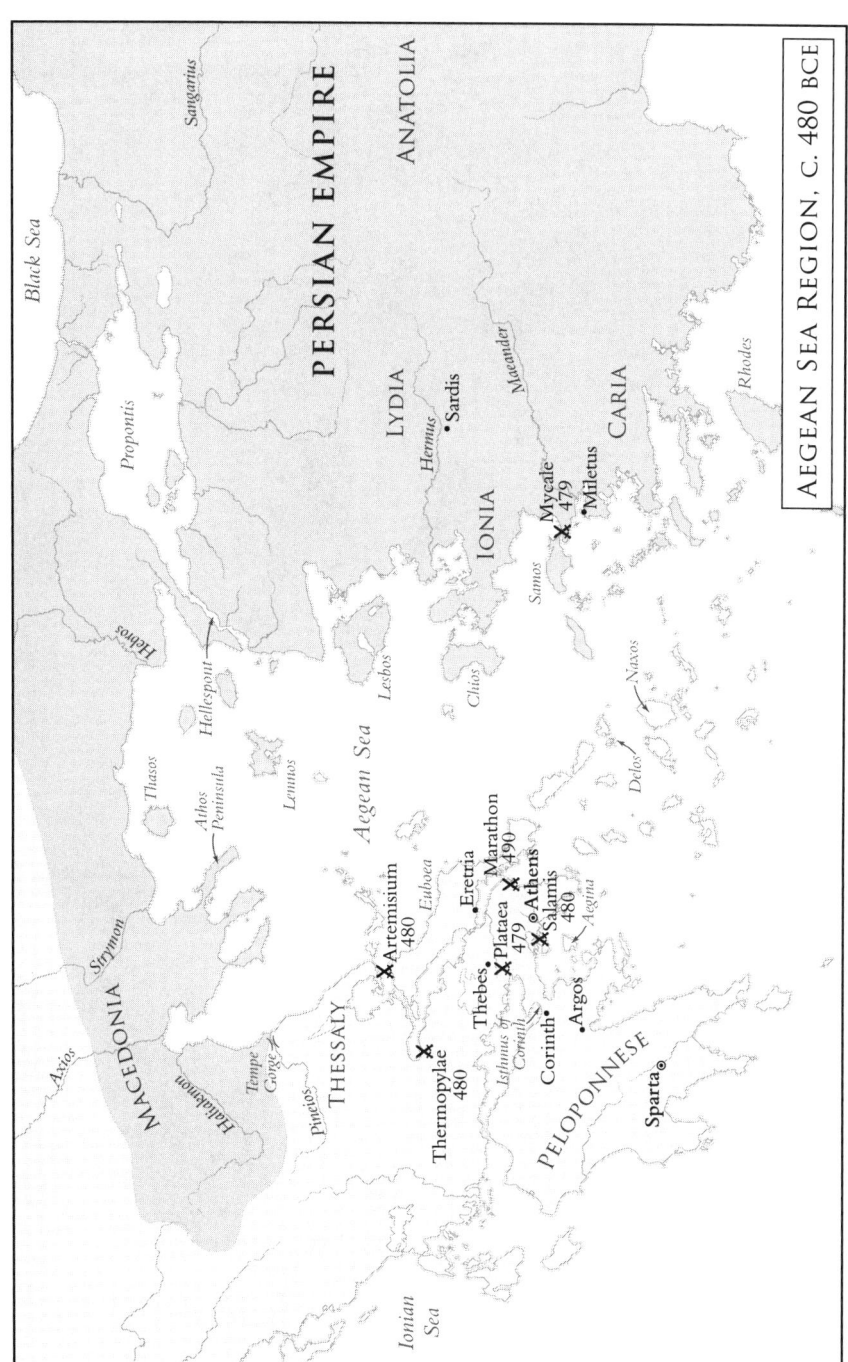

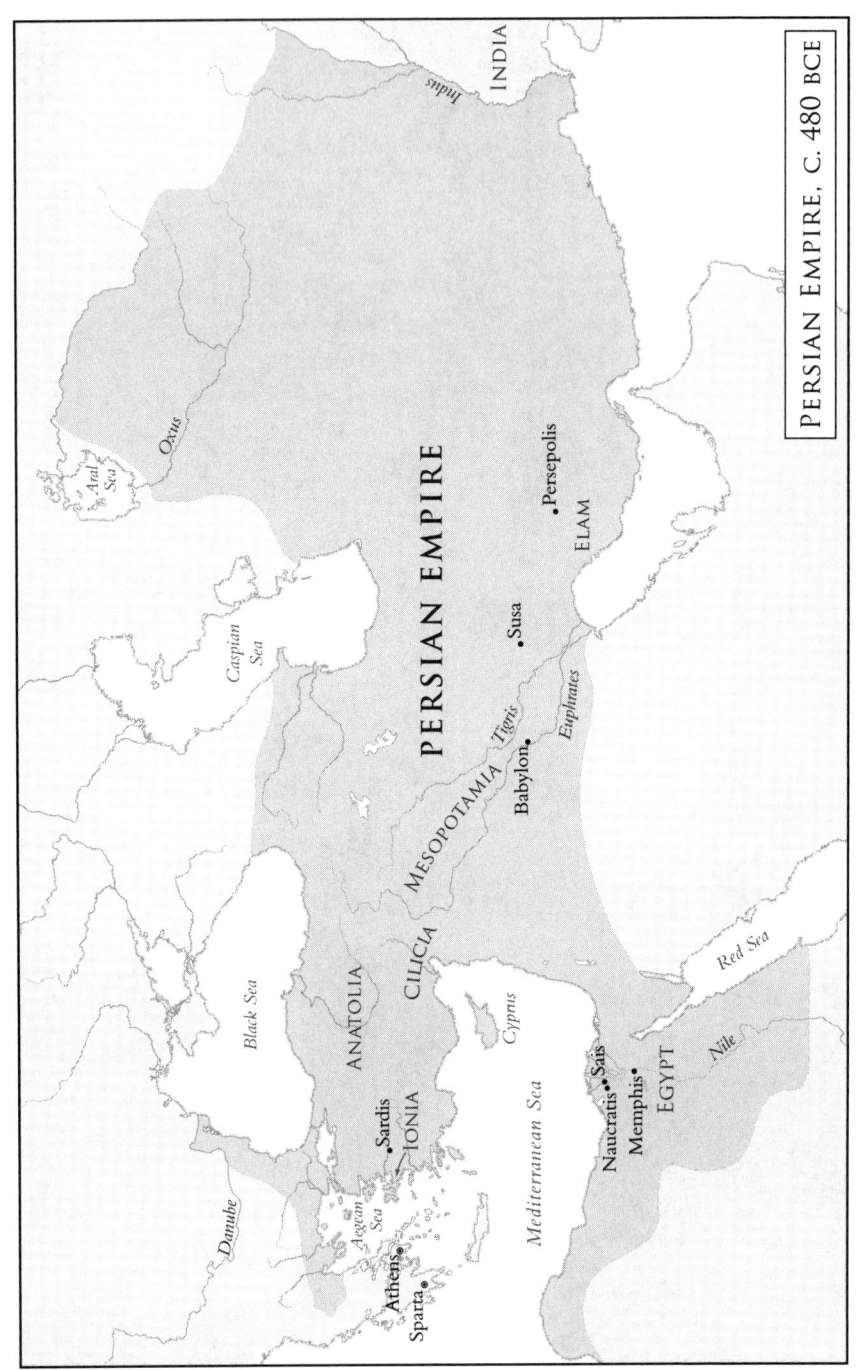

INTRODUCTION

> "When it was reported to King Darius that Sardis had been captured and burnt by the Athenians and the Ionians (. . .) it is said that he was unconcerned about the Ionians, knowing well that they would not escape retribution for their revolt, but he asked who the Athenians were. When he learned the answer, he called for his bow, nocked an arrow, and shot it into the sky. As the arrow sailed towards the sun, he said: 'O Zeus, may I have my vengeance upon the Athenians!' He then assigned one of his attendants to say to him three times, whenever dinner was set before him: 'Sire, remember the Athenians.'"
>
> —Herodotus, *Histories* 5.105

This tale about the Persian king Darius and his aggravation upon learning about the burning of Sardis—Persia's provincial capital in the Aegean—by Greek rebels in 498 BCE comes from the Greek historian Herodotus. Herodotus and other Greeks had many stories to tell about Persia. The Persian Empire was the superpower of its day—the largest empire in the world, indeed the largest empire that had ever existed up to that point in history. The Persian army had succeeded in every terrain from rugged mountains and barren scrubland to green river valleys. At the same time, many regions of the empire enjoyed exceptional prosperity and cultural flourishing as the Persian kings encouraged trade and respected local traditions. Some Greeks looked upon Persia with distrust, fearing its armies and calling its king a tyrant. Others saw it as an opportunity: a market for Greek trade goods; a source of patronage for mercenaries, artisans, and other skilled professionals; and a useful ally against other Greeks. Greeks could work for, trade with, ally with, or fight against the Persians; the one thing they could not do was ignore them.

Most Persians, on the other hand, had little reason to think about Greece at all. The Persian Empire was vast, powerful, prosperous, and largely peaceful. Persian literary sources have little to say about any foreign people, and there is no reason to suppose that the Greeks made more of an impression on the empire than any other culture on the frontier. Greece, from a Persian point of view, was a distant and insignificant backwater whose peoples were ignorant, impoverished, and plagued by petty squabbling. To the extent that Greece was of any concern to the Persian kings, it was because the internal conflicts of the Greek world repeatedly threatened to spill over into Persian territory and exacerbate problems elsewhere along the western frontier. Over the course of a century and a half, Persian kings and their local representatives tried different strategies for managing their Aegean frontier, but this activity was rarely a priority. Only one Persian king ever visited Greece in person. Most were content to leave matters to local subordinates. The most accurate part of Herodotus' fanciful story about Darius' quarrel with Athens may be that he had to rely on his staff to remind him about it.[1]

The Persians attempted to handle their problems in Greece by direct military intervention only twice. The first occasion was a series of operations in the late 490s BCE culminating in a targeted strike against the cities of Athens and Eretria in 490. The second was a large-scale invasion in 480–479. Although neither campaign achieved all its goals, both left an impression on the Greek world. These military confrontations, known today as the Greco-Persian Wars, were major events in the history of Greece. Many generations of Greeks celebrated the victories against Persian forces as heroic accomplishments that proved the superiority of Greece over Persia. Many modern historians have followed the Greek sources in portraying the wars of the 490s and 480–479 as important confrontations with far-reaching consequences, even going so far as to cast the events as the opening engagement of an enduring clash between East and West. From the Persian point of view, however, these expeditions were of far less importance. Although they did not achieve everything the kings had hoped for, their defeat did not provoke a crisis in Persia but simply led Persian authorities to find new ways of pursuing the same strategic goals.

Persia's main concern on its western frontier was not Greece but Egypt, which the empire conquered in 525 BCE and then struggled to hold for the next two centuries. Egypt was a wealthy, populous land whose people had a rich cultural history and resented being ruled by outsiders. Resistance and revolt in Egypt were major problems for the Persian kings. The imperative of maintaining control of Egypt—or regaining it after a

---

1. John O. Hyland, *Persian Interventions: The Achaemenid Empire, Athens, and Sparta, 450–386 BCE* (Baltimore: Johns Hopkins University Press, 2018), 1–8.

revolt—set the basic conditions of Persian policy in the Mediterranean as a whole. Persia's actions in Greece were tangled up in its relations with Egypt for two reasons: first, because dealing with problems at one end of the western frontier diverted attention and resources from the other; second, because Egyptians regularly recruited mercenaries from Greece for their struggle against Persian rule. When the Persians dealt with Greece, they were primarily thinking of how their actions there would affect their position in Egypt.

In the century following their two campaigns in Greece, Persian kings adapted their approach to their western frontier, pursuing through diplomacy what they had not accomplished militarily. Greece and Egypt continued to be linked, as Egyptian rebels made alliances in Greece and recruited Greek soldiers to bolster their ranks. By 387, Persia's patient management of Greece paid off when the king was able to dictate terms to Greeks who had worn themselves out in internal fighting. With the Aegean frontier secure, the Persian army marched once again on Egypt and brought the wayward province back under control.

The imbalance between the Greeks' preoccupation with Persia and the Persians' general indifference to Greece is typical of imperial frontiers. At the center of any empire, many different concerns compete for official attention. Unimportant frontier-dwellers rarely make an impression unless they become wrapped up in larger initiatives. On the other hand, those who live at the edge of an empire can feel the effects of imperial power and policy at all levels of society. This imbalance is also visible in the literary record. While Greeks wrote at length about their interactions with Persia, Persians barely wrote anything about the Greeks. As a result, modern historians' accounts of Greco-Persian relations have often tended to exaggerate the importance of Greece.

While the wars of the early fifth century in Greece dominate modern histories of Greco-Persian interaction, they were only part of a larger history in which the main actors were not Greeks but Persians, and in which the most important theater of events was not Greece but Egypt. Looking at a broader history allows us to put the Greco-Persian Wars into a more meaningful context. The story of Persia's engagement in Greece is not one of East-West cultural clashes or Greek ascendancy, but of Persia's success in adapting to the challenges of an unstable, frequently violent frontier region.

The Origins and Ideology of the Persian Empire

Persia was not the first empire to emerge in the ancient near east, but the Persians learned from and built on the experiences of those that had gone before. The Persian Empire's success depended on its ability to incorporate the strengths of earlier states.

Two of the first regions in the world to develop large-scale societies were Mesopotamia and Egypt. Both areas were centered on major rivers: Mesopotamia in the broad floodplain of the Tigris and Euphrates, and Egypt along the Nile. These two regions are linked by the drier but arable lands of the eastern coast of the Mediterranean Sea (a region known as the Levant) and surrounded in other directions by deserts, mountains, and scrublands. The agricultural wealth of Mesopotamia and Egypt, along with the easy transport afforded by the rivers, fostered the growth of large, stable, and cohesive societies. In the Levant, agriculture was productive but less reliable, leading to the development of numerous settled but contentious and unstable societies. The deserts and mountains of the surrounding hinterlands were home to small, sometimes nomadic cultures. The interactions of these many different kinds of societies created a long history of conflicts, tensions, alliances, and exchanges beginning as early as the 4000s BCE.

In the tenth century, the Assyrian kingdom of northern Mesopotamia began an aggressive campaign of imperial conquest. Assyrian expansion relied on a combination of advanced military technology, including siege machinery and iron weapons, and a policy of brutally repressing conquered peoples.[2] Massacre, enslavement, and forced relocation were the fates of many of Assyria's subjects. The Assyrian army's success allowed the kingdom to expand faster and farther than any state before it. At its greatest extent, Assyrian power stretched from the foothills of the Iranian plateau in the east to the Nile valley in the west.

---

2. Fabrice de Backer, "Some Basic Tactics of Neo-Assyrian Warfare," *Ugarit-Forschungen* 39 (2007); Fabrice De Backer, "Some Basic Tactics of Neo-Assyrian Warfare 2: Siege Battles," *State Archives of Assyria Bulletin* 18 (2009); Garret G. Fagan, "'I Fell upon Him Like a Furious Arrow': Toward a Reconstruction of the Assyrian Tactical System," in *New Perspectives on Ancient Warfare*, ed. Garret G. Fagan and Matthew Trundle (Leiden: Brill, 2010); Sarah C. Melville, *The Campaigns of Sargon II, King of Assyria 721–705 B.C.* (Norman: University of Oklahoma Press, 2016), 21–50.

Because of its rapid expansion, the Assyrian state faced challenges that no previous state had confronted. The greatest of these challenges was maintaining control over an enormous territory whose people were not united by culture, religion, language, or history. The Assyrians' brutality was a strategy calculated to instill terror and keep conquered peoples in line, but in the end it only fostered fiercer resistance. Around 664, Assyria's vassal ruler in Egypt, Psammetichus, led a rebellion and established himself as king of a newly independent Egypt. In the late 600s, when Assyria was weakened by civil war, an alliance of its neighbors and subject peoples, including the Babylonians of southern Mesopotamia and the Medes of the Iranian plateau,[3] overthrew Assyrian power. Egypt and Babylon exerted their power as new empires competing over the remnants of the Assyrian state while the Median chiefdoms expanded in the mountains. Pressure from nomadic peoples on the frontiers, no longer held back by Assyrian military might, added to the turmoil in the region. The Persian Empire arose out of these turbulent times.

In the second millennium BCE, nomadic groups speaking various Iranian languages had migrated into the mountains along the eastern fringe of Mesopotamia. As these newcomers mingled with local inhabitants and interacted with the larger, more organized states to their west, they developed new ethnic identities. The Medes were one of the cultures who emerged out of these interactions. Another people, whose culture developed in the southern region called Elam, came to be known as the Persians. The earliest documented ruler of the Persians, Teispes, ruled the Elamite city of Anshan in the second half of the seventh century. He was succeeded by his son Cyrus I and grandson Cambyses I, who ruled the same small territory. The early Persian state was a small and relatively weak one in the orbit of larger and more powerful states like Babylon and the Elamite kingdom. The son of Cambyses I, Cyrus II, changed his people's place in the world.[4]

---

3. The history of the Medes is a matter of uncertainty. Although Greek sources described them as an empire, evidence from Mesopotamian traditions and from archaeology seems to point more to a loose confederation of chiefdoms. See Mario Liverani, "The Rise and Fall of Media," in *Continuity of Empire(?): Assyria, Media, Persia*, ed. Giovanni B. Lanfranchi, Michael Roaf, and Robert Rollinger (Padua: S.A.r.g.o.n., 2003), 4.
4. Greek historians generally disregarded Teispes, Cyrus I, and Cambyses I, and saw Persian history beginning with Cyrus II. Greek sources refer to Cyrus II and his son Cambyses II simply as Cyrus and Cambyses. In this book, names of kings given without numbers refer to the most recently mentioned king of that name.

Around 550 BCE, when much of the larger Mesopotamian world was recovering from incursions by nomadic groups from the north, Cyrus began a campaign of conquest that subsumed the Babylonian and Median kingdoms. Then he led his forces even farther afield to build a kingdom stretching from Central Asia to the shores of the Aegean Sea.

In many ways, the Persian Empire was the heir to the states that had come before it. Cyrus' armies incorporated the Assyrians' military professionalism and expertise in siege warfare, which allowed them to capture fortified cities like Babylon. The management of the empire required a bureaucratic state whose operations, and even language, came largely from the Elamite kingdom. In other ways, however, the Persians adopted new strategies for managing such a large territory.

The Persian Empire followed a policy of accommodation and multiculturalism. Conquered peoples were not routinely massacred or enslaved. Forced relocation was used rarely and only on subjects who had proven particularly troublesome. Indeed, the Persians helped some peoples who had been expelled from their homelands by previous empires to return home—most famously the Jews, whom Cyrus restored from Babylon to Judea and whose temple in Jerusalem he ordered rebuilt. As long as subjects of the empire paid their taxes and provided soldiers for the Persian army, they were largely left alone with their own local governments. Persian kings took particular care to respect native religious practices throughout their empire, supporting local religious institutions and presenting themselves as loyal servants of local gods. No one was compelled to adopt the Persians' religion, customs, or language.[5]

The Persian kings claimed a right to rule the world as delegates of the god Ahura Mazda. According to Persian belief, Ahura Mazda stood on the side of light and truth against darkness and lies.[6] The king was regarded as Ahura Mazda's agent on earth, both empowered to extend his rule over all peoples and required to rule them with wisdom, justice, and compassion.[7]

No empire in history has ever entirely lived up to the ideals it espouses. The Persian ideology of benevolent multicultural tolerance was a

---

5. M. A. Dandamayev, "Achaemenid Imperial Policies and Provincial Governments," *Iranica Antiqua* 34 (1999).
6. It is not clear how widely Ahura Mazda was worshiped even among Persians, and it is possible that the god's cult was particular to the kings themselves.
7. Lori Katchoudorian, *Imperial Matter: Ancient Persia and the Archaeology of Empires* (Oakland: University of California Press, 2016), 1–24.

pragmatic tool of empire and it could be discarded when it got in the way of imperial objectives. The swift expansion of the empire under Cyrus and the further campaigns under later kings were unavoidably violent, in some cases rivaling the brutality of the Assyrians. In unruly frontier areas, Persian kings and generals could be quick to resort to destructive reprisals against rebels and the noncompliant. The fact that periods of weakness at the top, such as when a new and untested king came to power or during struggles for control among claimants to the throne, were frequently accompanied by revolts in the provinces shows that in some places the acceptance of Persian rule was similarly pragmatic and conditional.[8]

Nevertheless, the ideal that Persian kings articulated and broadly endeavored to achieve was one of peace and stability with minimal intrusion into local affairs.[9] Within the limits of political practicality, the Persian Empire created for its peoples a realm in which many cultures could flourish and many peoples could enjoy peace and prosperity.[10]

The Organization of the Empire

The Persian Empire was larger than any state that had come before. Keeping such a massive state under control required a sophisticated system of administration.

In the empire as it developed under Cyrus' successors, the king was at the center of the state, surrounded by the royal family, a professional bureaucracy, and individuals of special skill or political usefulness who were formally known as "Friends of the King." The king traveled with his court, rotating his peacetime residence between the main capital at Susa and other important ceremonial and administrative centers including Ecbatana, Pasargadae, Babylon, and later Persepolis. The progress of the court from one city to another was a spectacle which allowed the

---

8. Thomas Harrison, *Writing Ancient Persia* (London: Bristol Classical Press, 2011), 73–90.
9. Elspeth R. M. Dusinberre, *Empire, Authority, and Autonomy in Achaemenid Anatolia* (Cambridge: Cambridge University Press, 2013), 49–82.
10. On the history and organization of the Persian Empire, see Pierre Briant, *From Cyrus to Alexander: A History of the Persian Empire*, trans. Peter T. Daniels (Winona Lake, IN: Eisenbrauns, 2002), 357–511; Maria Brosius, *The Persians* (London: Routledge, 2006), 6–78; Matt Waters, *Ancient Persia: A Concise History of the Achaemenid Empire, 550–330 BCE* (Cambridge: Cambridge University Press, 2014), 92–113.

ordinary people of the empire's core Mesopotamian and Iranian regions to glimpse and even briefly interact with the king in person.

The empire was divided into provinces, called satrapies, each administered by a governor, or satrap, appointed by the king. Satraps were often members of the royal family, especially in frontier provinces where larger concentrations of military forces were stationed, but members of the local elite could also be chosen for the job. Satraps commanded detachments of the Persian army, collected taxes, and oversaw the administration of their satrapies, while in most places day-to-day governance was left to the locals in whatever form they were accustomed to. Satraps were answerable to the king for the maintenance of peace, stability, and security in their provinces.

Satraps commanded their own local military forces, made up of a core of professional soldiers, which could be augmented with local levies when needed. Detachments of troops were stationed at key points around the empire to help maintain order and control. These could include not just ethnic Persians, but also hired soldiers from various parts of the empire and around its frontiers. Greece was a prime recruiting ground for mercenaries, but many other peoples also served the Persians for pay, such as a garrison of Jewish soldiers stationed at Elephantine in southern Egypt—some of whose affairs are documented in surviving papyrus records.[11] Satraps' military and financial resources allowed many of them to operate with a degree of independence. In some cases, this independence allowed them to respond more effectively to local problems without burdening the overall administration of the empire. In other cases, satraps were more invested in building up their own local power bases and competing with neighboring satraps than in serving the policies of the kings.

Some of the tax revenue raised in the provinces was spent locally to supply Persian troops, pay satrapal officials, and maintain infrastructure, while some was delivered to the royal treasury. The revenue from some cities or regions was assigned to certain individuals such as Friends of the King or members of the royal family, including women. The management of these finances was part of the satraps' responsibilities, but local people were also involved. The annual ceremonial delivery of tribute goods by delegations from all parts to the empire to the king at Persepolis was one of the rituals that helped connect the disparate parts of the empire.

---

11. Christopher Tuplin, "Xenophon and the Garrisons of the Achaemenid Empire," *Archäologische Mitteilungen aus Iran* 20 (1987).

A highway known as the Royal Road ran from Susa to the westernmost satrapal capital at Sardis, in western Anatolia. Along this route, messenger stations were maintained to provide lodging, food, and fresh mounts both to messengers carrying reports from one end of the empire to the other and to officials traveling on state business. To further connect the empire, Darius I initiated a project to build a canal between the Nile River and the Red Sea. Darius and later kings also issued gold and silver coins of standardized weight. These initiatives for transport and common currency encouraged the growth of trade within the empire and beyond. The Persian court was also a major center of patronage for skilled crafters and other specialists, such as entertainers and physicians, from around the empire. Administrative records show that workers from many different regions were paid out of the royal treasury, including Greeks.[12]

The records of the imperial bureaucracy document a vast pool of workers on royal estates, doing everything from manual labor to skilled crafting. These workers were paid primarily in grain and other foodstuffs, but sometimes also in silver. Administrative documents show that female workers were often paid as much as men doing the same work, sometimes even more. On many estates, workers were managed by an *arashshara*, a female supervisor who ranked among the highest-paid laborers.[13]

The origins and working conditions of these laborers could vary widely, and the question of exactly how to describe this workforce is a vexed one. Persian ideology declared an abhorrence for the practice of slavery. Greeks, writing from the periphery of the empire, described the Persian king as a slave master who ruled over a people not fit for freedom.[14] The reality seems to have been more complicated.

Persian armies did not customarily make slaves of the people they conquered, nor was the buying, selling, and exploitation of enslaved individuals common among Persians, although surviving documents show that it did occur. Persia did not interfere with slave systems among the peoples of its empire or make any effort to halt the slave trade on its frontiers (a significant portion of which, in the Mediterranean, was run by

---

12. Henry P. Colburn, "Connectivity and Communication in the Achaemenid Empire," *Journal of the Economic and Social History of the Orient* 56, no. 1 (2013).
13. Maria Brosius, *Women in Ancient Persia, 559–331 BC* (Oxford: Clarendon, 1996), 84–97, 124–79.
14. Herodotus, *Histories* 7.135; Aristotle, *Politics* 3.14 (=1285a).

Greek merchants).[15] At the same time, defeated peoples and rebels were sometimes subject to forced relocation and were not allowed to return to their homelands. In the places where these groups were resettled, they were allowed to live as communities with their own languages, customs, and religions. Such forced resettlement must have been traumatic to those who experienced it, but the lives that they and their descendants lived afterward were not like the experiences of most slaves in the ancient world, torn away from their homes and families, bought and sold, and forced to labor without pay. The lives of workers on royal estates were humble ones—they were dependent on the more powerful members of their society and they had comparatively little autonomy—but the same might be said of peasant populations in any pre-modern society.[16]

Persia's Westward Expansion

Cyrus' conquests stretched as far as the kingdom of Lydia in western Anatolia, which came under Persian rule in 546 BCE. Since Lydia had conquered the Ionian Greek cities on the Aegean coast of Anatolia around 560, its conquest by Persia brought Greek cities under Persian rule for the first time. Like most Greeks of the time, the Ionians lived under a variety of types of government allowing some degree of citizen participation. Although it was Persian custom to leave local governments untouched, Cyrus and his subordinates found the volatile, often violent nature of Greek politics frustrating and feared it could destabilize the new northwestern frontier. To replace it, they supported the rise of local aristocrats to rule the Ionian cities and maintain order. These local rulers were termed tyrants, a word for sole rulers in the Greek world that did not originally have negative connotations.[17]

---

15. David Lewis, "Near Eastern Slaves in Classical Attica and the Slave Trade with Persian Territories," *Classical Quarterly* 61, no. 1 (2011).
16. Briant, *From Cyrus to Alexander*, 429–39.
17. The origins of the Greek word *tyrannos*, "tyrant," are uncertain, but it was clearly borrowed into Greek from another language, possibly Hittite, Luwian, Phoenician, or Phrygian. All of these possibilities point to Greeks deriving not just the word, but also the idea of a sole ruler, from contacts with peoples to their east. See Victor Parker, "Τύραννος. The Semantics of a Political Concept from Archilochus to Aristotle," *Hermes* Bd. 126, H. 2 (1998); Aren M. Maeir, Brent Davis, and Louise A. Hitchcock, "Philistine Names and

Cyrus was succeeded by his son Cambyses II in 530. In 525, Cambyses turned his attention to the big prize in the West: Egypt. Since the mid-seventh century, when Egypt broke away from Assyrian domination, the descendants of Psammetichus had ruled as the Twenty-Sixth Dynasty, also known as the Saite Dynasty because of their origins in the delta city of Sais. The Saite kings had established themselves in the city of Memphis, from which they controlled Upper Egypt, the long Nile valley south of the delta. In Upper Egypt, settlement was concentrated close to the river and hemmed in by the desert. A Memphis-based administration could readily monitor and respond to problems in the south. The delta was different. The delta, or Lower Egypt, was a broad expanse of marshlands, islands, and mud flats broken up by watercourses and canals. The river's annual flood created new channels and shifting sand bars that impeded navigation. Despite coming from the delta themselves, the Saite kings found Lower Egypt hard to govern. In the turbulent years before and after Assyrian rule, many local aristocrats in the delta had built up their own power bases, supported by their own small armies. These aristocrats resented interference even from other Egyptians and resisted the Saite kings' efforts to reunify Egypt.

As Cambyses' invasion approached Egypt, the Saite kings and the delta rulers were unable to resolve their differences in time to mount a coordinated defense. Peoples of the Levant, who had traditionally looked to Egypt for support against Mesopotamian aggression, saw that Egypt was in no shape to come to their defense and submitted to Cambyses without a fight. The last Saite king, Psammetichus III, met the Persian army with his forces at Pelusium in the eastern delta and was decisively defeated. After this battle, Persian armies rapidly moved through the delta, where local aristocrats either surrendered or remained neutral, and conquered Upper Egypt.

Cambyses followed his father's precedents by accommodating Egyptian traditions rather than imposing Persian customs. He was formally crowned Pharaoh of Egypt and carried out the traditional ritual prerogatives of the role, including honoring Egyptian gods and overseeing the economic activity of temples. He also sent an army to campaign on Egypt's southern and western borders, evidently a token effort that achieved little in practice but was the sort of show of strength that was expected of a

---

Terms Once Again," *Journal of Eastern Mediterranean Archaeology and Heritage Studies* 4, no. 4 (2016): 334–35.

new Egyptian king. Cambyses was advised on his management of Egypt by Udjahorresne, a priest and former admiral under the Saite kings who went over to Cambyses and became a Friend of the King. Cambyses kept many other lower-level Egyptian officials in their posts to demonstrate the benevolence of Persian rule and continuity with the past. Despite these efforts, Persian rule was never widely accepted in Egypt. Egyptian memories, preserved in later Greek sources, recast Cambyses as a mad tyrant who mocked the gods of Egypt and desecrated their temples.

The instability of Egypt in the sixth century made it easy for Persia to conquer, but that same instability made it hard to hold. Egypt and the Ionian coast of Anatolia marked the southern and northern extremes of Persia's western frontier. The entanglement between these two regions posed one of the lasting problems for Persian imperial policy.[18]

The Greeks and Egypt

The Greeks began to emerge out of relative isolation around 750 BCE. As Greeks engaged in the broader currents of Mediterranean trade, Egypt and Greece struck up a special relationship. The land of Greece was rocky, mountainous, and dry—poor for growing grain, but excellent for producing high quality wine and olive oil. Greek traders also had ready access to metal deposits in nearby Macedonia, Thrace, and northern Italy. Egypt was poor in metals but produced grain in abundance. Egypt's agricultural surplus supported an elite that craved luxury products like Greek oil and wine. The natural compatibility of their economies formed the basis of long-lasting good relations between Greeks and Egyptians.

Another resource Greece could offer was mercenary soldiers. Life in the city-states or poleis (singular polis) of Greece was unpredictable and often violent. Competition for scarce farmland fueled near constant warfare between neighboring poleis, while power struggles within poleis frequently escalated into bloody clashes between rival families and factions. The result was a large number of experienced soldiers who found themselves on the losing side of one conflict or another. Many of these soldiers left Greece to take paying service in the wealthier, more stable powers around the Mediterranean, including Lydia, Carthage, Persia, and Egypt.

---

18. On the Persian conquest of Egypt, see Stephen Ruzicka, *Trouble in the West: Egypt and the Persian Empire 525–323 BCE* (Oxford: Oxford University Press, 2012), 14–25.

Egyptian kings and delta aristocrats recruited soldiers from Greece, as well as from other nearby regions including Judea, Libya, and Nubia, to supplement their own armies. Greek troops were particularly favored in Egypt. Along with Greek merchants, they were granted special accommodations, including the right to found a polis of their own at Naucratis in the Nile delta. The Saite kings made especial use of Greek troops, not because Greeks were braver or tougher than Egyptians (however much Greeks liked to tell themselves so), but because their loyalty was not complicated by local ties; they didn't require time-consuming training; and they were, ultimately, expendable.[19] In the sixth century, Egyptian kings began to bring Greece into their larger sphere of influence by establishing relationships with local leaders and funding public building projects, including helping to finance the rebuilding of the temple of Apollo at Delphi after a fire.[20]

The relationship between Egypt and Greece posed a conundrum for Persia. Instability in Greece often spilled over into Persian territory and drew troops and resources away from Egypt, but stability in Greece freed up troops to fight on Egypt's behalf. Controlling Egypt required managing Greece. From the late sixth century to the early fourth century, Persian policy in the Mediterranean evolved as Persia tried different approaches to the problem of the western frontier.

The Greeks and Persia

The Greeks' history with Persia was complicated. In the aftermath of Darius' and Xerxes' invasions in the early fifth century, Greek thinkers tended to project the recent hostilities into the past and to portray the earlier history of Greece and Persia as the buildup to an inevitable clash. The reality, both before and after the wars, was less clear-cut.[21]

---

19. Matthew Trundle, *Greek Mercenaries: From the Late Archaic Period to Alexander* (London: Routledge, 2004), 101–15; Jeffery Rop, *Greek Military Service in the Ancient Near East 401–330 BCE* (Cambridge: Cambridge University Press, 2019), 88–114.
20. Herodotus, *Histories* 2.180, 2,182, 3.40, 3.47.
21. Pierre Briant, "History and Ideology: The Greeks and 'Persian Decadence,'" trans. Antonia Nevill, in *Greeks and Barbarians*, ed. Thomas Harrison (New York: Routledge, 2002); Joseph Wieshöfer, "From Achaemenid Imperial Order to Sasanian Diplomacy: War, Peace, and Reconciliation in Pre-Islamic Iran," in *War and Peace in the Ancient World*, ed. Kurt Raaflaub (Malden, MA: Blackwell, 2007), 122–23; Janett Morgan, *Greek*

Persia offered stability in the perennial turbulence of Greek life. Competition over limited resources, often violent, was common both within the Greek poleis and between them. Wars between poleis were frequent, largely fought over the control of scarce farmland and access to trade routes. Some poleis had long-lasting rivalries with their neighbors, such as those between Sparta and Argos, or Athens and Thebes, but alliances and antagonisms could shift from one year to the next. Many poleis also went through cycles of factional strife. A major source of contention was the struggle between those who favored limited, oligarchic regimes and those who wanted more expansive democratic governments, but conflicts could also arise between families or popular leaders. In many places, opportunistic aristocrats took advantage of these conflicts to seize sole power in their cities and rule as tyrants, but most tyrants were quickly ousted by rival aristocrats or their own disillusioned followers.

The only major city to largely avoid internal strife was Sparta, which had adopted a culture of extreme militarism early in its history. Spartan boys were taken from their parents at the age of seven and raised by the state in a brutal system designed to instill both physical hardiness and social conformity. Any Spartan who failed to live up to their society's exacting norms could be reduced to a life of poverty and humiliation. The primary purpose of Spartan militarism was to maintain control over the neighboring territory of Messene, which Sparta had conquered in the eighth century and whose people were reduced to helots, unfree laborers forced to work the land to supply Sparta with food. Even in conformist Sparta, though, individuals and factions struggled for power.[22]

Embroiled in these ongoing and overlapping conflicts, individuals and cities were constantly looking out for potential allies against their rivals. As the Persian Empire established itself as the major economic and military force in the Aegean, Greeks came to look to Persia for support in their internal struggles. Persia also became the main place of refuge for political leaders forced out of their homes by competing factions. These relationships could be as volatile as Greek politics. When the tyrant

---

Perspectives on the Achaemenid Empire: Persia through the Looking Glass (Edinburgh: Edinburgh University Press, 2016), 67–124.
22. Nigel M. Kennel, *Spartans: A New History* (Chichester: Wiley-Blackwell, 2011); Stephen Hodkinson, "Sparta: An Exceptional Domination of State over Society?" in *A Companion to Sparta*, ed. Anton Powell (Hoboken, NJ: Wiley-Blackwell, 2017).

Hippias was forced out of Athens in 510, for instance, he found refuge at the Persian court. The newly democratic Athens soon petitioned for admission to the Persian Empire as a bulwark against Spartan interference, but when the threat from Sparta passed, the submission to Persia was repudiated. In the 470s, both the Athenian Themistocles and the Spartan Pausanias, who had led Greek forces against Xerxes' invasion, fell out of favor at home and sought to make deals with Xerxes.

Personal relationships complicated the political relationships on Persia's Aegean frontier. Greek aristocrats had long formed links with one another through the custom of *xenia*, or guest-friendship, in which individuals and their families pledged mutual support and hospitality across the boundaries of poleis. As the Persian Empire became a major player in Aegean politics, many Greeks from elite families sought to form the same sorts of relationships with Persian kings, satraps, and generals.[23] These relationships did not always play out in the Greeks' favor. The tyrant of Samos, Polycrates, for instance, fell victim to shifting political forces when an earlier alliance with Egypt fell apart and he tried to switch his allegiance to Persia: the attempt ended with Polycrates dead and Samos conquered by Persia.[24] The interplay of competing interests could make Greco-Persian relations complicated, even downright contradictory: in the early 380s, the Athenians, at that time allied with Persia, were also supporting anti-Persian rebels in Cyprus, while the Spartans, then at war with Persia, intervened to stop Athenian aid from reaching Cyprus.[25]

Not all Greco-Persian relations were political or diplomatic, however. Like Egypt, Persia was a large market for goods that Greeks could produce themselves or deliver from farther west and north. Both the royal court and the regional elite provided patronage for skilled workers such as artisans, entertainers, courtesans, physicians, and mercenaries.[26] The royal court recruited skilled workers from throughout the empire as a reflection of the unity of all peoples under the king. Greek stonemasons, for example, left graffiti in the Persian quarries where they worked, and their families received distributions of food from the royal treasury. An

---

23. Lynnette G. Mitchell, *Greeks Bearing Gifts: The Public Use of Private Relationships in the Greek World 435–323 BC* (Cambridge: Cambridge University Press, 1997), 111–33.
24. Herodotus, *Histories* 3.120–25, 139–49; Philip Kaplan, "The Ring of Polycrates: Friendship and Alliance in the East Mediterranean," *Journal of Ancient History* 4 (2016).
25. See Document 13.7.
26. Rop, *Greek Military Service*.

administrative document written in Greek even shows that at least one Greek-speaking official worked in the imperial bureaucracy.[27]

Some Persians also made a home in Greece, such as Zopyrus, the grandson of a Persian general by the same name who lived in exile in Athens.[28] Trade, diplomatic exchange, and the movements of professionals like mercenaries and artisans also brought Persian goods into the Greek marketplace, where they were eagerly adopted and imitated. A variety of Persian and Persian-inspired products ranging from tunics and drinking cups to peacocks and parasols became part of the material culture of Greece, often paraded as signs of luxury and wealth.[29] Even Persian architecture had an influence on Greece in examples like the *odeion*, or concert hall, built in Athens by Pericles, which was thought to be an imitation of a Persian royal pavilion.[30]

After Cyrus' conquest of Lydia in 546, the Greek cities of the Aegean straddled the Persian frontier. The Ionian cities on the coast of Anatolia were inside the empire while the mainland cities west of the Aegean were outside it, but connections of culture, trade, and family continued to bridge the Aegean Sea. These interconnections kept the Greek world entangled with Persia, but until the end of the sixth century, tensions were low. The Ionian cities flourished culturally and economically under Persian rule, and while the mainland cities' relationships with Persia could be complicated, there was little sign of hostility from either side under Cyrus and Cambyses. The first major disturbances on this frontier came under the following king, Darius I.

The Rise of Darius

Cambyses died unexpectedly in 522. He had spent much of his short reign in Egypt solidifying Persian control over the country. The Persian Empire was still a young state working out how to realize Cyrus' vision

---

27. Kostas Vlassopoulos, *Greeks and Barbarians* (Cambridge: Cambridge University Press, 2013), 34–65. See Documents 7.5, 7.6, 7.7.
28. Herodotus, *Histories* 3.160.
29. Margaret C. Miller, *Athens and Persia in the 5th Century BC: A Study in Cultural Receptivity* (Cambridge: Cambridge University Press, 1997), 135–258; Erich S. Gruen, *Rethinking the Other in Antiquity* (Princeton: Princeton University Press, 2011), 9–75.
30. Plutarch, *Parallel Lives*, "Life of Pericles" 13.6.

of a world in which people of many cultures, languages, and traditions were united under one king. When that king himself was the only thing the disparate peoples had in common, his prolonged absence threatened the cohesion of the empire. Most likely in an effort to help shore up this cohesion, Cambyses' younger brother Bardiya had been appointed satrap of several northern and eastern regions. In his brother's absence, it appears that Bardiya had expanded his claim to power. A few Babylonian documents from the period even name Bardiya as king.[31] If Cambyses had lived any longer, he may have had a civil war on his hands.[32]

Bardiya assumed the throne on his older brother's death, but not all of the Persian aristocracy was content with him as king. A conspiracy took shape, led by one of Cambyses' military aides, Darius. Darius and his allies entered the palace, stormed Bardiya's chambers, and assassinated him. To justify their coup, the conspirators claimed that the real Bardiya had been secretly murdered before Cambyses' death and replaced with an impostor, one of the magi (singular magus), a class of priests. Backed by his allies, Darius proclaimed himself king.

The reaction in the empire was swift and strong. There had been unrest in the transitions from Cyrus to Cambyses and Cambyses to Bardiya, but Darius faced revolt on a much wider scale. He spent the first several years of his reign fighting rebellions in numerous satrapies. When his hold on the throne was finally secure, Darius celebrated his victories with a monumental inscription on a high cliff face at Bisitun (also called Behistun) in which he presented the official version of events.[33]

Despite the success of the coup and his victories on the battlefield, Darius felt the need to solidify his position as king. To this end, he publicly emphasized his ancestry, which tied him to Cyrus' family line through a common ancestor named Achaemenes (from whom the ruling family of the Persian Empire is known as the Achaemenid dynasty). It is impossible to say now how accurate this genealogy was, but much of it may have been fabricated to suit Darius' political needs. Darius also engaged in many of the traditional prerogatives of kingship, including extensive building projects and new conquests.

---

31. See Documents 6.1, 6.2.
32. See Document 13.6 for an example of a later Persian king who faced a revolt led by a younger brother who had been posted to oversee a volatile frontier region.
33. See Documents 6.3, 6.5, 6.7.

Darius campaigned ambitiously on most of the empire's frontiers. In the east he pushed the frontier toward India. In the north, he extended Persian control farther along the shores of the Caspian and Black Seas. In the southwest he extended Persian rule from the Nile valley west along the Mediterranean Sea, and in the northwest he expanded the frontier to encompass Thrace, Macedonia, and some Aegean islands. Not all these campaigns were successful, particularly in the north where Persian armies struggled to come to grips with the nomadic peoples of the steppe, but in many places Darius could boast of his success in the mission of bringing more lands and peoples under the rule of Ahura Mazda's chosen king.

The Ionian Revolt

Darius' campaigns in the northwest began a chain of events with serious consequences for the Greeks and for Persian policy on the whole Mediterranean frontier. Since Cyrus' conquest of Lydia in the 540s, there had been no major Persian military operations in the Aegean Sea region. Darius' push for northwestern conquests in the last decade of the sixth century put a new strain on the Ionian cities. Part of Persian subjects' obligations to the king was to provide soldiers, supplies, and support to military operations in their region. These obligations had fallen only lightly on the Ionian Greeks in the past generation, but Darius' expansionist activities demanded significantly more of his Ionian subjects. Ionians were also becoming frustrated with the rule of Persian-backed tyrants, who stifled the sort of free-wheeling political experiments that poleis were engaging in across the Aegean in mainland Greece.[34]

In 499, the accumulated resentment at Persian demands and the rule of the tyrants burst out in a rebellion known as the Ionian Revolt. The Ionian Greeks tried to recruit help from the Greek cities across the Aegean, but only two, Athens and Eretria, agreed to send troops. Eretria was a small city of little significance and its reasons for getting involved in Ionia are uncertain, but the Eretrians may have feared that Persian expansion in the Aegean would threaten their trade routes. Athens was

---

34. Mabel Lang, "Herodotus and the Ionian Revolt," *Historia* Bd. 17, H. 1 (January 1968); J. Neville, "Was There an Ionian Revolt?" *Classical Quarterly* 29, no. 2 (1979).

a far more significant player in the Greek world and had troublesome political relations with Persia. The former Athenian tyrant, Hippias, had been trying to bring about a return to the city with Persian help. In the turmoil after the ouster of Hippias, the Athenians had faced the threat of invasion by Sparta and had sought Persian protection. Now the Athenians wanted neither to submit to Persia nor to have Hippias back again, and helping to push the Persian frontier farther away from the Aegean seemed like a good strategic move.[35]

The revolt caught Persian forces by surprise as the joint army of Ionians, Athenians, and Eretrians marched inland and attacked the satrapal capital at Sardis. The Greek forces quickly captured part of the city while the Persian garrison held out in the citadel. The city soon began to burn, although it is not clear whether the fire was intentionally set or accidental, and Greek forces retreated. Over the next few years, the revolt spread over the whole northwestern frontier from the Hellespont to Cyprus while Persian forces in the region tried to suppress it. The Ionians were able to move supplies and forces by sea, which at first gave them an advantage over Persian armies moving overland in the mountainous terrain of western Anatolia. By 493, however, Persia had brought in a strong fleet to support its land operations. The revolt was defeated and Ionia returned to Persian control.

In the immediate aftermath of the revolt, Persia treated the Ionian cities harshly as a punishment. The people of Miletus, where the revolt had first taken off, were forcibly resettled in southern Mesopotamia. Fairly soon, however, the local satrap took steps to restore stability and ease some of the tensions that had provoked the revolt. The tribute assessments demanded of each city were reevaluated and standardized, and the tyrants were removed, allowing the Ionian cities to govern themselves democratically.

The Persian Empire learned three important things from the Ionian Revolt. First, that the Aegean frontier required a more coherent strategic approach. Second, that controlling the Aegean was impossible without

---

35. We are almost entirely dependent on Greek sources for the details of the Ionian Revolt and the following Persian invasions of mainland Greece, primarily Herodotus' *Histories*. The *Histories* is a complicated source. Herodotus was a serious and conscientious historian, but he also had a pro-Greek bias and a love of the dramatic. Almost every detail in his narrative has been debated by scholars and many questions remain unsettled. The narrative presented here represents one broadly accepted interpretation, but alternative interpretations can be found by consulting the Select Bibliography.

naval superiority. And finally, that dealing with Greece would require dealing with Athens. Darius' policy in the northwest in the following years built on these lessons.

Darius' Aegean Campaigns

After the defeat of the Ionian Revolt, Darius began a series of military and diplomatic operations to try to bring the Greek world under better control. In 492, he ordered an invasion of Greece, but this plan ended in disaster when the ships carrying much of the invasion force were wrecked in a storm off the Athos peninsula in the northern Aegean. The next year, he turned to diplomacy and sent ambassadors throughout Greece asking for gifts of earth and water, the traditional symbols of submission to Persian rule. Several peoples, especially those who lived on the Aegean islands and had seen the effectiveness of the Persian fleet, peacefully submitted. Among these territories was the island of Aegina, which lay south of Athens and whose people often competed with the Athenians over trade routes. The Aeginetans no doubt saw Persia as a bulwark against Athens.

With diplomatic footholds established in Greece, Darius next ordered a targeted strike against Eretria and Athens, the cities that had participated in the Ionian Revolt. In 490, a small fleet ferried Persian forces, led by the generals Datis and Artaphrenes, across the southern Aegean. This fleet first captured the island of Naxos, which had been involved in the Ionian Revolt, and stopped at the sacred island of Delos, where Datis and Artaphrenes made an enormous offering of incense to the Greek god Apollo. These early moves signaled the Persians' intentions in Greece: to take reprisal against those who resisted Persian authority, but not to do violence to local customs or institutions.

The fleet sailed on from Delos to attack Eretria, where the Persian forces succeeded in capturing the city after a brief siege. Like the people of Miletus, the captured Eretrians were rounded up to be forcibly relocated to a region near Susa. The Persian fleet next landed at Marathon, a small village on the coast east of Athens. Hippias was with the Persians, and since his family was originally from Marathon, the Persian plan was probably to gather local support for Hippias' return, then march on Athens and reinstall him as tyrant. Destroying Athens was not the

Persians' goal. As one of the major local powers, it would serve Persian interests much better as an ally than as a depopulated city.

The Athenians had sent out a call for aid, but few cities were willing to commit to a fight against the Persians. The Spartans promised to come, but delayed on religious grounds. Delay was a sensible policy from the Spartan perspective. Their overriding priority was to maintain control of the helots, a cause that would not be advanced by getting entangled with Persia. Only the small city of Plataea sent troops to join the Athenian forces. Plataea stood near the border between Attica, the region surrounding Athens, and Boeotia, a neighboring region whose major polis Thebes had been expanding its hegemony. The Plataeans saw Athens as a useful ally against Theban expansion and took the opportunity to put the Athenians in their debt. The Athenian army, with a small Plataean contingent, took up a position in the hills above Marathon, blocking the Persians' route toward Athens.

Greek soldiers primarily fought as hoplites, heavily armored infantry equipped with a shield and spear. Individually, hoplites were slow-moving and unwieldy, but massed into a tight formation called a phalanx they presented a formidable front. Hoplite tactics were straightforward, pitting one body of heavy infantry against another.[36] Persian forces were more sophisticated, combining skilled archers and cavalry with light, mobile infantry. Persian troops typically opened a battle with a barrage of arrows to soften up enemy forces and disrupt their order, followed by an infantry charge while the cavalry harassed the enemy's weak spots.[37] At Marathon, the Greeks hoped to fight in the narrow confines of the hills, where the solidity of the hoplite phalanx would be more effective, while

---

36. The details of hoplite warfare remain a subject of ongoing debate. See Hans van Wees, *Greek Warfare: Myths and Realities* (London: Duckworth, 2004), 177–91; Victor Davis Hanson, *The Western Way of War: Infantry Battle in Classical Greece* (Berkeley: University of California Press, 2009), 19–26; Peter Krentz, *The Battle of Marathon* (New Haven: Yale University Press, 2010), Ch. 2; Peter Krentz, "Hoplite Hell: How Hoplites Fought," in *Men of Bronze: Hoplite Warfare in Ancient Greece*, ed. Donald Kagan and Gregory Viggiano (Princeton: Princeton University Press, 2013).

37. George Cawkwell, *The Greek Wars: The Failure of Persia* (Oxford: Oxford University Press, 2005), 237–54; Brosius, *Persians*, 58–63; Christopher Tuplin, "All the King's Horse: In Search of Achaemenid Persian Cavalry," in *New Perspectives on Ancient Warfare*, ed. Garret G. Fagan and Matthew Trundle (Leiden: Brill, 2010); Michael B. Charles, "The Persian Καρδακες," *Journal of Hellenic Studies* 132 (2012).

the Persians hoped to fight on the coastal plain, where their maneuverability would favor them.

After several days of waiting, Persian supplies were running low, and Hippias had not been able to gather the hoped-for local support. The Persian force decided to change tactics. Rather than try to push through toward Athens overland, they began to load their troops back into their ships to sail around Attica, land at Athens, and capture the largely undefended city. Once the Persian forces were occupied with that task, the Athenians seized the opportunity to strike. Advancing at a swift pace to close with the Persians before suffering too many losses to their arrows and cavalry, the Athenians engaged and defeated the Persian forces that had not yet embarked.[38] Meanwhile, the troops already aboard ship carried on with their plan. They may have had contact with pro-Persian factions in the city, which encouraged them to make the attempt on Athens with a reduced force, but the Athenian army ran overland from Marathon back to Athens, a distance of forty-two kilometers, and drew up outside the city prepared for another fight. The Persian ships turned back rather than chance a landing.

Darius prepared another army to attack Greece, but events in Egypt intervened. A large part of the Persian fleet in the Mediterranean was crewed by Egyptians, and the decade of fighting in the Aegean had become a strain on them. Furthermore, Egyptian interests in Greek trade and mercenary recruitment were threatened by the ongoing turmoil in the Aegean. Neither Cambyses nor Darius had ever fully brought the semi-independent delta aristocrats and their armed retinues under control, and in 487 these local leaders began to cause problems for the Persian administration in the province. The army intended for the Aegean was diverted to Egypt where a show of strength was sufficient to quell the revolt. The delta aristocrats chose not to make a stand against this force but to save their resources for a better opportunity.

---

38. See the detailed reconstructions of the battle in Richard A. Billows, *Marathon: How One Battle Changed Western Civilization* (New York: Overlook Duckworth, 2010), 203–33; Krentz, *Marathon*, Ch. 6. Also note the problems raised by N. Whatley, "On the Possibility of Reconstructing Marathon and Other Ancient Battles," *Journal of Hellenic Studies* 84 (1964). Hyland's review of Billows and Krentz provides an excellent summary of the unresolved questions in the study of this battle and Persian-Greek conflicts in general: John O. Hyland, "Contesting Marathon: Billows, Krentz, and the Persian Problem," *Classical Philology* 106, no. 3 (July 2011).

Xerxes' Aegean Campaign

Darius died in 486 before he could take any further steps on the northwestern frontier. He was succeeded by his son Xerxes I, whose legitimacy, unlike his father's, was never in doubt. Xerxes accordingly felt less bound to prove himself by traditional standards of kingliness and freer to experiment with new policies.[39] In particular, he took a harder line in Egypt. While Cambyses and Darius had presented themselves as Egyptian pharaohs and largely worked within local tradition, Xerxes relied more on armed force to keep Egypt in line. He also adopted a new approach to Greece, setting aside his father's strategy of diplomacy and limited military intervention for a concerted campaign of conquest.

A revolt in Babylon in 484 required his attention first and may have diverted some troops and supplies from the Aegean, but preparations were soon under way for a major operation in 480. The king mustered an army, and his western satraps assembled a fleet. The Persians reasserted their authority in the northern Aegean, where King Amyntas I of Macedonia confirmed his status as a Persian vassal by arranging marriages between women of the Macedonian court and Persian nobles.[40] A bridge of boats was constructed across the Hellespont for the army to cross, while a canal was dug across the Athos peninsula to allow the fleet to bypass the treacherous waters at the headland. Xerxes intended to make a swift and decisive conquest in Greece.

Such a campaign required a substantial force. The size of Xerxes' army has been a matter of great debate among historians, but a cautious reading of Herodotus and comparison with archaeological evidence suggests a force of between 50,000 and 100,000, with the number most likely at the lower end of that range.[41] The ten thousand professional troops called the Immortals—because the unit was always replenished

---

39. Robert J. Littman, "The Religious Policy of Xerxes and the *Book of Esther*," *Jewish Quarterly Review*, new series 65, no. 3 (January 1975).
40. Marek Jan Olbrycht, "Macedonia and Persia," in *A Companion to Ancient Macedonia*, ed. Joseph Roisman and Ian Worthington (Malden, MA: Blackwell, 2010), 342–69, esp. 343.
41. F. Maurice, "The Size of the Army of Xerxes in the Invasion of Greece in 480 B.C.," *Journal of Hellenic Studies* 50, no. 2 (1930); Cuyler T. Young, "480–479 BC: A Persian Perspective," *Iranica Antiqua* 15 (1980); Peter R. Barkworth, "The Organization of Xerxes' Army," *Iranica Antiqua* 27 (1993); Cawkwell, *Greek Wars*, 247–52.

with fresh troops after suffering any casualties—formed the core of the army.[42] Additional forces drawn from the empire's peoples made up the rest. The fleet was composed of Egyptian, Phoenician, and Ionian ships.

The limiting factor on the size of the army was supplies, most importantly food.[43] People performing demanding physical labor, like soldiers at war, need a steady intake of calories and protein. In the ancient world, this meant a ration of grain, consumed as bread, biscuits, or porridge. At a minimum, each soldier required one kilogram of grain each day. Cavalry horses needed at least nine kilograms of fodder for each day of marching or fighting, when they could not graze.[44] At a conservative estimate of 45,000 infantry and 5,000 cavalry, Xerxes' army would have required a bare minimum of ninety-five metric tons of grain each day. It would have been impossible for the army to carry all these supplies on the march along with its gear, weapons, tents, and other baggage. While Persia's allies in the Greek world contributed to feeding the army, the only way to reliably deliver such quantities of supplies was by ship. Xerxes' army could not survive without its supply fleet, and the supply fleet could not operate without an armada of warships to protect it from the Greeks. These two facts largely dictated the progress of the campaign.

As Xerxes prepared his army, the Greek world was far from unified in its response. Greece had always been fragmented, as neighboring cities competed over control of farmland and access to trade routes, and the internal politics of most Greek poleis were fraught with sometimes violent conflict between powerful families and factions. Ever since Cyrus' conquests had brought Persian power to the shores of the Aegean Sea, diplomatic relations between Greeks and Persians had been tangled in these local politics, and the attitudes Greek cities took toward the Persian Empire often had more to do with local concerns than with any sentiments about Persia. In the decades before Xerxes' invasion, the island of Aegina had sought Persian protection against Athens, and Athens had sought Persian aid against Sparta. The Plataeans joined the Athenians

---

42. Michael B. Charles, "Immortals and Apple Bearers: Towards a Better Understanding of Achaemenid Infantry Units," *Classical Quarterly*, new series 61, no. 1 (May 2001).
43. Jack Martin Balcer, "The Persian Wars Against Greece: A Reassessment," *Historia* Bd. 38, no. 2 (2nd quarter 1989): 127–43.
44. Donald W. Engels, *Alexander the Great and the Logistics of the Macedonian Army* (Berkeley: University of California Press, 1978), 123–30.

at Marathon less out of animosity against Persia than in the interest of securing Athenian support against Thebes. Exiled politicians, like the Athenian tyrant Hippias or the Spartan king Demaratus, sought refuge and support in Persian territory, while factions in Greece, like the influential Alcmaeonid family in Athens, contemplated the value of aligning themselves with Persia as a tool against their rivals. These same local power dynamics were as strong in 480 as they had been in the decades before, and they did much to shape how the Greek world responded to the advance of Xerxes' forces.

Some Greek cities organized a defensive alliance, which historians refer to as the Hellenic League (although this alliance was temporary and ad hoc, unlike the Delian and Peloponnesian leagues that would come to dominate Greek politics in the following century). No inter-polis organization on the scale of the Hellenic League had been attempted in Greece before, and the alliance was plagued with internal dissension.

Many Greek states remained neutral, and some of those that joined the alliance later dropped out, while still others chose to side with Persia. Argos, for one, remained neutral because of its long-running conflict with Sparta, and Athens's perennial rival Thebes switched sides from the league to Persia once Xerxes' army reached their city. Major forces in northern Greece, including the Macedonians and the Thessalians, sided with Persia. All told, the Hellenic League's forces represented only a small fraction of all the Greeks. Indeed, considering the Ionians under his rule and the cities that went over to the Persians, Xerxes could count more Greeks on his side than in the opposing alliance.

As the major forces in the Hellenic League, Sparta took the lead on land and Athens at sea. Further rancorous debates followed as the alliance hammered out a strategy. The first move was to station land and sea forces at natural choke points to delay the Persian advance. An early attempt to fortify the Tempe Gorge in the far north was abandoned as impractical. The next suitable site on land was at Thermopylae, where only a narrow strip of coastal plain lay between the rugged mountains and the sea. A small contingent of Greek forces led by the Spartan king Leonidas assembled there. A Greek fleet led by the Spartan commander Eurybiades, assisted by the Athenian Themistocles, based itself at Cape Artemisium nearby to guard the channel between the mainland and the northern tip of the long, narrow island of Euboea. It is unlikely that either position was expected to hold out indefinitely, but by slowing the

Persians down they put pressure on Xerxes' supply lines and made a swift conquest more difficult.[45]

On land, the Persian advance was blocked for several days as the Hellenic League forces at Thermopylae resisted Persian attempts to break through. Then the Persian forces were shown a mountain path by a local guide that allowed a small contingent of Immortals to get behind the Greek position and threaten to envelop them. Most of the Greek troops withdrew while a small force of Spartans, Thebans, and Thespians remained behind to cover the retreat.

At the same time, Persian and Greek naval forces clashed off of Cape Artemisium. The primary type of ship used on both sides was the trireme, a long, low warship propelled by oars. Although triremes were equipped with rams at their prows and were capable of striking and sinking other ships, ramming had not yet become the main method of naval warfare. Instead, most naval battles were fought by crews of archers and skirmishers on the upper decks who tried to board and capture enemy vessels. The Greek rowing crews were inexperienced in combat, but they maintained defensive positions that the Persians failed to penetrate. A trireme could not remain at sea indefinitely, however. Both fleets needed safe harborage on a friendly shore each night. Once the Greek land forces withdrew from Thermopylae, the Greek fleet had to fall back as well.

There was no other natural choke point between Thermopylae and the Isthmus of Corinth. Spartan-led forces took up a defensive position at the Isthmus and began constructing a wall there. Thebes, Athens, and the regions around them had to be abandoned to the Persians. Thebes surrendered rather than try to fight a siege against the Persians, who were experts at capturing cities. Xerxes treated the Thebans leniently, and Theban soldiers were incorporated into the Persian forces. The Athenians, expecting harsh treatment because of their history of antagonism with Persia, chose instead to evacuate their people. Only a small group held out in the temples on the acropolis, a rocky hill in the midst of the city where they expected the goddess Athena to protect them. Xerxes' forces captured the acropolis easily. Intentionally or accidentally, its temples were burned.

The obvious way forward was for the Persians to use their fleet to land troops in the Peloponnese behind the Spartans' defenses at the Isthmus,

---

45. J. A. S. Evans, "Notes on Thermopylae and Artemisium," *Historia* Bd. 18, no. 4 (August 1969).

but such an operation would be risky with the Greek fleet still in play. When Xerxes found the Greek fleet bottled up in the narrow straits between the Attic coast and the island of Salamis, it seemed like a perfect opportunity to eliminate this threat. Persian ships attacked at dawn, only to find that in the narrow waters of Salamis, Greek knowledge of local tides, winds, and currents mattered more than the superior rowing skill and maneuverability of the Persian ships. The Persian fleet was severely depleted in the ensuing battle.[46]

Defeat at Salamis changed the strategic picture. Ferrying troops to the Peloponnese was no longer an option, and, without a protecting fleet, supply ships could not safely bring in the food the Persian army counted on. In addition, fall was coming on and soon the stormy Mediterranean winter would make any sailing hazardous. Xerxes had no choice but to adapt his strategy. He withdrew along with part of the army, leaving the rest under the command of his general Mardonius. A swift conquest was now out of the question. Mardonius' forces fell back to Thessaly where they spent the winter with their local allies.

The next year, 479, Mardonius' army marched south unopposed. Attica was once again evacuated. The Hellenic League was fraying at the seams, and Mardonius encouraged its collapse by offering Athens a separate peace, but the Athenians rejected this offer and remained in the alliance. A Greek army led by the Spartan regent Pausanias marched out to confront Mardonius in southwestern Boeotia near Plataea.

Neither side was confident of victory. Their forces appear to have been about evenly matched numerically, but both were under strain. The Persians were running low on supplies while the Greek alliance was growing more disorganized. Both sides took up defensive positions and tried to induce the other side to attack first. For several days the Persians harassed the Greeks and attacked their supplies, and the Greeks repositioned their forces in response. Then an attempted Greek nighttime maneuver went awry and left their lines in disarray at daybreak. Mardonius misread the battlefield and thought that the Greek army was breaking up. He ordered a swift attack to try to catch the Greeks unprepared,

---

46. N. G. L. Hammond, "The Battle of Salamis," *Journal of Hellenic Studies* 76 (1956); W. Kendrick Pritchett, "Toward a Restudy of the Battle of Salamis," *American Journal of Archaeology* 63, no. 3 (July 1959); Barry Strauss, *The Battle of Salamis: The Naval Encounter That Saved Greece—and Western Civilization* (New York: Simon & Schuster, 2004), 157–208.

only to find that despite the confusion in their ranks they were ready for a fight. The battle was haphazard and poorly coordinated on both sides, but in the end the Greek forces prevailed.[47] At around the same time, the Greek fleet confronted the remnants of the Persian fleet at Mycale in Ionia and destroyed it. After their success at Plataea and Mycale, the allied Greeks pressed the attack and dislodged Persian garrisons from the northern Aegean, the islands, and Ionia.

The experience of the war was a traumatic one for the Greeks who fought against Xerxes, especially the Athenians who twice had to abandon their city and see it burned down. For generations afterwards, the member states of the Hellenic League claimed the legacy of resistance to Persia as a special honor. In typical fashion, this legacy itself became tangled up in the conflicts within and between cities as individual groups and peoples recast their versions of the story to magnify their own contributions to the war effort and disparage others. The Athenian-influenced narrative given by Herodotus, for instance, paints the Corinthians as cowards at Salamis and the Spartans as almost comically disorganized at Plataea.[48]

The weight given to the events of Marathon, Thermopylae, Salamis, and Plataea in Greek literature and art has influenced many modern scholars' perspectives as well. In recent centuries, many historians have accepted the Greek narrative at face value and asserted that Persian victory would have meant the extinguishing of Greek civilization, but this argument ignores the cultural policies of the Persian Empire. The consequences of a Persian victory under Darius or Xerxes may have been devastating in the short term for some cities like Athens and Sparta, but they would have allowed other cities, like Thebes and Argos, to thrive, much as the Ionian cities did under Persian rule, despite the disrupting effects of the Revolt and its suppression.[49] The Persians had no interest in stamping out Greek culture.[50] Indeed, Persian kings and satraps patronized Greek professionals, and elements of Greek art were incorporated

---

47. Paul W. Wallace, "The Final Battle at Plataia," *Hesperia Supplements* 19 (1982); Roel Konijnendijk, "'Neither the Less Valorous nor the Weaker': Persian Military Might and the Battle of Plataia," *Historia* Bd. 61, H. 1 (2012).
48. See Documents 10.9, section 94; 10.13, sections 53–57.
49. Pericles B. Georges, "Persian Ionia under Darius: The Revolt Reconsidered," *Historia* Bd. 49, H. 1 (1st quarter 2000).
50. Jack Martin Balcer, "The Greeks and the Persians: The Processes of Acculturation," *Historia* Bd. 32, H. 3 (3rd quarter 1983).

into the multicultural Achaemenid court style.[51] A Greece under Persian rule would have had different centers of political and cultural influence, but there is no reason why the art, literature, and philosophy that the Western world has often looked to for inspiration should not have flourished there.

The Persians took one important lesson from Xerxes' campaign: the only thing that could induce Greek cities to work together in common cause was the threat of foreign invasion. The Persians never attempted such a move again. Instead, their approach to the Aegean shifted back to one of diplomatic engagement with limited military intervention.

Persia's Troublesome Frontier

With Athens and Sparta riding high after their victories and Persian forces on the back foot, the western frontier became a more insistent problem for the Persian kings. The decades from the 470s to the 450s were a time for the Persian Empire to retrench and reevaluate its strategy in the West.

The Greek wartime alliance was short-lived, but it gave birth to a new force in Aegean politics: the Delian League. The Delian League was originally founded as an anti-Persian mutual defense alliance in which numerous cities committed troops and ships to a joint force under Athenian leadership. In the 470s and 460s, the League succeeded in expelling the last remnants of Persian presence in the Aegean and resisting small-scale attempts to reassert Persian control. In 466, a Delian League fleet defeated a Persian fleet at Cyprus, then landed its troops at the Eurymedon River in southern Anatolia where they defeated a Persian land force. After this defeat, Persian attempts to project military power in the Aegean stopped for a time.

Despite the successes of the Delian League, Greek politics continued to be fractious. The united front against Persia, such as it was, did not last. Both Themistocles, the Athenian naval leader responsible for the victory at Salamis, and Pausanias, the Spartan commander at Plataea, were accused by their political rivals of conspiring with Xerxes. Pausanias died while under suspicion, while Themistocles fled to Persia and ended

---

51. Brosius, *Persians*, 72–76.

his life in the king's service. The Spartans had no interest in joining the Delian League's activities, but began to build up an earlier alliance of their own, the Peloponnesian League, to protect their interests against Athens's increasingly aggressive attitude toward their fellow Greeks.

Xerxes was killed in 465 in an attempted coup. While the Persian court was consumed with the power struggle that followed, an aristocrat in the Egyptian delta named Inarus raised a rebellion. Inarus reached out to the Athenians, envisioning an Egyptian-Athenian alliance that could sweep away all Persian presence from the Mediterranean coast. The Athenians enthusiastically pursued this alliance and sent a large force to back Inarus' revolt. The Egyptian and Athenian joint force secured control of the delta and besieged the surviving Persian garrison in Memphis.

Once Xerxes' son Artaxerxes had secured himself in power as Artaxerxes I, he turned his attention to the problems in Egypt. His first move was to attempt to split the Egyptian-Athenian alliance by inducing Sparta to make war on Athens in 458, but the Spartans rejected his overtures. Artaxerxes then raised an army to retake the delta and relieve the garrison at Memphis. In the mid-450s, this force entered Egypt, defeated Inarus, and routed both the Athenian troops already in the country and a force of additional troops that had arrived unaware of the defeat.

Diplomacy and Stability

Despite Persia's success in Egypt, it was clear that the western frontier problem had not been solved. The delta aristocrats were as restive as ever, and campaigning in Egypt demanded a level of investment that weakened Persian presence elsewhere. The Athenians continued to make attacks on Persia's Mediterranean territories, now focusing on Cyprus. The only way forward for Persia was to keep Greece and Egypt separated. Since the conquest of Greece had proven unfeasible, the solution to this problem would have to be diplomatic.[52]

Artaxerxes achieved this goal, at least in the short term, in 450. Some ancient sources cite a treaty between Persia and Athens, known as the Peace of Callias, but it is unclear how formal the agreement was.

---

52. Edward Rung, "War, Peace, and Diplomacy in Graeco-Persian Relations from the Fourth to the Sixth Century BC," in *War and Peace in Ancient and Medieval History*, ed. Philip de Souza and John France (Cambridge: Cambridge University Press, 2008).

Nevertheless, for the next few decades both sides observed a détente: Athens did not interfere in Persia's western provinces, and Persia did not send forces into the Aegean. This détente held as long as the Delian League, now a de facto Athenian empire, was the dominant power in the Aegean.[53] Egypt remained quiet, knowing that Greek aid would not be forthcoming and that the Persians could commit their entire western forces to suppressing revolt if necessary.

The détente began to crumble in 431 when Athens and the Delian League entered into a series of wars with Sparta and the Peloponnesian League, collectively known as the Peloponnesian War. This long conflict sapped the resources of both sides and destabilized the whole Aegean. The Persians were reluctant to intervene directly, but they saw Sparta as a useful check on Athens. Through the mediation of a younger son of Artaxerxes—a prince known as Cyrus the Younger—Persia provided money to Sparta for building up its fleet to more effectively challenge the Athenian navy, in return for a promise to restore Persian control over the Ionian cities. This infusion of money allowed Sparta to build up its fleet and counteract Athens's advantage at sea, enabling Sparta's victory in 404. In the aftermath of this war, Sparta then threw its support behind its benefactor Cyrus' attempted coup against his older brother, Artaxerxes II. When the defeat of Cyrus' campaign soured relations between Persia and Sparta, the Spartans reneged on their pledge to hand over Ionia.

Meanwhile, Egyptians had been following the fortunes of the war in Greece, hoping for a distraction that would tie up Persian resources and open the way for another revolt. Cyrus' bid for the throne provided this opportunity. A revolt had begun in the western delta under the leadership of an aristocrat named Amyrtaeus in the last decade of the 400s. By dividing the Persian king's attention, Amyrtaeus and Cyrus benefited one another. While Cyrus' ambitions were quickly cut short, Amyrtaeus succeeded in ousting Persian troops and making himself king of an independent Egypt.

In the early 300s, Persia was faced with trouble in the West once more: an independent Egypt and an unstable Greece. Once again, these two regions had to be dealt with in relation to one another, but it was Greece that offered the opportunity. While Egypt, despite its internal conflicts,

---

53. Lisa Kallet, "The Origins of the Athenian Economic *Arche*," *Journal of Hellenic Studies* 133 (2013).

was broadly united in its opposition to Persia, Greeks were primarily occupied with their own problems. Greek cities' policies toward Persia were subordinate to their own rivalries with one another. The Persian Empire sought partners in the Greek world for establishing a stable order, sometimes financing one city's wars against others (although Greeks complained that Persian money was more often promised than delivered), and at other times acting as an arbiter and peacemaker between poleis.[54]

The Persians turned to diplomacy to reclaim Ionia from the Spartans. In 395, Athens, Corinth, Thebes, and Argos allied against Sparta in a conflict known as the Corinthian War. By shifting their patronage to the anti-Spartan alliance, the Persians accomplished the destruction of the Spartan fleet they had previously financed and the collapse of Sparta's position in Anatolia. By 387, Artaxerxes II was able to dictate the terms of a general peace treaty to be applied to all the states of Greece. The agreement, known as the King's Peace, restored Persian control over all of Anatolia and broke up the various alliances of cities that had been busy waging war against one another for the past decade. Artaxerxes empowered Sparta to enforce the terms of the agreement, with the threat that Persian forces would intervene against any polis that broke the peace.[55] While the King's Peace did not put a stop to all conflict in the Aegean, it did give Persia the stability it needed on its northwest frontier and finally freed up Persian resources to deal with Egypt. This peace deal became the model for future agreements among Greek cities down to the late 300s when the Macedonian kings Philip and Alexander followed its example as a way of organizing the Greek cities for their campaign against Persia.

The conflicts between Greeks and Persians, especially those of 490 and 480–479, remained a crucial part of Greek memory and self-definition for centuries. The narratives of these events were elaborated into a story of Greek triumph against Persian menace, which was eagerly deployed by Athenians, Spartans, and other Greeks for their own political purposes. For as long as Europeans and their colonial descendants have idolized

---

54. David M. Lewis, "Persian Gold in Greek International Relations," *Revue des Études Anciennes* T. 1, no. 1–2 (1989); Maria Brosius, "Persian Diplomacy between 'Pax Persica' and 'Zero Tolerance,'" in *Maintaining Peace and Interstate Stability in Archaic and Classical Greece*, ed. Julia Wilker (Mainz: Verlag-Antike, 2012).

55. Timothy T. B. Ryder, *Koine Eirene: General Peace and Local Independence in Ancient Greece* (London: Oxford University Press, 1965), 7–20.

ancient Greece, the legacy of Marathon, Thermopylae, Salamis, and Plataea has been claimed as a fundamental part of Western culture.[56]

While the Greek triumphalist narrative of the Greco-Persian Wars is still alive in popular Western memory, historians have returned to the period with more critical eyes. The discovery and interpretation of Persian texts, while not shedding any direct light on the conflicts in the Aegean, has led to a more nuanced understanding of the organization and ideology of the Persian Empire. Treating the wars in Greece not as unique events but as part of a larger imperial history has helped us understand Persian motivations in ways that go beyond simplistic ideas about a clash between "East" and "West."

Persia was not the first empire in the world, nor was Greece the first troublesome frontier region whose internal problems spilled over into an empire's affairs, but it is from Greece that we first get detailed accounts of the tensions and problems of an imperial frontier from the point of view of those on the outside who lived with the day-to-day consequences of imperial policies. The slow evolution of Persia's strategy for dealing with Greece is visible to us in ways that similar processes from other times and places often are not. Many states in history have had to learn the same lessons that the Persians learned in Greece: that the problems of one distant frontier region can spill over into another, that military force is not always a solution, and that an empire cannot simply make its own reality and ignore the facts on the ground even in seemingly insignificant and faraway places. The real legacy of the Greco-Persian Wars in world history is not the heroic legend of stalwart Spartans at Thermopylae but the insight it gives us into the complexities and consternations of an imperial frontier.

---

56. See the contributions to Emma Bridges, Edith Hall, and P. J. Rhodes, eds., *Cultural Responses to the Persian Wars: Antiquity to the Third Millennium* (Oxford: Oxford University Press, 2007).

ABOUT THE SOURCES

Our knowledge of the Persian Empire and its interactions with the Greek world comes from several different kinds of sources. These sources were created in different times and places, for different purposes, and with different intended audiences. Using these sources effectively requires recognizing their distinct characteristics.

Persian sources

A tradition of writing historical narratives, often to serve the purposes of royal propaganda, existed in Mesopotamia and Egypt for thousands of years before the rise of the Persian Empire. The Persians adopted this tradition and some examples of it survive, such as the Bisitun Rock inscription celebrating Darius' triumphs as king. Other examples may have been lost, having been recorded on more perishable materials. Since Greece was not a place of much concern to most Persian kings, however, relations with Greece figure very little in Persian historical texts. We turn instead to other types of sources which offer us insight into how the empire worked, how the Persian kings thought about themselves and their empire, and how the Persians wished to be perceived by others inside and outside their empire.

Administrative texts
The empire required a sophisticated bureaucracy to track the collection and spending of revenues, whether in coin or in goods. The Persian bureaucracy was modeled on the examples of earlier such systems among the Elamites and the various states of Mesopotamia. The Persians took on not only the record-keeping practices of these earlier models but also their languages. The primary languages of the Persian bureaucracy were Elamite and Aramaic.

Elamite was spoken in the southwestern mountains of the Iranian plateau where the Persian empire first began its expansion. It was written with a system based on Mesopotamian cuneiform. Cuneiform texts are written using symbols made up of wedge-shaped marks made in soft clay with a triangular stylus. These symbols can represent sounds, combinations of sounds, whole words, or concepts. Aramaic was a Semitic language originating in the northern Levant which had come to be widely used as a common language for trade in the Levant and Mesopotamia. It had its own writing system which was developed for writing with ink on papyrus or thin sheets of leather. Examples of both Elamite and Aramaic administrative texts have survived, with some significant collections coming from the reign of Darius I.

These texts are generally short and formulaic. They record essential information for managing the empire's finances such as the collection of taxes, the paying of wages to workers, and the distribution of goods to elite members of the royal household and administration. They were not intended to be public or necessarily to be kept for the long term. They do, however, indicate that the various parts of the empire and its administration were in regular contact through letters and memoranda, few examples of which survive. The peoples of the empire could also use the bureaucracy to communicate with the royal court in order to resolve local problems; an example of such communications is known from Aramaic records dealing with relations between Jewish mercenary soldiers stationed at Elephantine in Egypt and the local population.

Although administrative texts of this type provide little information about Persian relations with the Greeks, they give us important insights into how the empire functioned on a day-to-day basis.

Public inscriptions

Another important set of texts gives us a different view of the Persian Empire. Public inscriptions were carved into the walls of some buildings at administrative centers like Persepolis and Susa. Other inscriptions were carved into cliff faces near well-traveled roadways such as the major inscription at Bisitun Rock at the western edge of the Iranian plateau.

Many of these inscriptions contain the same texts carved in multiple languages, often including Elamite and Akkadian, one of the major languages of Mesopotamia. In the reign of Darius I, Persians also began to use a variation of cuneiform to write their own language, known today as Old Persian, which appears in public inscriptions from the time of

Darius on. In some regions like Egypt, where public inscriptions were part of the local tradition, local languages were also used.

These inscriptions were mostly statements of ideology and propaganda, setting out idealized visions of the kings' role as leaders of a unified and peaceful empire in harmony with the gods. Like all such political propaganda, these texts cannot be taken as objective reflections of the reality of the empire, but they provide valuable insight into how the Persian kings wished to be perceived by those they ruled over.

It is not clear how many people actually read these inscriptions. Throughout the ancient world, literacy rates were low. In addition, some of these inscriptions were on buildings that members of the general public would rarely, if ever, have had access to. On the other hand, there is evidence that some of these texts were also copied out and distributed in multiple languages. The target audience for such copies was probably limited to the elite among the empire's peoples, but they could themselves be a channel for disseminating the Persian kings' messages.

Greek sources

Most of our information about Persian actions in the Aegean come from Greek authors. Since Greeks had local knowledge of and a direct stake in the Aegean world—a region that was rarely a priority for the Persians—we may look to these sources for a more detailed reflection of Greco-Persian relations than we get from the Persian side. At the same time, Persian power was a problematic force in Greek politics. Some cities, like Argos and Thebes, had a history of cooperation with Persia. Others, like Athens and Sparta, made resistance to Persia a key part of their self-identity. Greeks who wrote about Persians and their history with the Greeks were never neutral observers.

This collection includes selections from numerous Greek authors who wrote in different times and for different purposes. Some have much to tell us about interactions between the Greek and Persian worlds; others provide small but useful insights.

Aeschylus (525–455 BCE)
An Athenian playwright and the only eyewitness to the Greco-Persian Wars of 490–479 BCE to have left a surviving account of any part of the

conflict. Aeschylus' tragedy *The Persians* is a fascinating work of imagination, an Athenian attempt to retell the story of Xerxes' campaign from a Persian point of view.

Bacchylides (c. 518–c. 451 BCE)
A Greek lyric poet. One of his poems gives us the earliest Greek mention of Cyrus' conquest of Lydia, which first brought Greek cities under Persian rule, although Bacchylides had nothing to say about the politics of this event and was more interested in it as an example of dramatic divine intervention.

Herodotus (484–425 BCE)
A historian from the Greek city of Halicarnassus and our most important source for the events from the Ionian Revolt in 499 to the end of Xerxes' campaign in 479. Herodotus wrote his *Histories* based on extensive personal research and interviews with eyewitnesses, including some Persian sources. Herodotus favored the Greek opposition to Persia, but he was also frequently critical of both individual Greek leaders and communities as a whole. His attitude toward Persia was similarly complex. While he opposed the Persian conquest of Greece, he was sympathetic to Persians as a people and made sure to point out examples of nobility and wisdom in their history.

Herodotus' accounts of the battles between Greek and Persian forces have caused no end of consternation among modern historians. Although he was an astute observer of politics and culture, in military matters he was an amateur and wrote with an amateur's love of drama and spectacle rather than a professional's appreciation of the practicalities of combat.

Thucydides (460–400 BCE)
An Athenian historian who wrote the *History of the Peloponnesian War*, a detailed narrative of events in Greece in his own lifetime, most crucially the war between the Athenian-led Delian League and the Spartan-led Peloponnesian League (431–404). A careful observer of politics and an experienced general in his own right, Thucydides provides valuable insights into the ongoing entanglement of the Greek world with the Persian Empire in the generations after Xerxes' campaign.

Xenophon (c. 431–354 BCE)
An Athenian writer, philosopher, and adventurer who left many works on a wide variety of subjects. Several of his works contain observations on the Persian Empire and its involvement in the Greek world, including *The Education of Cyrus*, a fictionalized biography of Cyrus II; the *Hellenica*, a continuation of Thucydides' *History* which covers the end of the Peloponnesian War and important military and political events in Greece in the following decades; and the *Anabasis*, an account of Xenophon's time as a mercenary soldier following the Persian prince Cyrus the Younger in his attempt to take the throne from his brother Artaxerxes II.

Ctesias (late fifth c.–early fourth c. BCE)
A Greek physician who lived in Persia and served as personal doctor to Artaxerxes II. Ctesias wrote a history of Persia based on what he had learned from living at the Persian court. The original text of this history, called the *Persica*, does not survive, and his work is known primarily through a summary written by the Byzantine scholar Photius in the ninth century CE. Ctesias dismissed the works of other Greeks who had written about Persian history, especially Herodotus, but his close relationship with the Persian court also sometimes led him to be less critical of the Persian Empire and its history than those who wrote from an outside perspective.

Plato (428/7–348/7 BCE)
The philosopher and student of Socrates was not much concerned with the Persian Empire, although it occasionally furnished examples for him to draw on in his philosophical dialogues.

Diodorus of Sicily (first c. BCE)
A Greek historian whose *Library of History* was an attempt to compile the work of earlier historians into a general history of the world. Diodorus had no direct knowledge of the Persian Empire, but he preserves the work of many earlier authors whose own writings are now lost, including works that cover events in Greco-Persian history that are not otherwise documented. The quality of Diodorus' historical writing is dependent on the quality of the sources he used. When it comes to the history of Greeks and Persians, Diodorus' sources were often full of pro-Greek, and specifically pro-Athenian, propaganda, but for some events no better sources survive.

Dio Chrysostom (40–115 CE)
A Greek writer from the period of the Roman Empire. Although he has little to say about the Greco-Persian Wars in general, one of his rhetorical essays includes a secondhand report of how the outcome of the wars was remembered in Persia.

Plutarch (46–120 CE)
A prolific Greek scholar and antiquarian who worked under the Roman Empire. One of his major works, the *Parallel Lives*, included biographies of famous figures from Greek history matched up with biographies of famous figures from Roman history who had similar lives and accomplishments. The Greek biographies include many individuals who were important in Greco-Persian relations. He also composed a biography of the Persian king Artaxerxes II. Since Plutarch drew on many sources that are lost today, he sometimes provides useful pieces of information we would not otherwise know.

Arrian (86–160 CE)
Author of a history of the Macedonian king Alexander the Great's conquest of the Persian Empire. Although he wrote many centuries after Alexander's campaign, which itself came long after the Persian wars in the Aegean, it preserves a few useful details about Persia at the time of the Macedonian conquest.

In addition to these literary sources, a number of inscriptions carved in stone provide information about the Greeks and their history with Persia. Some of these inscriptions provide narrative accounts similar to those given by the authors listed above, while others represent the wide variety of experiences that Greeks had in the larger world, such as graffiti left by Greek soldiers in the service of the Egyptian kings or the marks of stone-cutters in Persian quarries.

Other sources

Some of the other peoples who lived in or near the Persian Empire also had literary traditions and recorded details of their interactions with the Persians or the Greeks. The most important of these texts come from the

Egyptians and the Jews. These sources offer perspectives from outside the context of Greco-Persian relations, but they have complexities of their own.

Egypt was one of the Persian Empire's major rivals as a superpower in the larger sphere of eastern Mediterranean and southwestern Asian politics. After being conquered by the Persians under Cambyses, Egypt remained a persistent trouble spot and site of repeated revolts against Persian rule, but not all Egyptians felt the same way. Some worked with the Persians and supported Persian rule in Egypt. Egyptian sources on the Persians present a mixture of responses and attitudes.

The Jews had a different history with Persia. The Jews had suffered depredations and forced relocation at the hands of the Assyrian and Neo-Babylonian empires. Persian policies significantly improved the lot of the Jews, who were able to return to their homeland and rebuild their temple in Jerusalem. When Persians appear in the Jewish tradition, they tend to be seen in a positive light.

Egyptian and Jewish sources help fill out our picture of the Persian Empire and its relations with its neighbors and subjects. In addition, an inscription from Lycia, in southwestern Anatolia, records the accomplishments of a local king, which included his role in facilitating negotiations between Persia and the Greek city of Sparta, another glimpse at Greco-Persian interactions.

Notes on the translations

[. . .]   Text missing from the original
[text]   Text restored or supplied by the translator
(. . .)   Text omitted by the translator
(?)   Translation uncertain

Where dates and units of measure can be confidently converted to modern dates or measures, I have done so in the translations. Where there is uncertainty, I have left the original terms and added an explanatory note.

Names

Many of the languages of the ancient near east, such as Egyptian, Akkadian, and Old Persian, were lost to modern scholarship for many centuries. As a result, many important figures, such as Persian kings and satraps, were known only by the Hellenized or Latinized versions of their names used by Greek and Roman authors. Since the nineteenth century, scholars have made great strides in recovering and interpreting these lost languages, so that today we know what many of these historical figures were called in their own languages. Most such names, however, are still unfamiliar to those who are not specialists in the field, and students and scholars alike continue to use the more familiar classical names. These facts present a problem for historians and translators: while it would be more accurate to refer to the Persian king who invaded Greece in 480 as Khshayarsha, for instance, it would be hard for nonspecialists to recognize that he is the same person better known to us by the name the Greeks used for him: Xerxes.

I have tried to strike a balance in the translations in this book, aiming to use the name that would be most useful to the reader interested in looking for further research. For major figures, such as Persian or Egyptian kings, whose names are well known in Hellenized versions, I use the conventional names. For less significant figures, who are mostly known from documents interpreted from their original language, I use a transliterated version of the original name.

Nevertheless, since it may be useful for some readers to find the original names of figures mostly known through Greek or Roman sources, I include here a list of such figures mentioned in the text with both their conventional names and their original names. This list also includes alternative spellings of some Greek names, which may help readers find further scholarship. Names shared by several individuals are listed only once.

Some Persian names are known only from Elamite texts, which may not accurately reflect original Persian pronunciations. The transliteration of names from non-Western writing systems is a matter of scholarly convention.

Conventional name	Original/alternative name	Original language
Aeschylus	Aiskhylos	Greek
Amasis	Ahmose	Egyptian
Amyrtaeus	Amenirdisu	Egyptian
Apries	Wahibre Haaibre	Egyptian
Ariaramens	Ariyamana	Old Persian
Artabazus	Artavazhda	Old Persian
Artaphernes[1]	Artafarna	Old Persian
Artaphrenes	Artafarna	Old Persian
Artaxerxes	Artakhsharça	Old Persian
Artystone	Irtashduna	Old Persian/Elamite
Atossa	Utautha	Old Persian
Cambyses	Kabujia	Old Persian
Croesus	Kroisos	Lydian/Greek
Cyaxares	Uvakhshtra	Old Persian
Cyrus	Kurush	Old Persian
Darius	Daryaush	Old Persian
Datis	Datiya	Old Persian
Gobryas	Gaubaruva	Old Persian
Hydarnes	Vidarna	Old Persian
Hystaspes	Vishtaspa	Old Persian
Mardonius	Marduniya	Old Persian
Megabyzus	Bagabukhsha	Old Persian
Nabondius	Nabu-naid	Akkadian
Nebuchadnezzar	Nabu-kudurri-usur	Akkadian
Necho	Nekau	Egyptian
Otanes	Utana	Old Persian
Pharnaces	Parnaka	Old Persian
Phraortes	Fravartish	Old Persian
Pissouthnes	Pishishyoathna	Old Persian
Psammetichus	Psamtik	Egyptian
Tissaphernes	Chithrafarnah	Old Persian
Xerxes	Khshayarsha	Old Persian

ch can also be written as č
kh can also be written as x
sh can also be written as š

---

[1]. The names Artaphernes and Artaphrenes are sometimes used interchangeably in Greek sources for the same individuals.

DOCUMENTS

SECTION 1
Organization of the Persian Empire

1.1: Darius' inscription from Susa

DSe[1]

This inscription by Darius I lays out much of the Persian kings' fundamental ideology and claims to power. Signs of good rule such as victorious military campaigns and successful building projects are celebrated, as is the importance of establishing benevolent peace and order within the empire.

[1] Ahura Mazda is a great god, who created this earth, who created the sky, who created man, who created happiness for man, who made Darius king, one king of many, one lord of many.

[2] I am Darius, the Great King, king of kings, king of lands containing many men, king of this great earth far and wide, son of Hystaspes, an Achaemenid, a Persian, son of a Persian, an Aryan, having Aryan lineage.

[3] King Darius says: "By the favor of Ahura Mazda these are the countries which I seized outside Persia. I ruled over them, and they brought me tribute. They did what I told them. My law held them firm. Media, Elam, Parthia, Aria, Bactria, Sogdiana, Chorasmia, Drangiana, Arachosia, Sattagydia, Gandara, Sind, Amyrgian Scythians, Scythians with pointed caps, Babylonia, Assyria, Arabia, Egypt, Armenia, Cappadocia, Sardis, Ionia, Scythians from across the [Black] Sea, Skudra, Ionians who wear shield-shaped hats,[2] Libyans, Ethiopians, men from Maka, Carians."

---

1. Translation adapted from Brosius, *Persian Empire*, no. 46.
2. Ionians who wear shield-shaped hats: Macedonians (referring to a flat, broad-brimmed hat called a *petasos*).

[4] King Darius says: "I changed many bad things that had been done to good things. By the favor of Ahura Mazda I dealt with the countries which fought against each other, where peoples were killing each other, so that their people do not kill each other any more, and I returned everyone to their place. And in the face of my decisions, they respected them in such a way that the strong neither beats nor deprives the weak."

[5] King Darius says: "By the favor of Ahura Mazda, I completed many building projects which had previously been abandoned. I saw that the fortification walls [of Susa], which had previously been built, had fallen into disrepair from age, and I rebuilt them. These are the fortification walls which I rebuilt."

[6] King Darius says: "May Ahura Mazda and the [other] gods protect me, and my royal house, and what I have inscribed."

1.2: Darius' account of the empire

DPe 1–2[3]

This inscription from Persepolis lists the lands over which Darius I asserted power. Starting with the core territories of Elam, Media, and Mesopotamia (Babylonia and Assyria), the list then moves to the outer provinces, following a loose clockwise trajectory from Egypt through Anatolia to Central Asia. This list mostly corresponds with the list given in Document 1.1, but the inclusion of both Ionian Greeks ("Greeks who are by the sea") and mainland Greeks indicates something of Darius' attitude to the northwestern frontier.

[1] I am Darius, the Great King, king of kings, king of many countries, son of Hystaspes, an Achaemenid.

[2] King Darius says: "By the favor of Ahura Mazda these are the countries which I received into my possession along with the Persian people, who feared me and who brought me tribute: Elam, Media, Babylonia, Arabia, Assyria, Egypt, Armenia, Cappadocia, Sardis, Greeks[4] who

---

3. Translation adapted from Brosius 133.
4. The Persians used the word *Yauna*, from the Greek word *Iones*, meaning "Ionians," to refer to all Greeks.

are on the mainland, Greeks who are by the sea, Sagartia, Parthia, Drangiana, Aria, Bactria, Sogdiana, Chorasmia, Sattagydia, Arachosia, Sind, Gandara, Scythia, Maka."

1.3: The Demotic Chronicle: Restoring the laws of Egypt

BN 215, C 6–16[5]

This account of Darius engaging with the laws of Egypt, though fragmentary, reflects the Persian attitude of accommodation. Local traditions were respected and continued, and members of the local elite were entrusted with important matters of governance in their territory.

The affairs which occurred after those which have been written in the book of laws since year 44 of the Pharaoh Amasis until the day when Cambyses became ruler of Egypt.

Cambyses died [. . .] before he reached his country. Darius became king, and the rulers of the entire earth obeyed him because of the greatness of his heart. He wrote to his satrap in Egypt in his third year and said:

"May the wise men be brought to me [. . .] among the warriors, the priests, and the scribes of Egypt [. . .] Have them write down the laws of Egypt up to year 44 of the Pharaoh Amasis."

The law [. . .] of the temples and the people was brought here [. . .] a papyrus up to year 19 [. . .] Egypt. They were [. . .] in year 27. They wrote a copy on papyrus, one in Assyrian script and one in documentary script.[6] It was completed in his presence. Nothing was omitted.

---

5. Translation adapted from Brosius 55.
6. "Assyrian script" is Aramaic, a language widely used for trade and administration in the Persian Empire; "documentary script" is the demotic form of writing used in Egypt.

1.4: Native rulers in Cilicia and Cyprus

Xenophon, *The Education of Cyrus* 7.4.1–2

Xenophon's account of the reign of Cyrus, although heavily fictionalized, includes some useful insights into the working of the Persian Empire, such as this story which conveys important aspects of the relationship between the king and his subjects.

[1] The Carians[7] fell into civil war and fought among themselves. Since both sides had well-defended strongholds, they both called upon Cyrus to intervene. While Cyrus himself stayed in Sardis to make rams and siege engines for battering down the walls of any who refused to surrender, he sent Andousius, a Persian who was neither foolish nor cowardly but a perfect gentleman, into Caria with an army.

The Cilicians[8] and Cypriots joined this expedition with great enthusiasm, [2] for which he never imposed a Persian satrap on them but was always content to have them governed by their own native rulers. He did, however, receive tribute from them, and he called on them whenever he had need of troops.

1.5: A royal woman requisitions wine and sheep

Women in the Persian royal family controlled substantial economic resources, as suggested by these records of Darius' wife Artystone requisitioning wine and sheep, perhaps as part of organizing a feast, or simply provisioning her household.

PF 1795

A message to Yamaksheda, the wine carrier, from Pharnaces: Issue 2,000 liters of wine to Princess Artystone.[9] By the king's order.

---

7. Caria: a region in southwestern Anatolia.
8. Cilicia: a region in southeastern Anatolia.
9. The Elamite word *dukshish* is conventionally translated as "princess," but can refer to any woman of the royal family. Artystone, in this case, was the daughter of one king (Cyrus), sister of another (Cambyses), and wife of a third (Darius).

March/April, 503 BCE.[10] Ansukka wrote the text. Mazara conveyed the message.

Fort. 6754[11]

A message to Harriena, the herdsman, from Pharnaces: King Darius commanded me in these words: "Issue 100 sheep from my estate to Princess Artystone."

Now Pharnaces says: As the king commanded me, I command you: Issue 100 sheep to Princess Artystone as the king ordered.

March/April, 503 BCE. Ansukka wrote the text. Mazara conveyed the message.

1.6: Estate workers receive their pay

These examples of records for the payment of workers' wages give us some insight into the Persian economy. Although the Persians did not interfere with slave economies among the peoples they governed, such as the Greeks, they made little use of slaves themselves. Workers on Persian estates were paid, usually in grain, wine, beer, sheep, or other commodities.

Workers of different ages and levels of skill or responsibility received different wages. Among the highest-paid workers on an estate we find the arashshara, a woman who oversaw the work of other laborers. Otherwise, male and female workers of comparable age and skill received equal pay. Women who gave birth received an additional allotment of food to help them recover from the rigors of childbirth.

---

10. The months of the Persian calendar do not exactly line up with the months of the Gregorian calendar used in the West today. In the original texts, the years are counted from the beginning of the current king's reign (in this case, Darius).
11. This text can be found in George G. Cameron, "Darius' Daughter and the Persepolis Inscriptions," *Journal of Near Eastern Studies* 1, no. 2 (April 1942): 216. Cameron interprets Artystone as Darius' daughter, a reading now known to be incorrect.

PF 1028

Those who work for Irdabama at Shiraz received a total of 11,100 liters of grain as their rations. Kuntukka supplied the grain. Rashda determined the allotments.

August/September, 500 BCE.
62 men received 30 liters each.
8 boys received 25 liters each.
34 boys received 20 liters each.
26 boys received 15 liters each.
19 boys received 10 liters each.
22 boys received 5 liters each.
190 women received 30 liters each.
32 women received 20 liters each.
11 girls received 25 liters each.
20 girls received 20 liters each.
24 girls received 15 liters each.
17 girls received 10 liters each.
25 girls received 5 liters each.
Total: 480 workers.
Sealed by Rashda.

PF 876

One *arashshara* of the female workers at Umpuranush received 30 liters of wine as her ration. Irtuppiya supplied the wine. Irshena determined the allotment.

April/May, 500 BCE.

PF 847

Female workers at Liduma received 2,615 liters of grain as their rations for one month. Irtuppiya supplied the grain. Irshena determined the allotments.

July/August, 501 BCE.

PF 1226

20 liters of grain was collected from Sharukba and provided to Lanunu, a woman who gave birth to a boy.

10 liters of grain was collected and provided to Parrukkizzish, a woman who gave birth to a girl.

A total of two women who had given birth received grain. Manzaturrush and his companions collected it and gave it to them.

June/July, 499 BCE. At Tikrakkash.

PF-NN 358

Lanunu, a woman who gave birth to a boy, received 10 liters of wine. Irkezza supplied the wine.

Parrukkizzish, a woman who gave birth to a girl, received 5 liters of wine.

A total of two women who had given birth received wine. Manzaturrush and his companions collected it and gave it to them.

June/July, 499 BCE. At Tikrakkash.

1.7: Royal women's property

The property of royal women included tracts of agricultural land. The revenues from these lands were conventionally designated to pay for rich garments for the ladies of the court, although in practice women seem to have had a fair amount of control over how they spent their money.

Plato, *Alcibiades* 1 123b–c

[b] I once heard from a very trustworthy man who had been to the Persian court that he had traveled through a stretch of fine country, nearly a full day's journey in length, which the local inhabitants called the Queen's Belt, and another that is called her [c] Veil. Many other rich and beautiful lands are similarly designated for her adornment, each being named for a different item of her apparel.

Herodotus, *Histories* 2.98

Anthylla [in Egypt] is a town worth mentioning, which has been given to the king's wife to furnish her with shoes, and has been so for as long as the Persians have ruled Egypt.

Xenophon, *Anabasis* 1.4.9

The country through which they marched[12] had been given to Parysatis[13] to pay for her belts.

1.8: Non-Persian workers in Persia

The workers in Persia included people of many ethnicities, such as these Lycians and Lydians, from western Anatolia, who received pay at the same scale as other workers (compare Document 1.6).

PF 1049

360 liters of grain provided by Puksha, as ordered by Irtuppiya in a sealed document. Umadadda received it and distributed it to Lycian crafters.

March/April, 500 BCE.
5 men received 30 liters each.
1 boy received 15 liters.
6 women received 30 liters each.
1 girl received 15 liters.
Total: 13 workers.

PF 873

1,215 liters of flour provided by Irishtimanka as rations to the men of Sardis,[14] blacksmiths, who work at Kurra. Irshena determined the allotments.

For a period of three months: January through March, 499 BCE.
9 men received 45 liters each.
Total: 9 workers.

---

12. Referring to the travels of a mercenary army raised by Cyrus the Younger in 401 BCE. See Document 13.6.
13. Parysatis: the principal wife of King Darius II.
14. Sardis: capital of Lydia.

SECTION 2
Persian ideology

2.1: Darius' second inscription from Naqsh-e Rustam

DNb 1–10[1]

In this inscription from Naqsh-e Rustam, Darius lays out the ideal qualities of a Persian king: justice, moderation, benevolence, and skill as a warrior and commander.

[1] Ahura Mazda is a great god, who created this excellent work which is seen, who created happiness for man, who bestowed wisdom and courage upon Darius the king.

[2] King Darius says: "By the favor of Ahura Mazda I am of such a kind that I am a friend of the Right, and not a friend of the Wrong. It is not my desire that the weak man should suffer injustice at the hands of the strong. It is not my desire that the strong man should suffer injustice from the weak.

[3] I desire what is right. I am not a friend of the man who follows the Lie.[2] I am not hot-tempered. I hold firmly in control the things that arise in me during a dispute. I am firmly in control of myself.

[4] I reward the man who seeks to contribute according to his efforts. I punish the man who does harm according to the harm done. I do not wish that a man should do harm, nor do I wish that he who does harm should go unpunished.

[5] What a man says against another man does not convince me until I hear the testimony of both.

---

1. Translation adapted from Brosius 103.
2. the Lie: the force of evil opposed by Ahura Mazda and his chosen representative, the king of Persia.

[6] I am content with what a man brings [as tribute] according to his abilities. My pleasure is great, and I am well disposed toward him.

[7] Of such a kind is my understanding and judgment. When you see or hear of what I have done in the palace and on the battlefield, this is the power which I possess over my mind and my understanding.

[8] This indeed is my courage as far as my body possesses the strength. As a commander, I am a good commander. The right decision is immediately taken according to my understanding when I meet a rebel or when I meet [someone who is] not a rebel. By my understanding and judgment, I know that I am above panic when I meet a rebel or when I meet [someone who is] not a rebel.

[9] I am trained in my hands and in my feet. As a horseman, I am a good horseman. As a bowman, I am a good bowman, both on foot and on horseback. As a spearman, I am a good spearman, both on foot and on horseback.

[10] These are the skills which Ahura Mazda has bestowed upon me, and which I have been strong enough to exercise. By the favor of Ahura Mazda, what I have done, I have achieved with the skills that Ahura Mazda has bestowed upon me.

2.2: Xerxes' *daiva* inscription

XPh[3]

Xerxes made a more forceful assertion of his royal power than his father Darius did, as seen in this inscription. Here Xerxes portrays himself as defender of order and justice, like Darius (see Document 2.1), but also lays out what happens to those who upset the order established by the kings.

The hostile acts described here against local religious institutions in some unspecified province of the empire do not contradict the general policy of religious tolerance. Rather, this inscription makes clear that tolerance for local religions had a political dimension: tolerance could be a reward for keeping the

---

3. Translation adapted from Brosius 191.

peace, and it could be rescinded as a punishment for resistance or rebellion.

[1] Ahura Mazda is a great god, who created this earth, who created the sky, who created man, who created happiness for man, who made Xerxes king, one king of many, one lord of many.

[2] I am Xerxes, the Great King, king of kings, king of countries containing many men, king of this great earth far and wide, son of King Darius, an Achaemenid, a Persian, son of a Persian, an Aryan, son of an Aryan lineage.

[3] King Xerxes says: "By the favor of Ahura Mazda, these are the countries of which I am king outside Persia. I ruled over them, they brought me tribute, and they did what I told them. My law held them firm. Media, Elam, Arachosia, Armenia, Drangiana, Parthia, Aria, Bactria, Sogdiana, Chorasmia, Babylonia, Assyria, Sattagyida, Sardis, Egypt, Ionians—those who dwell by the sea and those who dwell across the sea—men of Maka, Arabia, Gandara, Sind, Cappadocia, Dahae, Amyrgian Scythians, Scythians who wear pointed caps, Skudra, men of Akaufaka, Libyans, Carians, Ethiopians."

[4] King Xerxes says: "When I became king, there was one among these countries inscribed above where there was turmoil. Afterward, Ahura Mazda brought me aid. By the favor of Ahura Mazda, I struck that country and subdued it.

[5] "Among these countries there was a place where previously *daivas*[4] had been worshiped. Afterward, by the favor of Ahura Mazda, I destroyed that sanctuary of *daivas*, and I made a proclamation 'The *daivas* are no longer worshiped.' Where the *daivas* had previously been worshiped, there I worshiped Ahura Mazda reverently, in accordance with Truth.

[6] "And there were other matters which had been done badly. I made these good. All that I did, I did by the favor of Ahura Mazda. Ahura Mazda brought me aid until I had completed the work.

[7] "You who will be there after me, if you want to be happy while you are living and blessed when you are dead, have respect for the law which Ahura Mazda has established, and worship Ahura Mazda reverently in accordance with Truth. The man who has respect for the law which

---

4. *daivas*: divine entities of some kind; here apparently some sort of evil spirits or false gods.

Ahura Mazda has established and worships Ahura Mazda reverently in accordance with Truth will be happy while living and blessed when dead."

[8] King Xerxes says: "May Ahura Mazda protect me from harm, and my house, and this land. This I pray of Ahura Mazda. May Ahura Mazda give me this."

2.3: The king's relationship to Ahura Mazda

DSk[5]

The Persian king had a special relationship with the god Ahura Mazda, as expressed in this inscription by Darius from Susa. It is not clear how widely Ahura Mazda was worshiped among Persians outside the royal family. Other peoples within the empire were not expected to worship any Persian gods.

[1] I am Darius, the great king, king of kings, king of countries, son of Hystaspes, the Achaemenid.

[2] King Darius proclaims: Ahura Mazda is mine, and I am Ahura Mazda's. I worshiped Ahura Mazda. May Ahura Mazda come to my aid.

2.4: Maintaining the religions of non-Persian peoples

These two documents record the provision of wine for religious ceremonies including those for Humban, the Elamite sky god, and those performed by a magus, a Median priest. Since the Elamites and Medes were among the earliest peoples under Persian rule, these provisions for their religious traditions suggest that the Persian policy of religious accommodation goes back to the beginnings of the empire.

---

5. Translation adapted from Amélie Kuhrt, *The Persian Empire* (London: Routledge, 2007), Ch. 11, no. 38.

PF 339

57 liters of wine provided by Urshaya, received by the priest Turkama.
7 liters for Ahura Mazda.
20 liters for Humban.
10 liters for ceremonies at the river Huputish.
10 liters for ceremonies at the river Rannakarra.
10 liters for ceremonies at the river Shaushaunush.
Used for the gods.

PF 759

300 liters of wine provided by Ashbashtiya, received by the magus Hatrabanush for offering in the *lan*[6] ceremony for one year.

499–498 BCE. At Ankarakkan.

2.5: Stamped brick of Cyrus as patron of Babylonian temples[7]

This text, stamped on bricks found at the Babylonian city of Uruk, identifies Cyrus as a patron of Esagil and Ezida, two major Babylonian temples, in accordance with the Persian custom of accommodating local religious traditions.

I am Cyrus, king of the lands, the one who loves Esagil and Ezida, son of Cambyses, the strong king!

---

6. *lan*: a religious ceremony possibly associated with Humban. See Wouter Henkelman, "The Other Gods Who Are: Studies in Elamite-Iranian Acculturation Based on the Persepolis Fortification Texts" (PhD diss., University of Leiden, 2008), 181–304.
7. Translation by Guy Ridge.

2.6: Jews in the Babylonian Captivity

2 Chronicles 36:15–20[8]

The Neo-Babylonian Empire that arose in Mesopotamia after the collapse of the Assyrian Empire was aggressive and expansionist. Under King Nebuchadnezzar II (ruled 604–562 BCE), Babylonian armies captured Jerusalem in 598 and forcibly relocated thousands of Jews to Mesopotamia. Further deportations followed in the 580s and the temple in Jerusalem was destroyed in 586. This period of Jewish history, known as the Babylonian Captivity, lasted over fifty years until 539. In that year, the Persian king Cyrus defeated the Neo-Babylonians and permitted deported peoples to return home (see Document 2.7).

[15] And the Lord, the God of their fathers, sent His messengers to them, often and repeatedly, out of compassion for His people and His dwelling place, [16] but they mocked the messengers of God, despised His words, and scoffed at His prophets, until the wrath of the Lord against His people became too great for any remedy. [17] Therefore He brought upon them the king of the Chaldeans,[9] who slew their young men with the sword in their sanctuary and had no compassion upon young men or women, old men or the white-haired. He gave them all into the king's hand.

[18] He brought to Babylon all the vessels of the house of God, great and small, and the treasures of the house of the Lord, and the treasures of the king, and of his princes. [19] They burnt the house of God, broke down the wall of Jerusalem, burnt all the palaces with fire, and destroyed all the precious vessels. [20] He carried away to Babylon those who had escaped from the sword. They were slaves to him and his sons until the rise of the kingdom of Persia.

---

8. Translation adapted from *The Holy Scriptures, According to the Masoretic Text* (Philadelphia: Jewish Publication Society of America, 1917).
9. king of the Chaldeans: Nebuchadnezzar II, king of the Neo-Babylonian Empire. The Neo-Babylonians are called Chaldeans in biblical sources.

2.7: Persian kings support rebuilding in Jerusalem

Ezra 1:1–7, 6:1–5[10]

Cyrus supported the restoration of the deported Jews to their homeland and the rebuilding of the temple in Jerusalem. To demonstrate respect for local tradition, Cyrus presented himself as the agent of the Jews' god, Yahweh, much as he presented himself as the champion of Marduk in Babylon, and Cambyses would later adopt Egyptian titles (see Document 2.8).

The book of Ezra preserves documents that purport to be copies of royal decrees in support of the rebuilding efforts in Jerusalem. While these documents may not be authentic, they reflect the positive reception the Persian kings received among the Jews (compare with Document 2.9).

[1:1] In the first year of Cyrus, king of Persia,[11] in order that the word of the Lord by the mouth of Jeremiah[12] might be accomplished, the Lord inspired Cyrus to make a proclamation throughout all his kingdom, and also put it in writing, saying: [2] "The Lord, the God of heaven, has given me all the kingdoms of the earth, and He has assigned me to build Him a house in Jerusalem in Judah. [3] Any among you of His people—may your God be with you—are now free to go up to Jerusalem in Judah and build the house of the Lord, the God of Israel, the God who is in Jerusalem. [4] Whoever remains, wherever they may be, the people who live there are to help them with silver, gold, goods, and animals, in addition to the voluntary offering for the house of God in Jerusalem."

[5] Then the heads of the houses of Judah and Benjamin, the priests, the Levites,[13] and all whose spirit God had stirred prepared to go and build the house of the Lord in Jerusalem. [6] Those they lived among aided them with vessels of silver, with gold, goods, and animals, and with other precious things, in addition to all that was voluntarily offered. [7]

---

10. Translation adapted from *The Holy Scriptures, According to the Masoretic Text* (Philadelphia: Jewish Publication Society of America, 1917).
11. Not the first year of Cyrus' reign (559–530 BCE), but the first year in which he ruled Babylon (539).
12. A prophecy given to the Jews through Jeremiah promising a return to their homeland from exile in Babylon. See Jeremiah 29:10.
13. Levites: a Jewish tribe whose members traditionally performed certain religious and administrative duties.

Cyrus himself brought forth the vessels of the house of the Lord, which Nebuchadnezzar had taken from Jerusalem and put in the house of his gods.

(...)

[6:1] Then King Darius[14] issued a decree, and a search was made in the house of the archives where the treasures were stored in Babylon. [2] Then a scroll was found at Ecbatana, in the palace in the province of Media, in which was written: "A record. [3] In the first year of his reign, King Cyrus issued a decree: Concerning the house of God at Jerusalem, let the house be rebuilt, and the place where they offer sacrifices. Let the foundations be laid to the height of sixty cubits and the breadth of sixty cubits,[15] [4] with three courses of stone, and one of timber. The king's treasury shall pay the expenses. [5] Also let the gold and silver vessels of the house of God, which Nebuchadnezzar took from the temple at Jerusalem and brought to Babylon, be returned to the temple at Jerusalem, each one to its proper place; you shall put them in the house of God."

2.8: Inscription from the temple at Hibis[16]

Darius supported the building and rebuilding of temples in Egypt. The only example still surviving today in good condition is the temple of Amun at Hibis, in the Kharga Oasis in the western desert. There an inscription on the outer wall gives Darius pharaonic titles[17] and celebrates the building work in traditional Egyptian terms.

The Good God, Lord of the Two Lands, lord of the cult, King of Upper and Lower Egypt, Son of Re, Lord of the Crowns of Egypt, given eternal life like the sun forever, beloved of Amun, the Lord of Hibis, Great God, mighty of strength, beloved of Mut, the Lady of Hibis, and beloved of Khonsu [...] in Hibis.

---

14. Darius I.
15. Cubit: a unit of measure based on the length of a man's forearm from elbow to fingertip. The exact length varied in different cultures and times, but most were around half a meter.
16. Translation adapted from Brosius 195.
17. Although Darius is not named in this inscription, he is identified in another inscription not translated here because of its more fragmentary condition.

He has made this monument for his father Amun-Re, Lord of Hibis, Great God, mighty of strength, together with the nine gods,[18] building for him this temple anew, in fine limestone of Meska, and erecting the gates made of pine wood from the western mountains (...) and covering [their fittings with bronze] from Asia; renovating his temple as it had been originally. May they give him hundreds of thousands of anniversaries, and celebrate the jubilees on the throne of Horus, at the head of the living, like the sun forever and ever!

2.9: Letter to Gadatas

SIG 13 no. 22

This inscription purports to record a letter from Darius to an official on the Greek frontier, ordering him to stop interfering with local religious practices. The authenticity of the letter is debated. The inscription appears to have been carved in the second century CE, about seven hundred years after the reign of Darius. The text may be a relatively accurate version of an original letter, which had been preserved in some other way, or it may have been fabricated at a time when Greek cities felt the need to assert their traditional local privileges against the interference of another empire, this one based in Rome. In either case, this text is a useful reflection of how Persian religious policies were perceived and remembered among the empire's peoples.[19]

---

18. Nine gods: Atum, Shu, Tefnut, Geb, Nut, Osiris, Isis, Seth, and Nephthys.
19. For the debate on the authenticity of the text, see Pierre Briant, "Histoire et archéologie d'un texte. La lettre de Darius à Gadatas entre Perses, Grecs et Romains," in *Licia e Lidia prima dell' ellenizzazione*, ed. Mauro Giorgeri et al. (Rome: Consiglio nazionale delle ricerche, 2003); Christopher Tuplin, "The Gadatas Letter," in *Greek History and Epigraphy: Essays in Honour of P. J. Rhodes*, ed. Lynette Mitchell and Lene Rubinstein (Swansea: Classical Press of Wales, 2009). For a broader perspective on Persian interactions with Greek sacred spaces, see Simone Oppen, "Comparative Perspectives on Persian Interactions with Greek Sanctuaries during the Greco-Persian Wars" (PhD diss., Columbia University, New York, 2019).

From Darius, King of Kings, to his slave,[20] Gadatas: I have learned that you are not following my orders faithfully. I commend your plan for working my land and seeding the farthest parts of Asia with fruit trees from Across-the-Euphrates,[21] and you will have great favor in my court for this. But since you are ignoring my orders respecting the gods, if you do not change your course, you will feel the power of my displeasure. For you were forcing the sacred gardeners of Apollo to pay tribute and dig up unhallowed ground, ignoring the customs of my ancestors toward the divine, who instructed the Persians in strict justice and [...]

2.10: The king receives gifts

Plutarch, *Life of Artaxerxes* 4.4–5.1

These anecdotes about King Artaxerxes II may or may not be true, but they reflect the ideals of affability and generosity that the Persian king was meant to uphold (see Document 2.1).

[4.4] There was no gift so small that he did not receive it with great appreciation. When a man named Omisus presented him with one particularly large pomegranate, he said: "By Mithra![22] Entrust this man with a small city and it would soon be a large one!"

[5.1] Once, when people were presenting him with various gifts along the road, a poor farmer, who could come up with nothing else at the moment, ran to the river, scooped up water in his hands, and offered it to the king. Artaxerxes was so delighted that he sent the man a golden cup and a thousand darics.[23]

---

20. Persian kings and officials customarily referred to one another with the language of master-slave relationships, which Greek authors sometimes mistakenly took literally. These forms of address were conventional expressions of politeness and are not to be taken any more literally than, for instance, when people of the nineteenth century signed their letters with "Your obedient servant." See Anna Missiou, "Δοῦλος τοῦ βασιλέως: The Politics of Translation," *Classical Quarterly* 43, no. 2 (1993).
21. Across-the-Euphrates: the Persian name for the region of Syria and Palestine.
22. Mithra: a Persian god associated with light and truth.
23. daric: a gold coin minted by the Persian kings. One daric's value was approximately equal to a month's pay for a soldier.

2.11: The Persian king rewards a loyal Jew

Esther 6:1–11[24]

The Book of Esther recounts the troubles and triumphs of Esther and Mordecai, two Jews close to the Persian court. Although this story cannot be connected with any known historical events, it reflects details of how the Persian court worked and in particular how loyalty was rewarded, regardless of ethnicity.

Previously in the story, Mordecai had learned of a plot against King Ahasuerus[25] and warned the king. One of the king's courtiers, Haman, had then conspired against Mordecai and had plans to have him executed.

[1] On that night the king could not sleep, so he ordered that the book of records be brought and read to him. [2] It was found written there that Mordecai had given a warning about Bigthana and Teresh, two of the king's servants who guarded the door and who had been plotting to assassinate King Xerxes.

[3] The king said: "What honor and dignity has been bestowed on Mordecai for this?"

The king's servants who were attending him said: "Nothing has been done for him."

[4] The king said: "Who is in the court?"

Haman had come into the outer court of the palace, to speak to the king about hanging Mordecai on the gallows that he had prepared for him.

[5] So the king's servants said to him: "Behold, Haman is standing in the court."

And the king said: "Let him come in."

[6] So Haman came in. And the king said to him: "What shall be done for the man whom the king wishes to honor?"

---

24. Translation adapted from *The Holy Scriptures, According to the Masoretic Text* (Philadelphia: Jewish Publication Society of America, 1917).
25. The name Ahasuerus may be ultimately derived from the name Khshayarsha (known to the Greeks as Xerxes), but the king of Esther is a figure of folklore who cannot be confidently identified with any particular historical figure. See Stephanie Dalley, *Esther's Revenge at Susa: From Sennacherib to Ahasuerus* (Oxford: Oxford University Press, 2007), 191.

Haman said to himself: "Whom would the king wish to honor more than myself?"

[7] And Haman said to the king: "For the man whom the king wishes to honor, [8] let royal apparel be brought which the king has worn, and a horse that the king has ridden with a royal crown set upon its head. [9] Let the apparel and the horse be delivered to the hand of one of the king's most noble courtiers, and let them adorn the man whom the king is pleased to honor in that apparel. And let them lead that man on horseback through the streets of the city, proclaiming: 'Thus shall be done for the man whom the king wishes to honor.'"

[10] Then the king said to Haman: "Go quickly, take the apparel and the horse, just as you have said, and do all this for Mordecai the Jew, who sits at the king's gate. Do not fail to do a single thing you have said."

[11] Then Haman took the apparel and the horse, adorned Mordecai, and led him on horseback through the streets of the city, proclaiming: "Thus shall be done for the man whom the king wishes to honor."

2.12: Artaxerxes rewards a Greek friend

Plutarch, *Life of Artaxerxes* 22.5–6

Timagoras was an Athenian ambassador who was sent to negotiate with Artaxerxes II.[26] On his return to Greece, he was accused of having betrayed Athens and was condemned to death. Plutarch's indication that he communicated with Artaxerxes in secret suggests that Timagoras may have been positioning himself as a Friend of the King who could assist in Persian relations with Greece. Ostanes' remark about what Timagoras owed in return for his fine dinner is a reminder of the practical, reciprocal relationship between kings and their "friends." Timagoras' experiences highlight both the usefulness and the dangers of personal relationships across the Persian frontier (see also Document 7.8).

[5] [Artaxerxes] gladly gave ten thousand darics to Timagoras the Athenian, who had sent him a secret note by way of his secretary Beluris. Because Timagoras was sickly and needed milk, the king also sent him

---
26. For further details on this mission, see Xenophon, *Hellenica* 7.1.33–38.

eighty dairy cows to accompany him, as well as a bed and covers, plus servants to make the bed for him (as the king said, Greeks did not know how to do it properly) and bearers to carry him down to the sea, ill as he was. [6] When Timagoras was at court, the king used to send him such a magnificent dinner that the king's own brother Ostanes, remarked: "Remember this dinner, Timagoras; it is no small thing you will have to offer in return."

2.13: "Custom is king"

Herodotus, *Histories* 3.38

As is often the case, we cannot say whether there is any truth to this anecdote—and it has the ring of folktale more than history— but it conveys a Greek appreciation for the Persians' promotion of multicultural tolerance.

When Darius was king, he summoned the Greeks who were at his court and asked them how much money it would take to get them to eat the bodies of their deceased fathers. They replied that nothing would make them do so. Darius then summoned some Indians, called Kallatiai, whose custom it is to eat their dead parents,[27] and asked them—in the presence of the Greeks, who had an interpreter to explain the Kallatiai's words—how much money it would take to convince them to cremate their deceased fathers.[28] The Kallatiai exclaimed that he should not even mention such an abomination. Custom dictates such things, and it seems to me that Pindar[29] got it quite right when he said that custom is king.

---

27. The Kallatiai cannot be identified with any real people, nor is there any definite evidence that any culture in India has ever had a tradition of eating their deceased parents, although this custom has been documented among some other societies. See Beth A. Conklin, "'Thus Are Our Bodies, Thus Was Our Custom': Mortuary Cannibalism in an Amazonian Society," *American Ethnologist* 22, no. 1 (February 1995).
28. Cremation was the usual practice among Greeks.
29. Pindar: a Greek poet, famous for composing songs in honor of athletic victories. The passage Herodotus is referring to is not found among Pindar's surviving poems, but is quoted in Plato, *Gorgias* 484b.

SECTION 3
Cyrus' conquests

3.1: The Nabonidus Chronicle

BM 35382, column 3, lines 12b–22[1]

Cyrus' conquest of Babylon is recorded in the text known as the Nabonidus Chronicle, believed to have been composed by Babylonian priests who were hostile to the last Babylonian king, Nabonidus, and welcomed Cyrus as a replacement. The text is fragmentary and not all the events it refers to are described in detail, but the overall course of Cyrus' entry into Babylon is relatively clear: following his victory in battle at the nearby city of Opis in the fall of 539 BCE, Cyrus came into Babylon unopposed, demonstrated respect for Babylonian traditions and religious institutions, and was crowned king of Babylon.

[12b] In September/October,[2] Cyrus, while in combat at Opis, on [...] [13] the Tigris River, against the army of Akkad, when he did it, the people of Akkad [14] retreated(?). He carried off the plunder, he killed the people.

On the 10th of October, Sippar was seized without battle. [15] Nabonidus fled.

On the 12th of October, Ugbaru, the governor of Gutium, and the army of Cyrus, without battle, [16] entered into Babylon. Afterward, Nabonidus was seized in Babylon when he withdrew. Until the end of the month the leather shields [17] of Gutium encircled the gates of Esagil.[3]

---

1. Translation by Guy Ridge.
2. The months of the Babylonian calendar do not exactly line up with the months of the Gregorian calendar used in the West today.
3. Esagil: the temple of Marduk, at this time the principal god of Babylon.

Any cessation in Esagil and (other) temples [18] did not occur. And the appointed time was not transgressed.[4]

On the 29th of October, Cyrus entered Babylon. [19] They filled *haru* containers before him.[5] Peace was placed on the city. Cyrus spoke a greeting for Babylon [20] in its entirety. Gubaru, his provincial governor, appointed provincial governors in Babylon.

[21] From November/December to February/March, the gods of the land of Akkad whom Nabonidus had brought down to Babylon [22] returned to their shrines. On the night of the 6th of November, Ugbaru died.

3.2: The Cyrus Cylinder

BM 90920[6]

This text comes from a clay cylinder deposited as part of restoration work on a Babylonian temple carried out under Cyrus. Although portions of the text have been damaged, what remains lays out a more detailed version of Cyrus' conquest of Babylon that falls essentially in line with the one given in the Nabonidus Chronicle (Document 3.1). The text, written partially from the point of view of Cyrus, lays out a narrative that places Cyrus in a Babylonian royal and religious context while also celebrating the typical Persian royal virtues of warlike prowess tempered with benevolence and conspicuous respect for local religious customs.

[1–8] [When Marduk], king of all heaven and earth, the [. . . who through] his [. . .] lays waste [and through] his [. . . broad(?)] intelligence [. . . the one who inspects(?)] the world quarters, [. . .] his [offspring], a low-quality person was appointed for lordship of his land, [. . .] imposed upon them. He built a cheap replica of Esagil [. . .] for Ur and the rest of the sanctuaries, rites that were improper for them, [a *taklīmu*-offering that was not clean . . .] without reverence he plotted daily, and blasphemously he discontinued the regular food offering. [He delayed(?) the

---

4. I.e., there was no interruption in religious rituals.
5. Apparently part of the rituals for investing a new king of Babylon.
6. Translation by Guy Ridge.

cultic rites of . . .] he established permanently. In the midst of the sanctuaries, following his own plan, he eliminated worship of Marduk, king of the gods. He repeatedly produced misfortune for his city, daily [. . .] his people with the yoke, without rest, he destroyed them all.

[9–12] Concerning their complaint, Enlil-of-the-gods[7] was furiously angry and [. . .] their territory. The gods dwelling in their midst abandoned their cella(s), over [their] anger that he made (them) enter into Babylon. Supreme Marduk, Enlil-of-the-gods, relented. He changed his mind toward all of the settlements whose dwelling place(s) were turned into ruins and the people of the land of Sumer and Akkad[8] who became corpse-like, and he took pity on them. He examined and inspected all the lands, all of them, (and) sought for (them) a just ruler of his choice. He took Cyrus' hand, the king of the city of Anshan, and pronounced his call to rulership of the whole of totality, having named him (as king).

[13–15a] He made the land of Qutî, the totality of the enemy horde(s) (the Medes), bow at his feet, (while) he constantly shepherded the black-headed people,[9] (over) whom he had given him victory, with truth and justice. Marduk, the great lord, who nurtures his people, joyfully looked favorably upon his good deeds and his just heart, (and) he ordered him to go to his city, Babylon.

[15b–17] He caused him to take the road to Tintir,[10] like a friend and companion he was walking at his side. His extensive troops—whose number, like the waters of a river, could not be known—had their weapons equipped and were marching at his side. He caused him to enter the midst of Shuanna[11] without battle or combat; he saved his city Babylon from hardship. He handed over to him Nabonidus, the king, the one who didn't fear him.

[18–19] The people of Tintir, all of them, the entirety of the land(s) of Sumer and Akkad, the nobles and governor(s), bowed down beneath him (and) kissed his feet; they rejoiced for his kingship, their faces shone. They were gladly praising the lord who, through his aegis, revived the

---

7. Enlil-of-the-gods: Babylonian designation for the chief deity, using the highest god in the Sumerian pantheon, Enlil, as a metaphor for Marduk.
8. Sumer and Akkad: regions of southern Mesopotamia surrounding Babylon.
9. black-headed people: an idiomatic name for the ancient occupants of southern Mesopotamia.
10. Tintir: a Sumerian name for Babylon or Babylonia.
11. Shuanna: another Sumerian name for Babylon or Babylonia.

dead (and) spared all (of them) from hardship and trouble, extolling his name.

[20–22a] I am Cyrus, king of the world, the great king, the strong king, king of Tintir, king of the land(s) of Sumer and Akkad, king of the four quarters, son of Cambyses, the great king, king of the city of Anshan, grandson of Cyrus, the great king, king of the city of Anshan, descendant of Teispes, the great king, king of the city of Anshan, the eternal seed of kingship, whose reign Bel[12] and Nabu[13] loved, (and whose) kingship they desired for the happiness of their heart(s).

[22b–23] I took up residence in the palace of the king, the dwelling of lordship, when I entered into the midst of Tintir in a conciliatory manner, with delight and rejoicing. Marduk, the great lord, assigned to me a vast heart of one who loves Tintir as a mark (of ownership?) and daily I sought to ensure that he was being revered.

[24–28a] My extensive troops were marching into the midst of Tintir peacefully. I did not allow (any) troublemakers (for) the whole land of Sumer and Akkad. I sought the well-being of the city of Babylon and all of its sanctuaries. I eased the weariness of the citizens of Tintir, [upon] whom—as if without the heart of the gods—a yoke not destined for them was imposed, and I assuaged their *sarma'u*.[14] Concerning my good deeds, Marduk, the great lord, rejoiced, and he benevolently pronounced a blessing for me, Cyrus, the king who fears him, and Cambyses, the son, my offspring, and for the whole of my troops, so that we might gladly walk before him in well-being.

[28b–34a] Due to his excellent command, every king who sits on daises, who, [in] all regions, from the Upper Sea to the Lower Sea, inhabit distant districts, the kings of the land of Amurru who inhabit tents, all of them, their heavy tribute they brought here [to] the interior of Shuanna; they kissed my feet. From Shuanna to the city of Ashshur and Susa, Akkad, the land of Eshnunna, the city of Zamban, the city of Meturnu, Der until the border of the land of Qutî, the sanctuaries on the other side of the Tigris,[15] whose dwellings since earlier times were

---

12. Bel: an epithet for Marduk, meaning "lord."
13. Nabu: a Mesopotamian god of writing and wisdom.
14. *sarma'u*: the meaning of this word is uncertain.
15. These geographical references mark out an area encompassing greater Mesopotamia bounded by the Mediterranean Sea (the "Upper Sea"), the Persian Gulf (the "Lower Sea"), and the western reaches of the Iranian plateau.

deserted,[16] I returned the gods who dwelt within them to their places and I established an eternal abode (for them). I gathered all their peoples and I returned their dwellings (to them). And the gods of the land of Sumer and Akkad, whom Nabonidus—to the anger of the lord of the gods—made enter to the midst of Shuanna, I caused them to dwell in their living quarters, dwelling(s) of happiness, in well-being, at the command of Marduk, the great lord.

[34b–38a] May all the gods whom I caused to enter to the midst of their sanctuaries negotiate for my days to be long every day before Bel and Nabu. May they mention repeatedly my good words, and to Marduk, my lord, may they say: "Cyrus, the king who fears you, and Cambyses, his son [...] they or [...] the people of Tintir were showering praises (on) the kingship, I caused all the lands to dwell in a peaceful dwelling. [...] geese, two ducks, and ten pigeons on top of the geese, ducks, and pigeons [...] daily I supplied extravagantly.[17]

[38b–45] The wall of Imgur-Enlil, the great wall of Tintir, its defenses I sought hard to strengthen. [...] The quay of baked-brick that is on the bank of the ditch,[18] which a former king built but did not finish its construction, [...] did not surround the city outside, which an earlier king did not build, his work force, the levy of his country in Babylon, [...] with bitumen and kiln-fired brick I built anew and finished its construction. [...] I set outstanding doors of cedar with bronze plating, a threshold, and *nukushê-s* with a casting of copper in all their gates. [...] inscription [...] within it I discovered the name of Assurbanipal, a king who came before me. [...] forever. [... to] its place. O Marduk, great lord, [grant me] as gift a life [of long days, the fullness of age, the security of the throne and a long reign, so that I ... in] your heart forever.

3.3: The fate of Croesus

Bacchylides, *Epinikian Odes* 3.24–59

Cyrus' westernmost conquest was the kingdom of Lydia, in the mountainous inland regions of western Anatolia, ruled at that

---

16. Or "established."
17. It is unclear, due to the fragmentary nature of the text here, where the quotation ends.
18. Or "moat."

time by King Croesus. Since Croesus had conquered the Greek cities of the Ionian coast not long before, his defeat by Cyrus in 546 BCE brought some Greeks under Persian rule for the first time.

The story of Croesus appealed to many Greek authors as it featured some of their favorite themes, such as sudden reversals of fortune and the downfall of an overconfident ruler. The earliest known Greek account of the fate of Croesus comes from the lyric poet Bacchylides. In a poem composed for an Olympic victor in 468, Bacchylides recounts the fate of Croesus as an example of how extraordinary things can happen by the gods' will. This poem, though it makes no mention of Cyrus, shows how the Persian Empire's conquests had been incorporated into the common stock of Greek mythic and historic narratives.

Once, when Croesus, the king
of horse-taming Lydia,[19]   25
faced the fated
judgment of Zeus
and Sardis was sacked by the Persians' power,
Apollo of the golden lyre
saved him. On that somber   30
day, Croesus had no wish to wait
for sorrowful slavery. He ordered
a funeral pyre built before the bronze-walled
hall, and with his faithful wife
and weeping, fine-haired daughters   35
he mounted the mournful pyre. Raising
his arms to the deep sky,
he cried: "Imperious immortal!
Where is the gratitude of the gods?
Where is Leto's[20] kingly son?   40
Thus falls the house of Alyattes![21]
[...] numberless,
[...
...] the city,

---

19. The Lydians were famous for their cavalry.
20. Leto: the mother of the sun god Apollo and the moon goddess Artemis.
21. Alyattes: the father of Croesus.

the gold-churning Pactolus[22] runs red   45
with blood. Women are wantonly driven
out of the handsome halls.
What once was hated now is loved. Death is sweet!"
So he spoke, and signaled the timid slave
to light the wood. His dear daughters   50
cried out and clung to
their mother, for imminent death
is the most hateful thing to humans.
But when the terrible might
of the fire flashed,   55
Zeus sent a dark rain cloud
to put out the pale flame.
Nothing is unbelievable which the gods take care
to bring about.

---

22. Gold found in the sediments of the Pactolus River in Lydia was a source of the kingdom's wealth.

SECTION 4
Greek relations with Egypt

4.1: Psammetichus recruits Greek and Carian mercenaries

Diodorus of Sicily, *Library of History* 1.66–67

The Twenty-Sixth or Saite Dynasty began with Psammetichus I, who rebelled against Assyrian rule and made himself king of a united Egypt. Psammetichus began a practice followed by his successors of recruiting mercenaries from the Aegean region, including but not limited to Greeks.

[66] Psammetichus of Sais, who was one of the twelve kings[1] and ruled the coastal regions, dealt in cargo with all the merchants, especially the Greeks and the Phoenicians, and in the course of profitably trading the goods of his own land for those of others, he built up not only a store of wealth but also good relations with other peoples and their leaders. They say that because of this the other kings envied him and went to war with him.

Some of the old historians tell the story that the kings had heard an oracle that the first among them to make an offering to the gods in Memphis out of a bronze cup would rule all of Egypt. When a priest brought twelve golden cups out of the temple, Psammetichus took off his helmet and poured the offering out of that.[2] His fellow rulers were suspicious of him, but instead of killing him they banished him to waste his time in the marshes by the sea. At any rate, whether it was for this reason or because of the envy mentioned earlier, Psammetichus was divided from the others.

---

1. Referring to the numerous local warlords and dynasts competing for power in Egypt.
2. This legend is recorded by Herodotus (*Histories* 2.147, 2.151), who says that the priest mistakenly brought out eleven cups for the twelve kings, which is why Psammetichus used his helmet instead.

Psammetichus recruited mercenaries from Caria and Ionia and with these troops defeated the other kings in battle at the city of Momemphis. Some of the kings who opposed him were killed in this battle; the rest were banished to Libya and no longer had the strength to compete for power. [67] Once he was king of all Egypt, Psammetichus built the wall and the eastern gateway at the temple in Memphis, incorporating enormous statues twelve cubits[3] tall. He gave his mercenaries fabulous gifts over and above the promised rate of pay and settled them at the place called "The Camps,"[4] portioning out a great deal of land to them along the Pelusiac branch.[5] (Many years later, when Amasis was king, he moved them from here to Memphis.) Since Psammetichus owed his success to these mercenaries, he trusted them more than others in matters of importance, so he continued to maintain large numbers of mercenary troops.

4.2: Foundation of Naucratis

Herodotus, *Histories* 2.178–179

The Pharaoh Amasis extended the Twenty-Sixth Dynasty's diplomatic outreach to the Greeks by granting permission for a Greek colony, Naucratis, to be founded in Egypt. Unlike most Greek colonies, Naucratis did not belong to a single founding city but was established by a conglomerate of cities. Greek trade with Egypt was confined to this city as a way of keeping the Greeks close to the ruling dynasty.

[178] Amasis was friendly to the Greeks and, besides his other benefits to them, he gave the city of Naucratis to those Greeks who came to live in Egypt. To those who sailed there but did not want to settle, he gave land for setting up altars and sacred spaces for the gods. The largest, most famous, and most commonly used of these sanctuaries these days is called the Hellenion, which was jointly established by the Ionian cities

---

3. cubit: a unit of measure based on the length of a man's forearm from elbow to fingertip. The exact length varied in different cultures and times, but most were around half a meter.
4. Later to be the location of Naucratis. See Document 4.2.
5. Pelusiac branch: one of the western branches of the Nile delta.

of Chios, Teos, Phocaea, and Clazomenae; the Dorian cities of Rhodes, Cnidus, Halicarnassus, and Phaselis; and the Aeolian city of Mytilene.[6] The sacred enclosure belongs to them, and these cities likewise appoint the overseers of the trading port—no other cities have a claim there, even if they pretend to. The Aeginetans made a separate sanctuary of their own for Zeus, as the Samians have done for Hera and the Milesians for Apollo.

[179] In the old days, Naucratis was the only trading port in Egypt. There was no other. If anyone arrived at some other mouth of the Nile, they were required to swear an oath that they had not done so deliberately and then to sail to the Canopic mouth,[7] or, if contrary winds made that impossible, to unload all cargo onto barges and take it through the delta to Naucratis. That was how Naucratis was honored.

4.3: Graffiti by Greek mercenary soldiers in Egypt

SEG 16.863

This inscription was carved on the temple of Abu Simbel in Upper Egypt by mercenaries in the service of the Twenty-Sixth Dynasty Pharaoh Psammetichus II. The names listed here suggest soldiers whose families came from Greece and Caria (in southwestern Anatolia). The soldier Psammatichus was apparently named after the Egyptian king by his Greek father, Theocles.

When King Psammetichus came to Elephantine, this was carved by the companions of Psammatichus, son of Theocles, who sailed beyond Kerkis as far as the river went. Potasimto commanded those of foreign speech[8] and Amasis commanded the Egyptians. Archon, son of Amoibichus, and Pelekos, son of Oudamos, carved this.

---

6. Ionic, Doric, and Aeolic were distinct dialects of Greek whose speakers were concentrated in certain regions. All the cities listed here were on the Aegean coast of Anatolia, in the region known more generally as Ionia.

7. In the delta, the Nile branches into multiple channels, which then flow to the Mediterranean Sea. Seven major branches were named in antiquity, of which the Canopic was the westernmost. Naucratis was located on this branch, close to the Twenty-Sixth Dynasty's home city of Sais.

8. Most likely other mercenaries whose native languages were neither Greek nor Egyptian.

SECTION 5
Egypt under Persian rule

5.1: Autobiographical inscription of Udjahorresne

VM 158[1]

This inscription, from a statue set up by the Egyptian admiral and priest Udjahorresne, provides important insights into how the Persian kings managed conquered territories like Egypt. Udjahorresne served the last two kings of the Twenty-Sixth Dynasty of Egypt, Amasis and Psammetichus III, and two Persian kings, Cambyses and Darius. He tells us nothing about how he came into the Persians' service and is tactfully vague about the Persian conquest of Egypt, but he documents the Persian kings' practices of showing conspicuous respect to local religious traditions and relying on loyal provincials to manage their territories.

[a] An offering for the dead which Osiris-Hemag[2] brings: thousands of loaves of bread, beer, bulls, poultry, and all good, pure things for the soul[3] of the chief physician, Udjahorresne, who is honored by the gods of Sais. An offering for the dead that Osiris who presides over the sanctuary brings: an offering of bread, beer, bulls, and poultry, clothing, incense, ointment, and all good things for the soul of the chief physician, Udjahorresne, who is honored by all the gods. Osiris, lord of eternity, the chief physician has placed his arms about you as protection.[4] May your spirit

---

1. Translation adapted from Kuhrt, *The Persian Empire*, Ch. 4, no. 11.
2. Osiris-Hemag: a specific local version of the Egyptian god Osiris worshiped in Sais.
3. Egyptian: *ka*, the vital life force of an individual which was believed to survive after death.
4. Referring to the posture of the statue which held a model of a temple in its arms with a small statue of Osiris within.

command that everything useful be done for him, as he protects your chapel forever.

[b] The one honored by Neith-the-Great, the mother of god, and by the gods of Sais, the prince, count, royal seal-bearer, sole companion, true beloved, the king's friend, the scribe, the inspector of council scribes, chief scribe of the great outer hall, administrator of the palace, commander of the royal navy under the King of Upper and Lower Egypt, Amasis, commander of the royal navy under the King of Upper and Lower Egypt, Psammetichus III, Udjahorresne; engendered by the administrator of the chapels of Lower Egypt, chief-of-Pe priest, *rnp*-priest,[5] priest of the Horus Eye, prophet of Neith who presides over the nome[6] of Sais, Peftuaneith.

He says: [c] "The Great Chief of all foreign lands, Cambyses, came to Egypt, and the foreign peoples of every foreign land were with him. He conquered this land in its entirety. They established themselves in it, and he was the Great Ruler of Egypt and the Great Chief of all foreign lands.

"His majesty assigned to me the office of chief physician. He made me live at his side as a friend and administrator of the palace. I composed his titulary, his name as King of Upper and Lower Egypt: Mesuti-Re.[7]

[d] "I caused his majesty to recognize the greatness of Sais, that it is the seat of Neith-the-Great, the mother who bore Re and inaugurated birth when birth did not yet exist; and the nature of the greatness of the temple of Neith, that it is heaven in its every aspect; and the nature of the greatness of the chapels of Neith, and of all the gods and goddesses who are there; and the nature of the greatness of the sanctuary of Osiris, that it is the seat of the Sovereign, the Lord of Heaven; and the nature of the greatness of the Resenet and Mehenet sanctuaries; and of the House of Re and the House of Atum, and the mystery of the gods.

[e] (. . .) "I asked his majesty, the King of Upper and Lower Egypt, Cambyses, about all the foreigners who had set themselves down in the

---

5. *rnp*-priest: a religious and administrative position connected with the management of the western delta region under the Saite kings. See Elena Tiribilli, "New Documents of the *Renep*-Priest of the Delta Horemheb, Son of Ankhpakhered," *Egitto e Vicina Oriente* 41 (2018), 140–42.
6. nome: an administrative region of Egypt.
7. Mesuti-Re: the Egyptian name that Cambyses used as his formal name as king of Egypt. As these documents and others indicate, he was known by both his Persian and Egyptian names in Egypt.

temple of Neith, that they should be expelled from it, so that the temple of Neith should be in all its splendor, as it had been earlier. Then his majesty ordered that the foreigners who dwelt in the temple of Neith be expelled and that all their houses and all their refuse that was in the temple be demolished.

"Then they brought all their belongings themselves outside the wall of the temple. His majesty commanded that the temple of Neith be cleansed and all its personnel return to it, the [. . .] and the hourly priests of the temple. His majesty commanded that offerings should be given to Neith, the great one, the mother of god, and to the great gods who are in Sais, as it was done earlier. His majesty did this because I caused his majesty to recognize the greatness of Sais. It is the city of all the gods, who shall remain there on their seats forever.

[f] (. . .) "The King of Upper and Lower Egypt came to Sais. His majesty went to the temple of Neith. He touched the ground before her, as every king had done. He organized a great feast of all good things to Neith, the great one, the mother of god, and to the great gods who are in Sais, as every excellent king had done. His majesty did this because I had caused him to know the greatness of Neith, for she is the mother Re himself.

[g] (. . .) "His Majesty completed all that is useful in the temple of Neith. He established the libation for Osiris in the temple of Neith, as every king did earlier. His majesty did this because I had caused him to recognize how everything useful had been fulfilled in this temple by every king, because of the importance of this temple, for it is the place of all the gods forever.

[h] (. . .) "I established the divine offering of Neith, the great one, the mother of god, on the command of his majesty for all eternity. I erected the monuments for Neith, mistress of Sais, as an excellent servant does for his lord.

"I was a man who did good in his city. I saved its people from the very great disaster, which befell the entire land.[8] There had been nothing like it in this land. I protected the weak from the strong. I saved the fearful man on the day of his misfortune. I did every useful thing for them when the time came to do it.

[i] (. . .) "I was one honored by his father, praised by his mother, beloved of his brothers. I established them in the office of prophet. I gave

---

8. Presumably referring to the Persian conquest.

them good fields at his majesty's command for all eternity. I prepared a beautiful burial for the man who had none. I maintained all their children in livelihood. I caused all their households to endure. I did every useful thing for them as a father does for his son, when the turmoil happened in this nome, at the time of the very great disaster that happened in this entire land.

[j] (...) "His majesty, the King of Upper and Lower Egypt, Darius, (may he live forever), commanded me to return to Egypt, when his majesty was in Elam and was the great king of all foreign lands and great ruler of Egypt, in order to set to rights the office of the House of Life[9] [...] and of the physicians, after it had collapsed. The foreigners brought me from land to land and delivered me safely to Egypt at the command of the Lord of the Two Lands.

"I carried out the command of his majesty. I furnished them with their personnel, each the son of a (wellborn) man, the son of a lowborn man was not among them. I placed a scholar at their head [...] for all their work. His majesty ordered that they be given all good things, so that they could carry out their work. I equipped them with all that was useful, supplied all their needs, as it was written, just as it was earlier.

"His majesty did this because he knew the usefulness of this art, for preserving the life of all who are sick, for preserving the names of all the gods and their temples, their offerings and their rituals forever."

5.2: Seal of Cambyses as Pharaoh of Egypt[10]

Cambyses' royal seal as king of Egypt uses traditional pharaonic titles and associates him specifically with the goddess Wadjet, a protective goddess associated with the union of Upper and Lower Egypt.

The King of Upper and Lower Egypt, Cambyses, beloved of the goddess Wadjet who is ruler of the city of Imet, the great one, Eye of the Sun, ruler of the sky, mistress of the gods, given life like that of Re.

---

9. House of Life: a term for the collective activity of learned priests in Egypt whose skills included medicine, study of the gods and their rituals, and the management of temples.
10. Translation adapted from Brosius 19.

5.3: Epitaph and sarcophagus inscription for the Apis bull

Ancient Egyptians believed that an aspect of the god Ptah could come to earth and be born as a black bull with certain markings (see Document 5.4, section 28). When an Apis calf was identified, it was brought to Memphis to live out its life in luxury in a special enclosure. Upon its death, the bull was mummified and buried in a dedicated necropolis. The spirit of Apis was then believed to return to the gods to be born again in a new calf. The death of an old Apis bull and the discovery of a new one were occasions for great religious celebration in Egypt. Apis was believed to have a special connection with the king of Egypt, and the king's religious responsibilities included ensuring that a dead Apis was buried with appropriate reverence.

An Apis bull died early in Cambyses' reign in Egypt. The bull's epitaph and sarcophagus inscription show that Cambyses carried out his royal responsibility conscientiously, in accordance with his effort to accommodate Egyptian tradition and behave as Egyptians expected their king to do.

The epitaph inscription is damaged, but parts of the text have been reconstructed based on other Apis epitaphs.

Epitaph for Apis[11]

November 524 BCE, under the Majesty of the King of Upper and Lower Egypt, Mesuti-Re[12]—may he live forever! The god was taken up [in peace toward the perfect West and was laid to rest in his place in the necropolis], in the place which His Majesty has made for him, [after] all [the ceremonies had been performed for him] in the Hall of Embalming. Sets of linen were made for him, [... his amulets and all his ornaments in gold] and in all precious materials were brought [to him ...] temple of Ptah, which is within Hemag [...] ordered [...] toward Memphis, saying:

---

11. Translation adapted from Brosius 21.
12. Mesuti-Re: the Egyptian name that Cambyses used as his formal name as king of Egypt. As these documents and others indicate, he was known by both his Persian and Egyptian names in Egypt.

"You may lead [...]" All was done that His Majesty had ordered [...] in the twenty-seventh year[13] [...] of Apis in the [...] year of Cambyses.

Sarcophagus inscription for Apis[14]

Horus, Uniter of the Two Lands, King of Upper and Lower Egypt, Mesuti-Re, Son of Re, Cambyses—may he live forever! He has made a monument for his father Apis-Osiris[15] with a great granite sarcophagus, dedicated by the King of Upper and Lower Egypt, Mesuti-Re, Son of Re, Cambyses—may he live forever, in perpetuity and prosperity, full of health and joy, as King of Upper and Lower Egypt forever.

5.4: Murder of the Apis bull

Herodotus, *Histories* 3.27–29

The reverential burial of Apis reflected in the epitaph and sarcophagus inscriptions is consistent with Cambyses' other efforts to present himself as a traditional Egyptian king. Egyptian oral tradition, by contrast, remembered Cambyses as a cruel tyrant. Propaganda by Cambyses' successor Darius also tarnished his memory. By the time Herodotus visited Egypt and interviewed local people about their history, around a century after Cambyses' reign, a story about the death and burial of the Apis bull was circulating that portrayed Cambyses as an impious murderer. Herodotus recorded this story, which became part of a larger Greek tradition denigrating Cambyses.

Herodotus sets this story just after Cambyses' return from an unsuccessful campaign in the south.

[27] When Cambyses returned to Memphis, Apis (whom the Greeks call Epaphus) appeared in Egypt. When Apis appears, the Egyptians at

---
13. This portion of the text is badly damaged, but it most likely records that the deceased Apis was born in the twenty-seventh year of a previous king, almost certainly Amasis, who ruled from 570–526 BCE.
14. Translation adapted from Brosius 22.
15. In life, the Apis bull was believed to represent the god Ptah. In death, Apis joined Osiris, the god of the dead. Since Osiris' son Horus was the god of the kings of Egypt, Osiris was the kings' spiritual father.

once dress in their best and hold a celebration. Seeing this, Cambyses was convinced that they were celebrating his misfortunes, so he summoned the leaders of Memphis. When they came to him, he demanded to know why the Egyptians were acting this way, which they had not done before, just when he was returning after losing so much of his army. They answered that a god had appeared, one who only came to them after long stretches of time, and that it was the custom for all Egyptians to rejoice on such an occasion. Cambyses accused them of lying and put them to death for it. [28] Next he summoned the priests, who told him the same thing. He replied that it would not have escaped his notice if a tame god had come to Egypt. He then ordered the priests to bring Apis before him, so they fetched him.

Apis, or Epaphus, is a calf born to a cow which then cannot become pregnant again. The Egyptians say that a ray of light from heaven strikes the cow, and this is how Apis is conceived. The Apis calf has these signs: he is black with a white triangular mark between his eyes and the shape of an eagle on his back, his tail hairs are doubled, and there is a beetle-shaped mark under his tongue.

[29] When the priests led Apis in, Cambyses—who was not quite right in the head—drew his dagger and stabbed Apis, aiming for the belly but hitting the thigh. Laughing, he said to the priests: "Are these your gods, you idiots? Gods of flesh and blood who can feel the bite of iron? This is a god fit for Egyptians, but I will show you what happens to those who make a laughingstock of me!" He ordered the priests whipped and decreed death for any other Egyptians who were celebrating. So the festival ended and the priests were punished.

Apis lay in the temple wasting away from the blow to his thigh. When he had died of the wound, the priests buried him in secret without Cambyses' knowledge.

5.5: The Demotic Chronicle: Cambyses' reorganization of Egyptian temples

BN 215, D 1–14[16]

The text known as the Demotic Chronicle was written in the third century BCE, at a time when Egypt was ruled by the descendants

---

16. Translation adapted from Brosius 24.

of the Macedonian general Ptolemy after Alexander the Great's conquest of the Persian Empire. As such, it reflects the negative sentiments about the Persians that had built up in Egypt. This account of Cambyses interfering in the economic life of Egyptian temples must be seen in that light, but it is also possible that Cambyses did give orders along these lines in the aftermath of a revolt backed by the priestly elite.

[1] Those matters which shall be discussed in the Court of Law concerning the rights of the temples.

[2] Concerning building wood, firewood, linen and shrubs (?), which used to be given to the temples of the gods [3] in the days of the Pharaoh Amasis, with the exception of the temple of Memphis, the temple of Wenkhem, and the temple of Perapis [. . .] [4] regarding these temples, Cambyses gave these orders: "It is not allowed to give these to them [. . .] Let [the temples] be given [5] a place in the marshes and in Upper Egypt to provide them with building wood and firewood [6] to offer to their gods."

Concerning the tribute to the three temples mentioned above, Cambyses gave these orders: "Let the tribute be returned to them, [7] as it used to be."

Concerning the cattle which used to be given to the temples of the gods [8] in the days of the Pharaoh Amasis, except for the three temples mentioned above, Cambyses gave these orders: [9] "Their share is what is given to them. What was given to the three temples mentioned above, let it be returned to them."

[10] Concerning the fowl which used to be given to the temples in the days of the Pharaoh Amasis, [11] except for these three temples, Cambyses gave these orders: "Do not give it to them. The priests should raise their own geese [12] and offer them to the gods."

Concerning the amount of silver, the cattle, the fowl, the grain, and the other things [13] which used to be given to the temples in the days of the Pharaoh Amasis, Cambyses gave these orders: [14] "Do not give it to them."

5.6: Statue inscription proclaiming Darius Pharaoh of Egypt

DSab[17]

A statue of Cambyses' successor Darius was set up in Egypt, inscribed with both cuneiform and hieroglyphic texts declaring Darius' rule over Egypt. Later, either this statue was moved to the royal palace at Susa in Persia, or a copy was made to be erected at Susa. Selections from the texts of the inscription show how Darius presented himself in a complicated interplay of Persian and Egyptian terms.

Cuneiform inscription

[1] Ahura Mazda is a great god, who created this earth, who created the sky, who created man, who created happiness for man, who made Darius king. Here is the statue made of stone which Darius ordered to be made in Egypt, so that whoever sees it in the future may know that the Persian man held Egypt.

Hieroglyphic inscription from right side of robe

[. . .] The strong king, great in his powers, lord of strength like him who presides in Letopolis, lord of his own hand, who conquers the Nine Bows,[18] excellent in counsel, outstanding in his plans, lord of the curved sword, when he penetrates the mass [of the enemy], shooting at the target without missing, whose strength is like that of Montu.[19]

The King of Upper and Lower Egypt, Lord of the Two Lands, Darius, may he live forever! The Great King, king of kings, the supreme lord of the lands, [son of] the god's father, Hystaspes, an Achaemenid, who has appeared as king of Upper and Lower Egypt on the seat where Horus rules over the living, like Re, the first of the gods, forever.

---

17. Translations adapted from Brosius 49, 50.
18. Nine Bows: a traditional term for the foreign enemies of Egypt.
19. Montu: an Egyptian warrior god associated with the city of Letopolis.

SECTION 6
The rise of Darius

6.1: Bardiya, heir of Cambyses

Little is recorded about Cambyses' brother Bardiya, no doubt because Darius had him erased from the record after his coup, but Bardiya is mentioned in a few Greek sources. Statements in some sources that he was appointed satrap of several northern and eastern provinces are consistent with Cambyses' focus on Egypt: perhaps Bardiya was tasked with keeping the eastern parts of the empire secure while Cambyses expanded the western frontier.

Xenophon presents an imagined speech in which Cyrus bequeathed the kingship to Cambyses and gave several provinces—with a warning against striving for more—to Bardiya. Ctesias lists a different set of provinces under Bardiya's authority, but with a similar eastern focus.

Xenophon, *The Education of Cyrus* 8.7.11–12

[11] "Tanaoxares,[1] I give you the satrapies of Media, Armenia, and Cadusia.[2] In doing so, it seems to me that while I leave the greater power and the title of king to your elder brother, to you I leave more happiness and fewer troubles. [12] For I cannot see any worldly pleasure that you will lack. Indeed, everything that seems pleasing to mortals will be yours. It is the king's role, rather than yours, to strive after difficult endeavors, to be weighed down with cares, to be ever restlessly spurred on by the ambition to rival my deeds, to plot and be plotted against—and, trust me, it brings more trouble than joy."

---

1. Tanaoxares: the name Xenophon uses for Bardiya. It is not clear where this name comes from or why Bardiya is known by so many different names in the Greek sources, but Darius' propaganda after Bardiya's death must have done much to confuse the historical record.
2. Cadusia: a region in northwestern Iran, around the shores of the Caspian Sea.

Ctesias, FGrH 688 F 9.8[3]

Cyrus, at the end of his life, established his elder son Cambyses as king and appointed his younger son, Tanyoxarkes,[4] as lord over the Bactrians and their land, and over the Chorasmians, the Parthians, and the Carmanians,[5] free from any obligation to pay tribute.

6.2: Bardiya as king in Babylon[6]

This document from Babylon, recording a loan and the terms of its repayment, is significant because the dating formula at the end mentions Bardiya ("Barziya" in Akkadian) as king of Babylon. This document shows that Bardiya was accepted as king, at least in Babylon, as early as April or May of 522 BCE, while Cambyses did not die until July of that year, suggesting that Bardiya may have already been making claims to royal power while his brother was busy with the conquest of Egypt.

[Obverse, lines 1–7] [Half(?) a ...] mina, eight shekels of white silver,[7] belonging to Nabu-shumu-uṣur, son of Shapik-zēri, son[8] of Miṣiraya, [is a debt] upon Nabû-shum-uṣur, son of Mushezib-Marduk, son of Shumu-libshi. Each month one shekel of silver shall increase upon one mina. From the first of Simānu (May/June), he shall pay interest. Monthly he shall pay interest.

[Reverse, lines 8–16] Witnesses: Nadin, son of Balaṭu, son of Mukallim; Marduk-shumu-iddin, son of Bel-nadin-apli, son of Mukallim; Muranu, son of Nabû-dannu-ilāni, son of Miṣiraya; Guzanu, son of

---

3. The works of Ctesias do not survive intact. This passage is from a summary of his *Persica* written by the Byzantine scholar Photius. The text can be found in Photius, *Bibliotheca* 72.37.
4. Tanyoxarkes: the name Ctesias uses for Bardiya. Though clearly from the same source as Xenophon's "Tanaoxares," we do not know what that source was.
5. Chorasmians, Parthians, and Carmanians: these peoples and regions are all in the eastern part of the Persian Empire, stretching across areas of what is today Iran, Afghanistan, Turkmenistan, and Uzbekistan.
6. Translation by Guy Ridge.
7. white silver: a low-quality silver alloy.
8. The word for "son" may also mean "descendant."

Nabû-na'id, son of Le'ea. Nabû-aḫê-iddin is the scribe, son of Nabû-shum-lishir, son of Saggilaya. Tintir,[9] month of Ayyāru (April/May), accession year of Barziya, king of Tintir, king of the lands.

6.3: The overthrow of Bardiya

DB 10–15[10]

After coming to power, Darius had a monumental inscription carved into the cliff face at Bisitun in Old Persian, Akkadian, and Elamite, giving an account of how he became king and secured his power. This narrative is generally seen as propaganda which attempted to justify Darius' coup by claiming that Cambyses' younger brother Bardiya had been secretly killed and replaced by an impostor.

[10] (. . .) A son of Cyrus named Cambyses, one of our dynasty, was king before me. Cambyses had a brother, Bardiya, by the same mother and father. Later, Cambyses slew this Bardiya. When Cambyses slew Bardiya, the people did not know that Bardiya was slain. Then Cambyses went to Egypt. When Cambyses had departed for Egypt, the people became corrupt and the Lie[11] multiplied in the land, even in Persia and Media, as well as the other provinces.

[11] (. . .) Then a certain man, a magus, named Gaumata, raised a rebellion in Paishiyauvada,[12] at a mountain called Arakadri. On the 11th of March, 522, he rebelled. He lied to the people, saying: "I am Bardiya, the son of Cyrus, the brother of Cambyses."

Then all the people were in revolt and went over to him from Cambyses, both Persia and Media, as well as the other provinces. He seized the kingdom on the 1st of July, 522. Afterward, Cambyses died.

---

9. Tintir: a Sumerian name for Babylon or Babylonia.
10. Translation adapted from L. W. King and R. C. Thompson, *The Sculptures and Inscription of Darius the Great on the Rock of Behistûn in Persia* (London: British Museum, 1907). Every numbered passage in the original text begins with "King Darius says," which has been omitted here for readability.
11. the Lie: the force of evil opposed by Ahura Mazda and his chosen representative, the king of Persia.
12. Paishiyauvada: a town in the vicinity of Pasargadae.

[12] (...) The kingdom which Gaumata the magus seized from Cambyses had always belonged to our dynasty. Gaumata the magus took it away from Cambyses. He took Persia, Media, and the other provinces, according to his will. He became king.

[13] (...) No man, no Persian or Mede nor anyone of our own dynasty took the kingdom from Gaumata the magus. The people feared him exceedingly, for he slew many who had known the real Bardiya. He slew them for this reason: "So that they may not know that I am not Bardiya, the son of Cyrus."

There was no one who dared to act against Gaumata the magus until I came. Then I prayed to Ahura Mazda, and Ahura Mazda came to my aid. On the 29th of September, 522, I, with a few men, slew Gaumata the magus, and the foremost men who were his followers. I slew him at the stronghold called Sikayahuvati, in the district of Nisaea in Media. I took the kingdom from him. Ahura Mazda gave me the kingdom.

[14] (...) I reestablished the kingdom that had been taken from our house. I put it back on its foundation. I restored to the people the temples which Gaumata the magus had destroyed, as well as the pastures, the herds, the dwelling places, and the houses which Gaumata the magus had taken away. I reestablished the people in their proper place, the people of Persia, Media, and the other provinces. I restored that which had been taken away, as it had been in days gone by. I did this by the favor of Ahura Mazda. I labored until I had reestablished our royal house, as it had been in days gone by. I labored so that Gaumata should not take away our royal house.

[15] (...) This is what I did after I became king.

6.4: Inscriptions of Ariaramnes and Arsames

Darius claimed to be descended from a branch of the Achaemenid royal family through his great-grandfather Ariaramnes, who, according to Darius, was the brother of Cyrus' grandfather. Outside of Darius' own propaganda, however, no evidence for this family relationship exists.

Two gold tablets supposedly found at Ecbatana (they were not professionally excavated and their real origins are uncertain) show us Darius' propaganda at work. They purport to record inscriptions by Ariaramnes and his son Arsames as kings of Persia, but there are good reasons to see these texts as forgeries created under Darius or his successors. The style of the inscriptions matches those written by Darius, not those of earlier kings. More tellingly, they are written in Old Persian, which was not a written language until the time of Darius.

AmH[13]

[1] Ariaramnes, the Great King, king of kings, king of Persia, son of King Teispes, grandson of Achaemenes. [2] King Ariaramnes says: "The great god Ahura Mazda has bestowed upon me this country of Persia, which I hold, and which possesses good horses and good men. By the favor of Ahura Mazda, I am king of this country." [3] King Ariaramnes says: "May Ahura Mazda bring me aid."

AsH[14]

[1] Arsames, the Great King, king of kings, king of Persia, son of King Ariaramnes, the Achaemenid. [2] King Arsames says: "Ahura Mazda, the great god, the greatest of gods, made me king. He bestowed upon me the country of Persia, with good men and good horses. By the favor of Ahura Mazda, I hold this land. May Ahura Mazda protect me and my royal house, and may he protect this country which I hold."

6.5: Rebellions against Darius

DB 52–54[15]

Evidently, not all Persians were convinced of Darius' right to rule, since he faced numerous rebellions as soon as he claimed power. In his inscription at Bisitun (see Document 6.3), Darius

---

13. Translation adapted from Brosius 2.
14. Translation adapted from Brosius 3.
15. Translation adapted from King and Thompson, *Sculptures and Inscription of Darius the Great*. Every numbered passage in the original text begins with "King Darius says," which has been omitted here for readability.

also detailed how many revolts he put down in his first year. This passage sums up the resistance.

[52] (...) This is what I have done by the grace of Ahura Mazda. After I became king, I fought nineteen battles in a single year and by the grace of Ahura Mazda I overthrew nine kings and took them prisoner.

One was a magus named Gaumata. He lied, saying: "I am Bardiya, the son of Cyrus." He made Persia revolt.

Another was an Elamite named Acina. He lied, saying: "I am the king of Elam." He made Elam revolt.

Another was a Babylonian named Nidintu-Bel. He lied, saying: "I am Nebuchadnezzar, son of Nabonidus." He made Babylon revolt.

Another was a Persian named Martiya. He lied, saying: "I am Imanish, king of Elam." He made Elam revolt.

Another was a Mede names Phraortes. He lied, saying: "I am Khshathrita, of the dynasty of Cyaxares." He made Media revolt.

Another was a Sagartian named Tritantaechmes. He lied, saying: "I am king of Sagartia, of the dynasty of Cyaxares." He made Sagartia revolt.

Another was a Margian named Frada. He lied, saying: "I am king of Margiana." He made Margiana revolt.

Another was a Persian named Vahyazdata. He lied, saying: "I am Bardiya, son of Cyrus." He made Persia revolt.

Another was an Armenian named Arakha. He lied, saying: "I am Nebuchadnezzar, son of Nabonidus." He made Babylon revolt.

[53] (...) I captured these nine kings in these wars.

[54] (...) These are the provinces which revolted. Lies made them revolt, because they deceived the people. Then Ahura Mazda delivered them into my hand, and I treated them according to my will.

6.6: Darius' foundation charter from Susa

DSf 3–4[16]

This portion of a building inscription from Susa, in which Darius celebrated the construction of his new palace in the city, details how materials and artisans were brought in from around the empire.

---

16. Translation adapted from Brosius 45.

The palace was thus not only a symbol of Darius' power but also a statement of the unity of the Persian Empire under his rule.

[3] The materials for this palace which I built at Susa were brought from afar. The earth was dug down deep until the rock was reached within the earth. When the excavation had been made, then rubble was packed down, some parts forty cubits deep, other parts twenty cubits.[17] On that rubble the palace was constructed. The Babylonian people dug that earth deep, packed down that rubble, and molded the sun-dried bricks.

[4] The cedar timber was brought from a mountain called Lebanon. The Assyrian people brought it to Babylon. From Babylon the Carians and Ionians brought it to Susa. The rosewood was brought from Gandara and from Carmania. The gold which was worked here was brought from Sardis and from Bactria. The precious stone lapis lazuli and carnelian which was worked here was brought from Sogdiana. The precious stone turquoise which was worked here was brought from Chorasmia. The silver and the ebony were brought from Egypt. The ornamentation with which the wall was adorned was brought from Ionia. The ivory which was worked here was brought from Ethiopia, from India, and from Arachosia. The stone columns which were worked here were brought from a village called Abiradu, in Elam.

The stone-cutters who worked the stone were Ionians and Sardians. The goldsmiths who worked the gold were Medes and Egyptians. The men who worked the wood were Sardians and Egyptians. The men who worked the baked brick were Babylonians. The men who adorned the walls were Medes and Egyptians.

6.7: Darius' military victories

DB 71–76[18]

A further text was added to Darius' monument at Bisitun (see Documents 6.3 and 6.5) later in his reign, detailing some of his major

---

17. cubit: a unit of measure based on the length of a man's forearm from elbow to fingertip. The exact length varied in different cultures and times, but most were around half a meter.
18. Translation adapted from King and Thompson, *Sculptures and Inscription of Darius the Great*. Every numbered passage in the original text begins with "King Darius says," which has been omitted here for readability.

military achievements. These include putting down another revolt in Elam and a campaign (or possibly multiple campaigns) against the steppe-dwelling Scythians of Persia's northern frontier. Interestingly, Darius describes his activities against the Scythians as a noteworthy success, in contrast to Herodotus, who portrays Darius' Scythian campaign as a humiliating failure (Herodotus, Histories 4.83–142).

[71] (...) The following is what I did in the second and third year of my rule.

The province of Elam revolted. They made an Elamite named Athamaita their leader. Then I sent an army into Elam. I made my servant, a Persian named Gobryas, their leader. Then Gobryas set forth with the army. He fought a battle against the Elamites. Then Gobryas destroyed much of the Elamite army and captured their leader Athamaita. He brought Athamaita to me, and I killed him. Then the province became mine.

[72] (...) Those Elamites were disloyal and did not worship Ahura Mazda. I worshiped Ahura Mazda. By the grace of Ahura Mazda, I treated them according to my will. [73] (...) Whoever worships Ahura Mazda, the divine blessing will be upon him, both while living and when dead.

[74] (...) Afterwards I went with an army to Scythia. Then the Scythians who wear the pointed cap came against me. When I arrived at the sea, I crossed it with all my army. Afterwards I utterly defeated the Scythians. I took captive one of their chiefs. He was led to me bound, and I killed him. My army seized another of their chiefs, named Skunkha, and led him to me. I made a different man their chief, as was my desire. Then the province became mine.

[75] (...) Those Scythians were disloyal and did not worship Ahura Mazda. I worshiped Ahura Mazda. By the grace of Ahura Mazda, I treated them according to my will. [76] (...) Whoever worships Ahura Mazda, the divine blessing will be upon him, both while living and when dead.

SECTION 7
Greek relations with Persia

7.1: Athens seeks an alliance with Persia

Herodotus, *Histories* 5.73

In the late 500s BCE, the Spartans, under their king Cleomenes, got involved in political infighting in Athens and invaded the city twice to support Spartan-friendly political factions. After the second invasion, the Athenians, led by the reformer Cleisthenes, went looking for useful allies against Sparta and made overtures toward the Persians.

After these events, the Athenians recalled Cleisthenes and the seven hundred households banished by Cleomenes. They then sent envoys to Sardis, hoping to make an alliance with the Persians, for they knew that Cleomenes and the Spartans were preparing for war. When the envoys had arrived at Sardis and presented their commission, Artaphrenes, son of Hystaspes, the governor of Sardis, asked them what sort of people they were and what land they came from, since they wished to become allies of the Persians. When the envoys answered his questions, he gave them this short response: if the Athenians gave earth and water to the king,[1] he would grant them an alliance; if they did not wish to give earth and water, they were to depart. The envoys agreed to make the gift, on their own authority, out of their desire to conclude the alliance. When they returned home, however, they were severely reproached for it.[2]

---

1. The gift of earth and water was the traditional ritual of voluntary submission to Persian rule.
2. Given the gravity of the situation, it seems unlikely that the emissaries would have made such an offer on their own initiative. It is more likely that the Athenians were willing, perhaps grudgingly, to accept Persian rule as an alternative to further interference from Sparta, but that in later years, with anti-Persian sentiment on the rise, they preferred

7.2: Hippias plans his return to Athens with Persian help

Herodotus, *Histories* **5.96**

Greek politicians who got themselves into trouble at home often looked to Persia as a refuge and potential ally. Hippias, the son of Peisistratus, ruled Athens as tyrant between about 527 and 510 BCE. After being driven into exile, he sought Persian backing for his return to Athens. Restoring Hippias as a Persian-friendly local ruler in Athens (rather than destroying the city) was no doubt a major aim of the Persian campaign in 490 (see Document 9.2).

[Hippias] did everything he could to turn Artaphrenes against the Athenians and to make Athens subject to himself and Darius. When the Athenians found out about what Hippias was doing, they sent messengers to Sardis urging the Persians not to listen to Athenian exiles, but Artaphrenes told them that if they wanted to be safe, they had better take Hippias back. The Athenians refused to accept these terms, and since they refused, it was understood that they were openly hostile to the Persians.

7.3: Demaratus goes over to Darius

Herodotus, *Histories* **6.70**

The Spartan king Demaratus was forced to flee Greece in 491 after losing a dynastic struggle. He was welcomed in Persia by Darius and later became an adviser to Xerxes. Installing Demaratus as a pro-Persian ruler in Sparta most likely featured among the goals for Xerxes' campaign in Greece in 480–479.

Taking supplies with him for a journey, Demaratus made his way to Elis while putting it about that he was on his way to the oracle at Delphi. The Spartans, though, suspected that he was trying to flee and set off in

---

to rewrite their own history and deny responsibility for the offer. It is, however, impossible to be certain on this point.

pursuit. Demaratus somehow got over to Zacynthus from Elis before they caught up with him. Crossing over after him, the Spartans seized Demaratus and his attendants, but the Zacynthians refused to let them take him, so he made it to Asia to the court of Darius. The king welcomed him with great dignity and granted him land and cities.[3]

7.4: Argos makes an alliance with Persia

Herodotus, *Histories* 7.150–151

When Xerxes was preparing to invade Greece in 480, some Greek cities formed a defensive alliance, headed by Athens and Sparta. Many cities refused to join the alliance. Among these was Argos, longtime rival of Sparta, which declined to join when the Spartans refused to allow them a share of the command. Herodotus reports a rumor that Argos had made already a separate peace with Persia and the demand for a share of the command was only a ruse.

[150] There is another story well known throughout Greece that Xerxes sent a herald to Argos before starting out on his campaign. When the herald arrived he said:

"Men of Argos, King Xerxes says these words to you: 'We believe that our ancestor Perses was the child of Perseus, son of Danae, and Andromeda, the daughter of Cepheus.[4] If that is so, then we are your kin. In that case, it would not be right either for us to march against the land of our ancestors, or for you to give aid and comfort to our enemies. You should instead remain at peace. If things go well for me, I will remember you above all others.'"

---

3. Demaratus' descendants were still in control of a few cities in western Anatolia at the end of the fifth century BCE. See Document 11.3.
4. Perseus, Danae, Andromeda, and Cepheus were all figures of Greek mythology. Perseus was a hero traditionally associated with the city of Argos. Perses was a figure invented by the Greeks to furnish a legendary ancestor for the Persians anchored in Greek mythology, a practice the Greeks often applied to foreign peoples. There is no reason to suppose that Xerxes believed this invented genealogy, but, if there is any truth to Herodotus' story, he seems to have been comfortable using the Greeks' own mythology as a way of communicating with them.

Upon hearing this message, it is said that the Argives decided not to make any claims at once, but later when the other Greeks invited them to join the alliance, since they knew for sure that the Spartans would not allow it, they demanded a share in the command so that they would have an excuse for remaining aloof.

[151] This story is confirmed, according to some Greeks, by what happened many years later. Some envoys from Athens, led by Callias the son of Hipponicus, had gone to Memnonian[5] Susa on another matter,[6] and it happened that emissaries from Argos were there at the same time. The Argives asked Artaxerxes, the son of Xerxes, whether the friendship they had made with Xerxes still held good, as they wished, or whether he regarded them as enemies. Artaxerxes answered that it certainly did hold good, and that he thought no city more well disposed to him than Argos.

7.5: Greek stone-cutters at Persepolis

Pugliese Carratelli I 1–3

Three short inscriptions in Greek were carved into the stone quarries at Persepolis, recording the presence of Greek-speaking stone-cutters.

[1] [This belongs] to Pytharchus.[7]

[2] [Dedicated] to the gods.

[3] Nico carved this.

---

5. Memnon: a legendary hero of the Trojan War whom Greeks thought of as coming from distant lands either to the east or the south. Herodotus connected Memnon with the royal palace at Susa. See Herodotus, *Histories* 5.53–54.
6. Most likely the "Peace of Callias" in the early 440s, although there is debate about the existence and nature of that agreement. See Document 13.1.
7. Probably carved by a stone-cutter to indicate that this particular stone face was his to work.

7.6: A Greek-speaking administrator at Persepolis

PF-NN 1771

A single administrative tablet written in Greek has survived from Persepolis, showing that at least one worker in the Persian bureaucracy knew Greek.

20 liters of wine, December/January.

7.7: Ionian women receive childbirth rations at Persepolis

PF 1224

This record of special rations for Ionian women who gave birth at Persepolis documents a community of at least twenty-three Greek women and their families working and receiving pay at the Persian ceremonial capital.

320 liters of grain provided by Ashbashuptis. Shedda, the agent for special rations, whose allotment is determined by Abetteya, received it at Persepolis and gave it as extra childbirth rations to Ionian women working on the irrigation channels at Persepolis. Their allotments are determined by Abetteya and Mishshabadda.
9 women who gave birth to sons received 20 liters each.
14 women who gave birth to daughters received 10 liters each.
February/March, 499 BCE.

7.8: Friendship and its complications

Xenophon, *Hellenica* 4.1.31–39

Relationships of xenia, or guest-friendship were a traditional way in which Greek aristocrats formed personal relationships across the boundaries of the polis. Similar relationships were also extended to Persians who dealt with the Greek frontier. While these relationships could be channels for diplomacy and political negotiation, they could also create conflicting loyalties. The exchange between the Spartan king Agesilaus—at that time ravaging the Persian-held territories in Ionia—and the satrap Pharnabazus in 395 or 394 BCE shows both the potentials of xenia *and its dangers.*

First they greeted each other and Pharnabazus held out his right hand. Agesilaus clasped it. Then Pharnabazus spoke first, since he was the elder.

"Agesilaus, and you other Spartans here," he said, "I became your friend and ally when you were fighting the Athenians. Not only did I support your fleet with money, but also I myself fought alongside you on horseback and we drove your enemies into the sea together. You cannot accuse me of ever having played you false, like Tissaphernes. Yet despite this, you have now left my land in such a state that I cannot even feed myself, unless I gather up the scraps you leave behind like an animal. All the beautiful houses and woods full of trees and beasts that my father left me, which I used to enjoy so much, I now see either cut down or burned up. Well, if I don't know what is righteous and just, you tell me how these are the acts of men who know how to repay favors."

The thirty Spartans were ashamed and said nothing, but then after a time Agesilaus spoke up.

"Pharnabazus," he said, "I think you understand that in the Greek cities, people also become guest-friends to one another. But when their cities go to war, such people fight on behalf of their homelands against their friends, and even kill them, if it should so happen. In the same way, since we are now at war with your king, we are compelled to treat everything of his as enemy territory. However, we would think it the best thing in the world to become your friends. Now, if it were a matter of throwing off the king to be ruled by us instead, I certainly would not advise it, but if you side with us now you will have the chance to flourish without having any master or humbling yourself to anyone. I think freedom is, after all, worth any amount of money. Even so, we are not urging that you should be free and poor. Rather, by taking us as your allies, you will increase your own power, not the king's, and by subduing those who are now your fellow slaves you will make them your own subjects. You will become both free and rich—what else could you need to have perfect happiness?"

"In that case," said Pharnabazus, "shall I tell you plainly what I will do?"

"That would be a good idea," said Agesilaus.

"Well then," he said, "if the king sends another general here and makes me subordinate to him, I will gladly become your friend and ally. On the other hand, if he gives the command to me, ambition is such a powerful force that I will fight you to the best of my ability."

When he heard these words, Agesilaus grasped Pharnabazus' hand and said:

"My dear friend, I hope you will be our ally! But know this: I will leave your territory now as quickly as I can, and in the future, even if the war continues, we will leave you and your land alone as long as we have other foes to fight."

That was the end of the meeting, and Pharnabazus mounted up and rode away, but his son Parapita, a fine young man, stayed behind. He ran up to Agesilaus and said:

"Agesilaus, I make you my guest-friend."

"For my part, I accept," Agesilaus replied.

"Remember it," said Parapita. He at once gave the beautiful javelin he was carrying to Agesilaus. In return, Agesilaus took a splendid decoration from the horse his secretary Idaeus was riding and gave it to Parapita. Then the young man leapt upon his horse and followed after his father.

SECTION 8
The Ionian Revolt, 499–493 BCE

8.1: Herodotus' narrative of the revolt

Herodotus, *Histories* 5.97–124

Herodotus is the only author to give an account of the Ionian Revolt (499–493 BCE). We are dependent on his narrative, even though it is clearly biased. Herodotus took a dim view of the revolt, presenting it as a disorganized and poorly planned spasm of violence stirred up by Histiaeus and Aristagoras, two Ionian aristocrats who feared falling out of favor with Darius and hoped to have better luck as rebels.

The actual causes of the revolt have been much debated by historians. One view sees the revolt arising from the Ionian Greeks' yearning to be free of the Persians and their local puppets; another sees it as the result of discontent caused by the demands for ships, soldiers, and supplies to support Darius' campaigns against the Scythians. There may be elements of truth to both positions.[1]

Herodotus begins his account with Aristagoras in Greece trying to drum up support for the Ionians in their struggle against the Persians. Having had no luck with King Cleomenes of Sparta, he turned next to Athens.

[97] At this moment, when the Athenians were on bad terms with the Persians,[2] Aristagoras of Miletus,[3] after he had been driven out of Sparta

---

1. K. H. Waters, "Herodotus and the Ionian Revolt," *Historia* Bd. 19, H. 4 (November 1970); Pericles B. Georges, "Persian Ionia under Darius: The Revolt Reconsidered," *Historia* Bd. 49, H. 1 (1st quarter 2000).
2. The Athenians were at odds with Persia because they had refused to take Hippias back as tyrant. See Document 7.2.
3. Miletus: a coastal city in southern Ionia. Aristagoras was tyrant of Miletus.

by Cleomenes, next turned to Athens, since it was the second most powerful city. When he came before the Athenian assembly, Aristagoras gave the same speech he had given to the Spartans about the wealth of Asia and the Persians' way of making war. He claimed that the Persians would be easy to defeat, since they were not accustomed to wielding shields or spears. To these things he added the claim that the Milesians were originally settlers from Athens,[4] and that it would be right for Athens to rescue such a mighty people. There was nothing he did not earnestly promise until finally they were persuaded.

It is easier to fool many people, it seems, than just one: Cleomenes the Spartan may not have fallen for his story, but thirty thousand Athenians did. Taken in by Aristagoras, they voted to send twenty ships to the Ionians' aid. Melanthius, a man of the city who was well regarded all around, was appointed admiral. These ships were the start of trouble for Greeks and barbarians alike.

[98] Aristagoras sailed on ahead, and when he got to Miletus, he hatched a plan which was not intended to do any good to the Ionians (nor did it), but rather to annoy Darius. He sent a man to the Paeonians who had been taken captive by Megabyzus and settled in Phrygia in a village of their own.[5] Upon reaching them the man said: "Men of Paeonia: Aristagoras, the tyrant of Miletus, sent me here to advise you how to reach safety, if you will just do as he suggests. All Ionia is now in revolt against the king and it is within your grasp to return safely to your own lands. You must make it as far as the sea on your own, but from there he will take care of you."

This was very welcome news to the Paeonians. Many of them gathered up their wives and children and made their way secretly to the sea, although some were too afraid to go and remained where they were. Those Paeonians who made the journey to the coast crossed over to Chios. When they had made it to Chios on foot, a large company of Persian cavalry came chasing after them. Unable to catch them, the Persians sent word to Chios, ordering the Paeonians to return, but the Paeonians

---

4. There is no historical or archaeological evidence that Miletus was settled by Athenians, but Greeks often found it useful to make arguments in terms of supposed shared ancestry. See Document 7.4; Holt N. Parker, "The Linguistic Case for the Aiolian Migration Reconsidered," *Hesperia* 77, no. 3 (July–September 2008).
5. Paeonians: a loose collection of peoples who lived in the mountainous regions north of Macedonia. Some Paeonians had been forcibly resettled in Anatolia by Darius. See Herodotus 5.12–17.

refused. The Chians helped them get to Lesbos, and from there the Lesbians escorted them to Doriscus.[6] From Doriscus they walked all the way to Paeonia.

[99] The Athenians came to Ionia with twenty ships and the Eretrians[7] with five triremes. The Eretrians did not come out of any desire to curry favor with the Athenians, but feeling that they owed a debt to the Milesians. You see, the Milesians once helped the Eretrians when they were at war with the Chalcidians, when the Samians came in on the Chalcidian side. Once the Athenians and Eretrians had arrived and joined the other assembled allies, Aristagoras launched an expedition against Sardis. He did not lead the campaign himself but stayed behind in Miletus. Instead he appointed some other Milesians to head the expedition, his brother Charopinus and another citizen by the name of Hermophantus.

[100] When this army of Ionians reached Ephesus,[8] they left their ships there and marched inland in many small bands with Ephesians as guides. They marched first along the Cayster River, then crossed Mount Tmolus and fell upon Sardis unopposed. They seized all of the city except the citadel, which was defended by Artaphrenes himself with a sizable force.

[101] Although they captured the city, they had no opportunity to loot it. Most of the houses in Sardis were built of reeds, and even those built of brick had reed roofs. When one soldier set fire to a house, the flames quickly spread from house to house until the whole city was on fire. When the city began to burn, the Lydians and Persians in the citadel were cut off as the buildings all around them were consumed in flame, so they made a rush for the marketplace and the Pactolus River. (This river carries gold dust down from Mount Tmolus and runs right through the marketplace before flowing down into the Hermus River and finally to the sea.) The Lydians and Persians assembled in the marketplace where they had no choice but to stand their ground. When the Ionians saw some of the enemy assembled and ready to fight, and many more on their way, they were frightened and fell back to Mount Tmolus. From there, under cover of darkness, they returned to their ships. [102] When Sardis was burned, a temple of the local goddess Cybele was also burned down,

---

6. Chios and Lesbos are islands off the coast of Ionia. Doriscus is a town on the European mainland in the northern Aegean.
7. Eretria: a city on the coast of Euboea.
8. Ephesus: a coastal city in southern Ionia.

which was the pretext on which the Persians later burned temples in Greece.

When the Persians who governed the territories west of the Halys River[9] learned about these events, they assembled their forces and came to the Lydians' aid. Finding that the Ionians had left Sardis, the Persians followed their tracks and caught them at Ephesus. The Ionians drew up for battle but were thoroughly routed. The Persians slew many famous fighters, including Eualcides, the Eretrian commander, who had won a crown in the games[10] and whose praises had been sung by Simonides of Ceos. Those who escaped the battle dispersed to their own cities. [103] That was how the fighting went.

At this point, the Athenians entirely abandoned the Ionians, and although Aristagoras sent many messengers imploring them for aid, they said they would do nothing more to help the Ionians. The Ionians, though deprived of their Athenian allies, were no less determined to carry on the war that they had begun against Darius. They sailed to the Hellespont and brought Byzantium and the other cities of that region under their power. Then sailing out from the Hellespont, they won over most of Caria to their cause. Even the city of Caunus, which had not wanted to throw in its lot with them at first, joined in once they had burned Sardis.

[104] All the cities in Cyprus except Amathus[11] also eagerly joined the revolt against the Persians. It happened like this. There was a certain Onesilus, son of Chersis, grandson of Siromus, great-grandson of Euelthon, and he was also the younger brother of Gorgus, the king of Salamis.[12] This Onesilus had often in the past encouraged his brother to rebel against the Persians, and when he learned of the Ionians' revolt, he was all the more insistent in pressing his brother to join them. Since he could not convince Gorgus to act, he and his supporters kept watch until the king left the city and then shut the gates against him. When Gorgus found himself shut out of his own city, he took refuge with the

---

9. Halys River: the modern Kızılırmak, the eastern boundary of the kingdom of Lydia before it was conquered by Persia.
10. The Olympics or one of the other Panhellenic athletic competitions. Crowns of leaves were awarded to winners.
11. Amathus: a city in southern Cyprus. Amathus appears to have been a native Cypriot settlement with strong links to Phoenicia, unlike most of the cities that rebelled with Onesilus, which were Greek colonies.
12. Salamis: a Greek city in eastern Cyprus, not to be confused with the island off the coast of Athens where Greek and Persian naval forces clashed in 480.

Persians. Now king of Salamis, Onesilus called on all Cypriots to join him in revolt. The other cities followed his lead, but the Amathusians refused, so he laid siege to their city.

[105] When it was reported to King Darius that Sardis had been captured and burnt by the Athenians and the Ionians, and that Aristagoras of Miletus was the man responsible for hatching this plot, it is said that he was unconcerned about the Ionians, knowing well that they would not escape retribution for their revolt, but he asked who the Athenians were. When he learned the answer, he called for his bow, nocked an arrow, and shot it into the sky. As the arrow sailed towards the sun, he said: "O Zeus, may I have my vengeance upon the Athenians!" He then assigned one of his attendants to say to him three times, whenever dinner was set before him: "Sire, remember the Athenians."

[106] Darius then summoned Histiaeus the Milesian,[13] whom he had been keeping at court for some time, and said to him: "Histiaeus, I have learned that Aristagoras, the governor you appointed in Miletus, has been making trouble for me. He has led an army of men from across the sea against me and persuaded some of the Ionians to follow him as well, though they will not get away with it. They have taken Sardis from me. Well, does this seem right to you? How did this happen without you having anything to say about it? You had better keep your nose clean in the future."

Histiaeus replied: "Sire, what are you saying—that I should have had a part in a scheme to do you any harm, great or small? What reason could I have for doing such a thing when I owe everything to you and I am trusted to attend your counsels? No, be assured, if my underling has done what you say then he has done it all on his own. I can hardly believe that my deputy or any of the Milesians have done you any harm. However, if what you have heard is true, then you see what comes of having taken me away from the coast, for it seems that as soon as I was out of sight, the Ionians did what they have long had a mind to do. If I had been in Ionia, not one city would have made a move. Now, send me to Ionia and I will set everything in order and turn over to you that Milesian governor who

---

13. Histiaeus: a former tyrant of Miletus. According to Herodotus, Darius had brought Histiaeus to his court on the advice of one of his generals, who was suspicious of Histiaeus' activity as tyrant and thought the king should keep a closer eye on him. Histiaeus, looking for an excuse to be sent back to Ionia, had encouraged Aristagoras to stir up trouble. There is no telling how far Herodotus' account can be trusted when it comes to the motivations of Histiaeus and Aristagoras.

is behind these schemes. When I have satisfied you in these matters, I swear by the royal gods that I will not take off the tunic I have on when I get to Ionia until I have made Sardinia, the largest island in the sea, pay you tribute."

[107] Darius, deceived by Histiaeus' words, sent him off with orders to return to him at Susa once he had accomplished his task.

[108] Meanwhile—that is, during the time when the message about Sardis was sent to the king, and Darius did the bit with the bow, had words with Histiaeus, and finally sent him off to handle affairs on the coast—this is what was happening. While Onesilus was besieging Amathus, he received a report that a Persian, Artybius, was on his way to Cyprus by ship with a large army. Upon receiving this news, Onesilus sent a herald to the Ionians to call on them for aid. The Ionians, after brief deliberations, came to Cyprus with a large force. The Ionians were thus on Cyprus when the Persians sailed across from Cilicia and marched overland to Salamis. At the same time, the Phoenician ships were sailing around the headland known as the Keys of Cyprus.[14]

[109] The tyrants of Cyprus, seeing this state of affairs, summoned the Ionian generals and said: "Ionians, we Cypriots will let you choose whether you would rather face off against the Persians or the Phoenicians. If you prefer to take on the Persians on land, now is the time for you to land your troops and get them into order while we board your ships and sail out to oppose the Phoenicians. If you prefer to face the Phoenicians, get to it, but whatever you choose it is up to you to ensure that both Cyprus and Ionia are free."

To this, the Ionians said: "We were sent here by the common council of the Ionians to guard the sea, not to turn our ships over to the Cypriots and face the Persians on land. Now it is time for us to prove that we are up to the task and for you to show yourselves worthy men, remembering how you suffered under Persian oppression." [110] That was the Ionians' answer.

When the Persian forces arrived on the plains around Salamis, the kings of Cyprus arranged their troops for battle. The best of the Salaminians and Solians were stationed to oppose the Persians while the other Cypriots faced the rest of the attacking force. Onesilus voluntarily placed himself to confront Artybius.

---

14. Keys of Cyprus: the northeastern extremity of Cyprus now known as the Karpass Peninsula.

[111] Artybius' horse had been trained to attack foot soldiers by rearing up. When he learned about this, Onesilus said to his shield-bearer (a Carian, a courageous and experienced veteran): "I hear that Artybius' horse rears up and kicks and bites whoever faces him. Think about it and tell me which of the two you would rather confront on the field, Artybius or his horse."

The squire answered: "Sire, I am prepared to do either or both, however you command me, but I'll tell you what I think you should do. I say a king and general should fight a king and general. You see, if you kill a general, that is a great thing. On the other hand, if he kills you—heaven forbid!—it is not nearly so bad an end to be killed by such a worthy enemy. It's better for us servants to fight other servants, or a horse. Never you fear his tricks: I'll see to it he never rears up against another man again." [112] No sooner had he given this answer than the fighting broke out both on land and at sea.

The Ionians in their ships were in fine form that day, with the Samians standing out as the best, and they defeated the Phoenicians. On land, once the armies came face to face they charged into battle. As for the two generals, Artybius attacked Onesilus from horseback, and Onesilus, as he had agreed with his shield-bearer, struck the Persian commander a blow as he charged. When the horse clashed on Onesilus' shield with its hooves, the Carian sliced its feet off with his scimitar. [113] Thus Artybius, the Persian general, died along with his horse.

In the midst of the battle, Stesenor, tyrant of Curium, who had a large force of soldiers, betrayed the rest of the army. (Curium is said to be an Argive settlement.[15]) Once the Curians had deserted, the Salaminian war chariots did likewise, and when that happened, the Persians gained the upper hand over the Cypriots. The Cypriot army was routed and many fell, including Onesilus, son of Chersis, who had started the revolt, and the king of Soli, Aristocyprus, son of that Philocyprus whom Solon,[16] when visiting Cyprus, had described in a poem as the best of all tyrants.

[114] The Amathusians, since Onesilus had besieged them, cut his head off and took it away with them to mount over the gates of the city.

---

15. Curium: a city on the southern coast of Cyprus. While it is not unusual for Herodotus to add in extra historical details, the mention of Argos may also have to do with the fact that Argos remained neutral during Xerxes' invasion (see Document 7.4). The Argive ancestry of the Curians might have made their choice to side with the Persians more understandable to Herodotus' audience.

16. Solon: famous Athenian lawgiver and poet.

Once the head was hung up and had become hollowed out, a colony of bees moved in and filled it with honeycomb. The Amathusians consulted an oracle about this marvel and were advised that, for their benefit, they should take the head down and give it a proper burial, then offer sacrifice to Onesilus as a hero every year. [115] The Amathusians took this advice, and they continue the custom even today.

Now, when the Ionians, after fighting at sea, learned that Onesilus' plans were utterly undone and that the cities of Cyprus were under siege (except for Salamis, which the people turned over to their former king, Gorgus), they sailed back to Ionia. Of the Cypriot cities, Soli held out against siege the longest, but the Persians captured it in four months after undermining its walls. [116] So the Cypriots, having been free for a year, were enslaved anew.[17]

Daurises, Hymaees, and Otanes, three Persian generals who were all married to daughters of Darius, pursued the Ionians who had attacked Sardis back to their ships. After defeating the Ionians, they divided up the cities among themselves to plunder. [117] Daurises advanced toward the Hellespont and captured the cities of Dardanus, Abydus, Percote, Lampsacus, and Paesus.[18] He took each of these cities in a single day.

As Daurises was marching from Paesus toward Parius, however, he received word that the Carians intended to throw in with the Ionians and rebel against Persia, so he turned away from the Hellespont and marched his army into Caria. [118] The Carians were somehow alerted before Daurises arrived and they assembled their forces at the place called the White Stones, near the Marsyas River, which flows from Idria to the Maeander. Once they were gathered together, they considered many different plans, the best of which, if you ask me, came from Pixodarus, son of Mausolus, who was married to the daughter of Syennesis, the king of Cilicia. He proposed crossing the river and fighting the Persians with the water behind them so that, having nowhere to flee to, they would be forced to stand firm and be braver than usual. But this suggestion did not carry the day. Instead it was decided that the Persians should be the ones

---

17. The people of Cyprus became subjects of the Persian king again and were required to pay tribute and participate in Persian military ventures. The reconquered cities were probably also looted by Persian troops. The Cypriots did not, however, become slaves subject to being bought, sold, and forced to labor without pay. Herodotus and other Greek writers often use the language of slavery to describe submission to Persian rule.
18. Cities on the Anatolian coast of the Hellespont.

to fight with the Maeander River at their backs so that if they were bested they would have nowhere to flee to and would perish in the river.

[119] Once the Persians had arrived and crossed the Maeander, the Carians met them in battle near the Marsyas. The Carians put up a hard fight for a long time, but in the end they were overwhelmed by superior numbers. The Persians lost about two thousand men, the Carians about ten thousand.

Those who fled the field were hemmed into the large sacred plane-tree grove of Zeus of the Armies at Labraunda. (The Carians are the only people we know of who sacrifice to Zeus of the Armies.)[19] The survivors debated how best to save themselves, whether they should surrender to the Persians or leave Anatolia for good. [120] While they were considering their decision, the Milesians and their allies came to their aid. At this the Carians put aside their plans and got back into the fight. They faced the Persians again and were beaten even worse the second time. Many Carians fell, but the Milesians got the worst of it.

[121] The Carians rallied after this defeat and kept up the fight. When they learned that the Persians were planning a strike against their cities, they set up an ambush along the road at Pedasa. The Persian forces stumbled into this trap at night and were destroyed, including their generals Daurises, Amorges, and Sisimaces. Myrsus the son of Gyges died with them. The commander of the ambush was Heraclides of Mylasas, son of Ibanilus. [122] That is how those Persians perished.

At this point, Hymaees, one of the Persians who had been pursuing the Ionians after their attack on Sardis, headed towards the Propontis and captured Cius in Mysia.[20] Having taken this city, he learned that Daurises had left the Hellespont to attack the Carians, so he took his army out of the Propontis to the Hellespont. There he subdued all the Aeolians[21] living in the region of Ilium and also the Gergithae, who are

---

19. Zeus of the Armies: evidently either a local version of Zeus or a Carian god whom Greeks like Herodotus equated with the Greek god Zeus.
20. Mysia: a region in northwestern Anatolia.
21. Aeolians: Greeks living along the central northern Aegean coast of Anatolia. Although they shared much culture and history with the Ionian Greeks, they spoke a slightly different dialect of Greek and shared some distinct social and religious customs. They are often lumped together with the Ionian Greeks and they also participated in the Ionian Revolt.

the descendants of the ancient Trojans. In the midst of these conquests, Hymaees fell ill and died in the Troad,[22] [123] and thus he ended his life.

Artaphrenes, who was in command of Sardis, and Otanes, the third general, were tasked with leading the fight against the Ionians and their Aeolian neighbors. They captured the Ionian city of Clazomenae and the Aeolian Cyme.

[124] When these cities were falling to the Persians, Aristagoras showed himself to be nothing but a coward who had thrown Ionia into chaos for his own purposes, for when he saw what was happening he began making plans to flee. It was clear that defeating Darius would be impossible.

8.2: Ration authorization for Datis

PF-NN 1809

In a rare case in which Persian sources refer to events on the Aegean frontier, this document records the general Datis making a swift return to Persepolis in the winter of 494. Datis' movements at this date are most likely related to the preparations for the Persian offensive against Miletus in 494 (see Document 8.4).[23]

70 liters of beer as rations for Datis. He carried an authorization with the king's seal. He traveled by the fast horse service from Sardis to the king at Persepolis.

January/February, 494 BCE.

---

22. Troad: the region in northwestern Anatolia on the south side of the Hellespont where the fabled city of Troy was located.
23. John O. Hyland, "The Achaemenid Messenger Service and the Ionian Revolt: New Evidence from the Persepolis Fortification Archive," *Historia* Bd. 68, H. 2 (2019).

8.3: The Lindos Chronicle

IG XII, Lindos II, 2, D.1.4–47

An inscription from the temple of Athena at Lindos, on the island of Rhodes, records significant events from the history of the city. Among them is an incident that may have happened during the Persian campaign to suppress the Ionian Revolt. The mention of Datis as commander places the events either in this period or during the campaign against Athens and Eretria in 490 (see Document 9.2).

This story, inscribed many centuries after the events in question, tells a dramatic tale of divine intervention, but behind it we can read a credible account of Persian tactics: a siege ends with negotiations and a peaceful settlement confirmed with a display of respect for local religious customs.

When Darius, king of the Persians, sent his mighty fleet to enslave Greece, it landed here [5] first of all the islands. When they landed, the people fled. Some took refuge in the fortresses while most gathered in Lindos. The barbarians blockaded and laid siege to the city [10] until, when the water supply ran low, the Lindians began to consider surrendering the city to them.

Then the goddess sent a message in a dream to one of the archons[24] to encourage him [15] to keep his spirits up, promising that she would persuade her father[25] to send them water. The man who saw this vision reported Athena's command to the rest of the citizens. They examined their reserves, and finding that they could only hold out for five more days, [20] they begged the barbarians for a truce for just that long. They said that Athena had promised that her father would send them rain, and that if the rain did not come by the appointed time, [25] they would surrender the city to them.

When Datis, Darius' admiral, heard this speech, he burst out laughing. But within the stated number of days, a darkness gathered around the city and [30] a torrent of rain unexpectedly fell upon it, leaving the

---

24. archons: magistrates either elected or appointed to govern a city, usually for a term of one year.
25. Zeus, god of the sky and storms.

besieged with an abundance of water while the Persian forces got hardly any.

Astounded by this manifestation of the goddess's power, the barbarian took [35] the adornments from his body and pledged his cloak, necklace, and bracelets, as well as his headdress and short sword, plus his carriage, as offerings to the temple. [40] These were preserved until the days when Eucles, son of Astyanax, was priest of Helios, when the temple burned down along with most of the offerings.

Datis lifted the siege, as he had promised, established friendly relations [45] with the besieged, and declared that the gods had protected these people.

8.4: The sack of Miletus

Herodotus, *Histories* 6.18–20

Persian naval forces confronted the rebels off the Ionian coast at the battle of Lade in 494 and won a decisive victory, effectively ending the Ionian Revolt. The city of Miletus was recaptured by Persia in that same year. As the original epicenter of the revolt, Miletus received a harsher treatment than most other cities in Ionia.

[18] Once the Persians had defeated the Ionian fleet, they laid siege to Miletus by land and sea. By undermining the walls and using every kind of siege engine against it, they captured the whole city in the sixth year after Aristagoras' uprising. They enslaved the city, and thus the oracle of the fall of Miletus was fulfilled.

[19] For when the Argives consulted the oracle at Delphi concerning the safety of their city, they were given a double oracle, one part for themselves and one part for the Milesians.[26] I will save the part concerning the

---

26. It is not entirely clear when the Argives received this oracle, but it may have come in response to Aristagoras soliciting Argive support for the Ionian Revolt. Herodotus does not mention Aristagoras going to Argos, but Argos was a major power in Greece and a perennial rival to Sparta. Having been rejected by Sparta, Argos would have been a natural next stop for Aristagoras (see Document 8.1).

Argives until I reach that part of the story and present it then, but the part given for the Milesians in their absence went like this:

> Miletus, you who scheme at evil deeds,
> will be a feast and splendid gifts for many.
> Your wives will wash the feet of long-haired men.
> Strangers will tend my shrine in Didyma.[27]

These words now caught up with the Milesians, as most of the men were slain by Persians, who wear their hair long. The women and children were treated as slaves,[28] and the temple at Didyma, both the shrine and the oracular site, were plundered and burned. I have made mention of the treasures of this temple in several other places in my story.[29]

[20] The captives from Miletus were taken to Susa. King Darius did no further harm to them, but settled them at the city of Ampe on the Persian Gulf, near where the Tigris River flows into the sea. The Persians themselves occupied the city of Miletus and the surrounding plains while turning over the uplands to the Pedasian Carians.

8.5: A peaceful settlement with the Ionians

Many other Ionian cities besides Miletus also suffered the ravages of war and siege, but once the fighting was done, the Persians were mostly concerned with restoring order. Their immediate goal was to stabilize Ionia while they launched strikes on Athens and Eretria, the two cities west of the Aegean that had contributed forces to the revolt. Herodotus records changes in the administration of the region that suggest the Persians recognized that stifling local politics and making arbitrary demands for tribute and supplies had been major causes of resentment. A fragment from Diodorus of Sicily, a later historian, gives a more colorful, less reliable version of events, but one that also suggests that Persians

---

27. Didyma: a site south of Miletus where there was a temple to Apollo with an oracle. Also called Branchidae.
28. Referring to the forced resettlement described below.
29. Herodotus, *Histories* 1.92, 2.159, 5.36.

were sensitive to local sentiment in their treatment of the Ionians after the revolt.

Herodotus, *Histories* 6.42–43

[42] In this year, the Persians did nothing more against the Ionians. Indeed, some things developed that were very much to the Ionians' benefit. Artaphrenes, the governor of Sardis, summoned representatives from the Ionian cities and compelled them to agree among themselves that they would settle their disputes through arbitration and would no longer fight or harass one another. He made them agree to this, and he also measured out their land in parasangs, which is a Persian measure equal to thirty *stadia*,[30] and ordered them to pay tribute according to this measurement, an arrangement which remained in force even to my day. This assessment was close to what they had paid before. These arrangements brought peace to the Ionians.

[43] The next spring, the king dismissed the other generals from their posts and sent Mardonius, the son of Gobryas, down to the sea at the head of a substantial army and fleet. Mardonius was a young man who had recently married the king's daughter, Artozostre. As soon as he reached Cilicia, Mardonius boarded ship and traveled with his fleet while his subordinates led the army to the Hellespont.

Sailing along the coast of Asia, Mardonius came to Ionia, where I will mention something that will astonish those Greeks who do not believe that Otanes proposed a democratic constitution for the Persians when the seven conspirators were debating: he removed all the Ionian tyrants and established democracies in the cities.[31]

---

30. The parasang was a Persian unit of length with a precise measure that is hard to define. It was apparently based not on actual distance but on the length of time it would take an army to march over terrain, so that a parasang of flat, dry road might be much longer than one of hilly or muddy ground. In general, it seems to have ranged between four and six kilometers. The *stadion* (plural *stadia*) was a Greek unit of length. There was no consistent standard for the length of a *stadion*, which could vary from around 160 to around 190 meters. Tim Rood, "Xenophon's Parasangs," *Journal of Hellenic Studies* 130 (2010).
31. According to Herodotus, seven Persian nobles conspired to overthrow the false Bardiya (see Document 6.3), then held a debate as to which form of government would be best for Persia, in which Otanes argued in favor of democracy (see Herodotus, *Histories* 3.80–82). Herodotus' Greek audience was probably right to be skeptical about the constitutional debate, which would be completely out of place in the Persian tradition, but it is

Diodorus of Sicily, *Library of History* 10.25 F 4

Hecataeus the Milesian, whom the Ionians had sent as their ambassador, asked Artaphernes what grounds he had to mistrust the Ionians. Artaphernes replied that he was sure the Ionians would bear a grudge, having been beaten so badly in the war.

"Why, surely," said Hecataeus, "if suffering breeds distrust, then it follows that being treated well by the Persians will make our cities well disposed to you."

Artaphernes approved of this argument, so he restored the laws in Ionia and imposed fixed tributes on the cities based on what they could afford.

---

plausible that local governments in Ionia were reorganized in the wake of the revolt, since the tyrants had proven incapable of assuring stability in their cities.

SECTION 9
Darius' Aegean campaigns, 492–490 BCE

9.1: Diplomatic initiatives

Herodotus, *Histories* 6.48–49

Darius' attacks on mainland Greece were coordinated with a diplomatic campaign intended to establish local alliances and divide the Greeks.

[48] Darius then attempted to ascertain the Greeks' intent, whether they meant to make war on him or surrender. Accordingly, he sent heralds to cities throughout Greece to demand earth and water.[1] While these heralds were on their way to Greece, he also sent word to the coastal cities that paid him tribute and ordered them to start building ships, both warships and horse transports. [49] These cities began the preparations as ordered.

Many of those on the mainland, and all of the islanders, gave the Persian heralds what the king demanded. Among the islanders who gave earth and water to Darius were the Aeginetans. The Athenians responded to this act immediately, on the belief that the Aeginetans had thrown in with the Persians just to join the war on Athens. They gladly seized upon this pretext and sent to Sparta to accuse the Aeginetans of betraying Greece.

---

1. The gift of earth and water was the traditional symbol of submission to Persian rule.

9.2: The Aegean campaign and the battle of Marathon

Herodotus, *Histories* 6.94–117

In 490 BCE, a small Persian force was sent over water to capture those Greek cities which had contributed to the Ionian Revolt or otherwise caused trouble for Persia in the preceding decade, above all Athens and Eretria. The Persian force raided or captured a number of cities on the Aegean islands, including Eretria, before landing at Marathon on the east coast of Attica.

The Athenian hoplite army, bolstered by a small contingent of Plataeans, fought the Persians at Marathon and drove them back to their ships. The surviving Persian forces then attempted to sail around the peninsula of Attica and make a strike at Athens before the Athenian army could march back overland to defend the city, but this attempt failed and the Persians ended their campaign.

The battle of Marathon was the first Greek victory over Persian forces in a pitched battle. In reality, a small Athenian-led army succeeded against a small Persian expeditionary force which had already accomplished the rest of its mission. In the Athenian imagination, however, Marathon took on a legendary status. Veterans of the battle considered it the high point of their lives while the dead were buried in an extraordinary public tomb on the battlefield. The memory of Marathon remained a crucial part of Athenian patriotic self-promotion for generations afterward.[2]

Herodotus' account of the battle and the campaign that led up to it is suffused with Athenian self-glorification and surrounded with divine portents. Under the surface, however, we find the outlines of a largely successful Persian diplomatic and military campaign that aimed both to make an example of those Greeks who resisted Persian rule and to demonstrate Persia's benevolence toward local tradition. The factional divisions that led to the capture of Eretria, and the fear of the same in Athens, give us a sense of how divided the Greek world was about how to

---

2. Hans-Joachim Gehrke, "From Athenian Identity to European Ethnicity—the Cultural Biography of the Myth of Marathon," in *Ethnic Constructs in Antiquity: The Role of Power and Tradition*, ed. Ton Derks and Nico Roymans (Amsterdam: Amsterdam University Press, 2009).

respond to Persia's power, even in the cities that had joined in the Ionian Revolt.

[94] The Persian king was attending to his concerns, since his servant was always reminding him about the Athenians and the descendants of Peisistratus were at his court, disparaging the Athenians.[3] Darius seized these pretexts for subduing all those Greeks who had not offered him earth and water. He dismissed Mardonius from command of the army, since he had accomplished so little, and dispatched new commanders for the campaign against Eretria and Athens: Datis,[4] a Mede, and his own nephew Artaphrenes, son of Artaphrenes. Their orders were to enslave Eretria and Athens and bring the slaves before him.[5]

[95] These generals set out on their mission and reached the Aleian plain in Cilicia, leading a large and well-equipped army. They encamped there and were met by the fleet that had been prepared for them. They were also joined by the horse transports that Darius had ordered his tributary subjects to prepare the previous year. They loaded their army and horses onto ships and sailed to Ionia accompanied by six hundred triremes. From here they did not take the coastal route to the Hellespont and Thrace but sailed out from Samos through the Icarian Sea[6] and along the islands. They took this route, I think, mostly out of fear of sailing around Athos, where a great fleet had been wrecked on the shore the year before.[7] Furthermore, since Naxos had not been conquered, they had another reason to choose this route.

[96] The Persians intended to attack Naxos first. When their fleet sailed across the Icarian Sea and landed on Naxos, the Naxians, remembering recent events, fled into the mountains. The Persians captured as

---

3. See Documents 7.2; 8.1, section 105.
4. The ration record for Datis (Document 8.2) places him in the Aegean region in 494, at the end of the campaign against the Ionian Revolt, which means the change of military leadership had most likely already happened before the new campaign against Eretria and Athens was launched.
5. Referring to the forced relocation of the populations of these cities.
6. Icarian Sea: the part of the Aegean roughly bounded by the Anatolian mainland and the islands of Samos, Icaros, Naxos, and Cos.
7. Athos: a large mountain at the end of a peninsula in the northern Aegean. A Persian fleet on its way to attack mainland Greece was wrecked there in 492 (Herodotus mistakes the year, placing the wreck in 491).

many of them as they could and burned the city and its temples. Then they set out for the other islands.

[97] Meanwhile, the Delians had abandoned Delos and fled to Tenos. While the Persian fleet was sailing toward shore, Datis sailed on ahead and had the fleet anchor not at Delos but off Rhenaea.[8] When he learned where the Delians had gone, he sent them this message by a herald:

"Why have you holy men misjudged me and fled? I mean no harm to the land where the twin gods[9] were born or to its people, and neither does my king. Come back to your island and your homes."

He made this proclamation to the Delians, then he piled up three hundred talents[10] of frankincense on the altar and burned it as an offering. [98] He then sailed his fleet on to attack Eretria, taking Ionians and Aeolians with him.

When Datis had put to sea, Delos was shaken by an earthquake, the first and the last that had occurred there down to my time, according to the Delians. I suppose the god sent this marvel as a sign to humanity of the evils that were to come, for in the three generations under the rule of Darius, son of Hystaspes, his son Xerxes, and his grandson Artaxerxes, Greece suffered worse than in the twenty generations before Darius. Some of these troubles were caused by the Persians, and some by the struggles for power among the leaders of Greece. It is no wonder that Delos, where earthquakes had been unknown, should feel one now. Indeed, there was an oracle that said:

Delos, the unshaken, I will shake.

Translated into our language, Darius means "The Doer," Xerxes means "The Brave," and Artaxerxes means "The Very Brave."[11] That is what the Greek would call these kings in their own tongue.

---

8. Delos and Rhenaea are two small islands separated by a narrow strait. Tenos is a larger island to their north.
9. Twin gods: Apollo and Artemis, who were born on Delos, according to Greek myth, which made Delos sacred.
10. talent: a unit of weight whose exact value varied from place to place. Herodotus probably means the Attic talent, which weighed approximately 26 kilograms, which would make Datis' offering around 7,800 kilograms.
11. These translations are wrong. In Old Persian, Daryaush (Darius) means "He who holds onto goodness," Khshayarsha (Xerxes) means "He who rules over heroes," and

[99] Upon leaving Delos, the barbarians landed on the islands. They gathered an army there by taking the children of the islanders as hostages. In their journey around the islands, they also put in at Carystus, where the Carystians refused to either turn over hostages or join in a war against their neighbors, by which they meant Eretria and Athens. The Persians besieged their city and ravaged their land until the Carystians came around to their way of thinking.

[100] When the Eretrians learned that the Persians were sailing against them, they asked the Athenians to come to their aid. The Athenians did not refuse this call but sent them the four thousand cleruchs who had taken over the land of the Chalcidian "horse-breeders,"[12] but the Eretrians had no sound plans. Despite having sent for aid from Athens, they could not agree on what to do. Some wanted to evacuate the city and retreat to the hills of Euboea while others were prepared to hand the city over to the Persians for their own gain.

Aeschines, son of Nothon, a man from one of the leading families of the city, learned about these plans and revealed how matters stood to the Athenians. He advised them to return to their homeland rather than stay and be destroyed along with the Eretrians. The Athenians took Aeschines' advice [101] and saved themselves by crossing over to Oropus.[13]

The Persians beached their ships in Eretrian territory at Temenos, Choereae, and Aegilea. They landed their cavalry and prepared to attack. The Eretrians decided not to march out and meet them in battle. Rather, they intended to carefully guard their walls since the proposal to evacuate the city had been voted down. The walls were heavily attacked for six days and there were many casualties on both sides. On the seventh day, Euphorbus, son of Alchimachus, and Philagrus, son of Cineas, betrayed the city to the Persians. When they entered the city, the Persians looted and burned the temples in revenge for the burning of the temples at Sardis.[14] The people of the city were enslaved in accordance with Darius' orders.

Artakhsharça (Artaxerxes) means "He who rules through truth." Rüdiger Schmidt, "Achaemenid Throne-Names," *Annali dell'Instituto Orientale di Napoli* 42 (1982).
12. cleruch: an Athenian settler on land seized from another city after an Athenian victory in war. Chalcis was a city near Eretria. The Athenians had settled citizens on Chalcidian land after defeating the Chalcidians in battle in 504. "Horse-breeder" was the Chalcidian title for the wealthy elite of their city. See Herodotus, *Histories* 5.77.
13. Oropus: a town on the mainland across the strait from Eretria.
14. See Document 8.1, section 102.

[102] The Persians waited a few days after subduing Eretria, then they sailed for Attica, eager to do to the Athenians what they had done to the Eretrians. Since the ground around Marathon was the most suitable place in Attica for cavalry and the nearest to Eretria, Hippias, son of Peisistratus, led them there.[15] [103] When the Athenians learned of their arrival, they also marched out to Marathon. The ten strategoi[16] were in command, and Miltiades was the tenth of them.

Miltiades' father, Cimon, son of Stesagoras, had been exiled from Athens by Peisistratus, son of Hippocrates. While he was in exile, it happened that he won the four-horse chariot race at the Olympic Games, the same race that his half brother Miltiades had also won. He won the same race again with the same horses in the next Olympics, but he allowed Peisistratus to be announced as the winner instead. By letting this victory go, he got a truce from Peisistratus that allowed him to return to his property in Attica. After he won a third Olympic victory with the same horses, he was killed by Peisistratus' sons (Peisistratus himself had died by then). They set men in ambush for him near the town hall at night.

Cimon was buried in front of the city, on the other side of the road known as "Through the Hollow." The horses he won his three Olympic victories with are buried opposite him. Only the horses of the Spartan Euagoras could compare with them in accomplishments.

At that time, Cimon's elder son Stesagoras was being brought up by his uncle Miltiades in the Chersonese.[17] His younger son was with him in Athens, and he gave his son the name Miltiades in honor of the founder of the Chersonese.

---

15. Hippias' father Peisistratus had seized power in Athens and ruled as tyrant there from 546 until he died in 527. On his death, he passed power down to his two sons, Hippias and Hipparchus. Hipparchus was assassinated in 514 and Hippias driven out in 510. Since his exile, Hippias had been trying to gather Persian support for his return to Athens (see Document 7.2). His presence with the Persian forces suggests that they intended to install him as a pro-Persian ruler in Athens. Since Peisistratus originally came from Marathon, the Persians may have hoped to find local support for Hippias there. These political considerations may have as much to do with the Persian choice to land at Marathon as military expediency.

16. strategoi (singular *strategos*): a board of ten generals annually elected by the citizens of Athens.

17. Chersonese: literally "peninsula," the name used for several different locations in antiquity. In this case, the peninsula on the European side of the Hellespont, known today as the Gallipoli Peninsula.

[104] This was the Miltiades who was now a general in Athens, having left the Chersonese and escaped death twice. The Phoenicians had pursued him as far as Imbros, thinking that it would be a great thing to catch him and send him to the Persian king. Once he had reached his family's estates in Athens and thought he was safe, his enemies hauled him into court on a charge of having ruled as tyrant in the Chersonese, but he was acquitted and chosen as strategos by the Athenians.

[105] First of all, before they set out from the city, the strategoi sent word to the Spartans by Philippides,[18] an Athenian professional long-distance runner. This Philippides reported to the Athenians that when he was near Mount Parthenium, above Tegea, he encountered Pan.[19] Pan, he said, called him by name and told him to ask the Athenians why they paid no attention to him, even though he was friendly to them, had often helped them in the past, and would again in the future. The Athenians believed that this report was true, so when they became prosperous they built a shrine to Pan under the acropolis, and ever since receiving that message they have honored Pan with annual sacrifices and a torch race.

[106] Philippides arrived in Sparta on the next day after leaving Athens (on the occasion when he was sent out by the strategoi and Pan appeared to him). He came before the magistrates and said:

"O, Spartans, the Athenians beg you to come to their aid and not to allow the most ancient city in Greece to be enslaved by barbarians. Eretria has just been captured and Greece is now poorer by one famous city."

When he had delivered his message as ordered, the Spartan magistrates resolved to come to Athens's aid, but they could not act immediately because they did not wish to break their own law. It was then the ninth day of the month, and they said that, it being the ninth, they could not march out until the full moon.[20] [107] So they waited for the full moon.

Meanwhile, Hippias, son of Peisistratus, was leading the Persians to Marathon. The previous night he had had a dream in which he seemed to be having sex with his own mother. He concluded that this dream was a

---

18. Some sources give the name as Pheidippides.
19. Pan: a god of the wilderness.
20. Greek cities used lunar calendars in which the days of the month were linked to the phases of the moon. The Persian attack occurred in late summer during the Spartan month of Carneius. From the seventh to the fifteenth of that month, the Spartans celebrated the festival of Carneia in honor of Apollo, and by custom they were forbidden from sending their army out of the city while the festival was under way.

sign that he would return to Athens, recover his position as ruler, and end his days in his own property as an old man. At any rate, that was what he reckoned the dream meant.

Acting as the Persians' guide, Hippias had the captive Eretrians landed on the island of the Styrians called Aegilia.[21] Then he had the ships anchor at Marathon, led the barbarians out and had them muster on the land. In this midst of this operation, he began to sneeze and cough more forcefully than usual. Since he was an old man and most of his teeth were loose, the force of his coughing dislodged one tooth and expelled it into the sand. He spent much effort searching for it, but the tooth could not be found. With a groan, he said to those nearby: "This land is not ours and we will not be able to bring it under our control. My tooth has as much of it as belongs to me." [108] Hippias figured that his dream had come true in this way.

While the Athenians were drawing up their troops in the sacred ground of Heracles, the full strength of the Plataean muster came to join them, since the Plataeans had placed themselves under Athens's authority, and the Athenians had already made great efforts on their behalf.

Here is how the Plataeans had come under Athenian protection: because the Thebans were putting pressure on them to accept Theban authority,[22] the Plataeans had first offered themselves to the Spartans through King Cleomenes, son of Anaxandridas, when he happened to be in the vicinity, but the Spartans did not think this was a good idea. "We live far away," they said, "and our help would be cold comfort to you. You could be enslaved many times over before we heard a thing about it. We recommend giving yourselves over to the Athenians, who are your neighbors and not bad as protectors."

The Spartans offered this advice less out of good will toward the Plataeans and more in an effort to cause trouble for the Athenians by getting them embroiled in Boeotian affairs, but the Plataeans took the advice seriously nonetheless. While the Athenians were making sacrifices to the

---

21. Aegilia: an island in the strait between Euboea and Attica.
22. Earlier historians identified this projection of power by the Thebans as part of the creation of a Thebes-centered alliance known as the Boeotian League, but more recent work has shown that the Boeotian League was created only in the fifth century. Thebes' interest in Plataea at this time probably had more to do with competing with Athens and building a less formalized regional hegemony. See Stephanie L. Larsen, *Tales of Epic Ancestry: Boiotian Collective Identity in the Late Archaic and Early Classical Periods* (Stuttgart: Steiner 2007), 169.

twelve gods,[23] the Plataeans came and sat at the altar as supplicants and offered themselves into the Athenians' hands.

When the Thebans learned what had happened, they launched an attack on Plataea, but the Athenians came to their defense. Just as the battle was about the start, the Corinthians, who happened to be there, intervened. Both sides appealed to the Corinthians to arbitrate, so they settled the boundary on the condition that the Thebans stop pressuring those Boeotians who did not want to join with the other Boeotians. Having rendered this decision, the Corinthians departed. As the Athenians were leaving, the Thebans attacked them, but the Athenians won the battle. The Athenians then extended the boundary the Corinthians had set, making the Asopus River the limit of Theban territory in the direction of Plataea and Hysiae. So that is how the Plataeans put themselves under the power of Athens, and why they came to help at Marathon.

[109] The strategoi at Marathon could not agree on a course of action. Some were against fighting, since their numbers were few compared with the Persian force. Others, including Miltiades, called for a battle. So they were at odds, and the side opposed to joining battle was winning, but there was an eleventh man, chosen by lot to be polemarch,[24] who had a vote. In the old days, the Athenians gave the polemarch an equal vote with the strategoi, and on this occasion the polemarch was Callimachus, from Aphidnae.

Miltiades came to Callimachus and said: "It is in your hands now, Callimachus, whether Athens is to be enslaved or to live free. You have a chance to leave behind a legacy for all who come after us, greater even than what Harmodius and Aristogeiton[25] did. For Athens is now in its hour of greatest danger since its founding. We know just what we will suffer under Hippias if we bow down to the Persians, but if our city

---

23. The twelve gods: Zeus, Hera, Poseidon, Demeter, Apollo, Artemis, Hephaestus, Athena, Ares, Aphrodite, Hermes, and Hestia.
24. Unlike the strategoi, who were elected to their position by the people, the polemarch was chosen by lot from among the eligible citizens, like other Athenian magistrates. The duties and powers of the polemarch are not entirely clear. The title means literally "war leader" and Herodotus' account suggests that in 490 the polemarch had some military powers. After reforms in 487 BCE, the polemarch's role was limited to judicial and ceremonial functions. See Aristotle, *Athenian Constitution* 58.
25. Harmodius and Aristogeiton: leaders of the conspiracy that killed Hipparchus in 514, although it failed to kill his brother Hippias. Harmodius and Aristogeiton were revered in Athens as symbols of resistance to tyranny.

prevails, it will become the first among all the cities of Greece. I will lay out for you how this can happen and how the power to decide has come into your hands. We ten strategoi are divided, some for an attack and others for holding back. If we do not attack now, I expect that the Athenians will be torn apart with internal fighting, and so we will end up giving in to the Persians, but if we attack before the cracks begin to show in our resolve, as long as the gods play fair with us, we will win the day. Everything depends upon you. If you side with me, your homeland will be free and rank first among the cities of Greece; if you side with those who are eager to avoid a fight, you will have the opposite of these good things I have described."

[110] This speech convinced Callimachus and with his vote he confirmed the decision to seek a battle. After that, the strategoi who had been in favor of fighting yielded their daily authority to Miltiades.[26] He accepted the command, but nevertheless he waited until it was his day in the rotation before launching the attack. [111] When his turn came, he marshaled the Athenians for battle. Callimachus was in command of the right wing, since it was the Athenian custom at the time that the polemarch should command the right wing. Once he took the position of command, the rest of the tribes were drawn up in order,[27] with the Plataeans at the end taking up the left wing. Ever since that battle, when the Athenians offer sacrifices on behalf of the whole community every four years, the Athenian herald prays for the good fortune of Athens and Plataea alike.

When the Athenian battle line formed up, it happened to be the same length as the Persians'. The Athenians' center was drawn out only a few ranks deep, making that the weakest part of the line, but the wings were strong in numbers. [112] Once the army had been drawn up and the sacrifices had proven favorable,[28] the Athenians advanced against the

---

26. Overall command of the army normally rotated each day among the ten strategoi.
27. The tribes, or phylae, were administrative divisions of the Athenian population. The units of the army were organized by tribe and there was a standard order in which they drew up on the battlefield.
28. Greek armies routinely offered sacrifices before engaging in battle, looking for signs of the gods' favor in the behavior of the sacrificial animals or the condition of their internal organs. Armies would not usually advance into battle without favorable signs. See Document 10.13, section 61.

barbarians at a running pace.[29] The distance between the two armies was at least eight *stadia*.[30]

When the Persians saw the Athenians coming on at run, they prepared to confront them. They thought the Athenians must have been seized with a suicidal madness, since they were so few and advancing so fast with no cavalry or archers among them. That was what the barbarians supposed, but the Athenians who swarmed upon them to fight at close quarters fought nobly. These were the first Greeks we know of to charge into battle, and also the first to look on men in Persian clothing unshaken, for up to this time even hearing the name of the Persians had struck the Greeks with terror.

[113] The fighting at Marathon went on for a long time, and in the center of the line, the Persians and the Sacae[31] who had been stationed with them defeated the Greeks. While the Persian center was chasing the remnants of the Greek center inland, the Athenian and Plataean wings both defeated the Persian wings. The victorious Greek wings first let their opponents flee and turned inward to crush the Persian center, then chased down the fleeing Persians, hacking at them as they went. When the Athenians reached the shore they began calling for fire and laying hold of the Persian ships.

[114] Callimachus the polemarch fell in the fighting, having proven himself a worthy man. One of the strategoi, Stesilaus, son of Thrasylaus, also died. Cynegirus, son of Euphorion, also fell when he seized hold of the stern of one ship and his hand was cut off with an axe. Many other famous Athenians died at Marathon.

[115] The Athenians overpowered seven ships, but the rest got away. The barbarians picked up the enslaved Eretrians from the island where they had been left, then sailed around Sunium,[32] aiming to reach the city before the Athenian forces could get back there. Accusations were made

---

29. For heavily armed hoplites to run into battle was unusual, since it would tire them out before the battle started and make it hard to maintain a good fighting order. It seems most likely that the army advanced at a walking pace, then charged the last distance once they were within the range of Persian arrows.
30. The *stadion* (plural *stadia*) was a Greek unit of length. There was no consistent standard for the length of a *stadion*, which could vary from around 160 to around 190 meters. Eight *stadia* would be around 1.5 kilometers.
31. Sacae: semi-nomadic peoples from the Eurasian steppe, some of whom were subjects of the Persian Empire.
32. Sunium: the southernmost tip of the peninsula of Attica.

in Athens that this was part of a plan hatched by the Alcmaeonids, who signaled the Persians by holding up a shield once they were back on their ships.[33]

[116] So the Persians sailed around Sunium. Meanwhile, the Athenians rushed back to the city as fast as they could and got there ahead of the barbarians. They departed from the sacred ground of Heracles at Marathon and made camp again in another sacred ground of Heracles, this one at Cynosarges. The barbarians anchored off Phalerum, which in those days was the official harbor of Athens, and kept their ships there for a time, but then they sailed back to Asia.

[117] 6,400 barbarians were killed in the battle at Marathon; of the Athenians, 192. That was the death toll on both sides.

---

33. The Alcmaeonids were one of the prominent aristocratic families in Athens. They could have signaled the Persians at sea by reflecting the sun's light off a polished shield from the hills. Herodotus later asserts that a signal was indeed sent to the Persians, but that it could not have come from the Alcmaeonids (Herodotus, *Histories* 6.121–24).

SECTION 10
Xerxes' Aegean campaign, 480–479 BCE

10.1: The accession of Xerxes

XPf[1]

This inscription from Persepolis records Xerxes' accession to the throne after the death of his father, Darius.

King Xerxes says: There were other sons of Darius, but it was the desire of Ahura Mazda that my father Darius should choose me to be crown prince. When my father Darius left the throne, by the will of Ahura Mazda I became king on my father's throne. When I became king, I built many excellent buildings. I protected what had been built by my father and I added other buildings. Moreover, all that I built and all that my father built we built by the favor of Ahura Mazda.

10.2: Revolt in Babylon

Ctesias, FGrH 688 F 13.25–26[2]

Xerxes' response to the situation in the Aegean may have been delayed by a revolt in Babylon. The revolt is not well documented but is mentioned by Ctesias.

---

1. Translation adapted from Brosius 107.
2. The works of Ctesias do not survive intact. This passage is from a summary of his *Persica* written by the Byzantine scholar Photius. The text can be found in Photius, *Bibliotheca* 72.38–39.

[25] Xerxes fought a campaign against the Greeks because the Chalcedonians had tried to destroy the bridge, as has already been mentioned, and had pulled down the altar erected by Darius, and because the Athenians had killed Datis and refused to return the body.[3]

[26] First, he went to Babylon where he was eager to see the tomb of Belitanas,[4] which he did with the help of Mardonius, but he was not able to fill the trough with oil, as had been written.[5] Xerxes departed to Ecbatana, where he received word that the Babylonians were in revolt and had killed his general Zopyrus. (That is what Ctesias says about these matters, but Herodotus disagrees. The things Herodotus attributes to Zopyrus[6]—apart from the story about his mule giving birth[7]—Ctesias says were actually accomplished by Megabyzus, who was the husband of Xerxes' daughter Amytis.)[8] So it was by Megabyzus' doing that Babylon was captured. Xerxes gave him, among many other treasures, a golden millstone weighing six talents, which is the greatest mark of honor the king can bestow.

---

3. The bridge is probably Darius' bridge across the Danube constructed during his campaign against the Scythians (see Herodotus, *Histories* 4.89). Darius' altar is not known from any other source. Datis was one of the commanders of the attack on Naxos, Eretria, and Athens in 490 (see Document 9.2), but nothing is known about how and where he died. This account of the war's causes is confusingly abbreviated—whether by Ctesias himself, his Persian sources, or Photius—but it suggests that a series of affronts to royal authority had built up on the northwestern frontier and the Persians felt it necessary to respond with force.

4. tomb of Belitanas: probably the temple of Bel-Marduk, the chief god of Babylon, which Ctesias misunderstood as a tomb.

5. Aelian, *Varia Historia* 13.3 preserves a more detailed version of the story of Xerxes failing to fill a trough with oil as a bad omen, but it is clearly a Greek legend. No such practice is known from Babylonian tradition. The Greek story may have been based on the practice of divination by gazing into the reflective surface of a vessel filled with oil. See Eric R. Dodds, "Supernormal Phenomena in Classical Antiquity," in *The Ancient Concept of Progress and Other Essays on Greek Literature and Belief*, ed. Eric R. Dodds (Oxford: Clarendon, 1973), 185–92.

6. Herodotus 3.153–58 recounts how Darius reconquered Babylon after a revolt; Ctesias places the events in Xerxes' reign.

7. Mules are hybrids of horses and donkeys and are normally infertile, but in rare cases mules can give birth. Because the event was so rare, it was often regarded as an omen from the gods.

8. The text in parentheses is Photius' comment on Ctesias.

10.3: Persian preparations

Herodotus, *Histories* 7.20–25, 36

Despite some rhetorical posturing, Herodotus' account of the preparations for Xerxes' campaign in Greece is largely plausible, focused on the stockpiling of supplies the army would need on the march and advance work on bridges and canals to ensure the safe and swift movement of both the army and its supply fleet. His account of bridge construction leaves some confusing gaps, but on the whole it accords with what we know about ancient engineering.

[20] Xerxes spent four full years after subduing Egypt[9] to prepare his army and its supplies. In the fifth year, he led out a mighty force, greater than any other army we know of. The force led by Darius against the Scythians was nothing compared to it.[10] Neither was the army of the Scythians which pursued the Cimmerians into the land of the Medes and subdued nearly all of inland Asia (for which Darius' campaign was a retribution).[11] Neither was the campaign said to have been led by the sons of Atreus against Ilium.[12] Nor yet was the army of the Mysians and Teucrians which, before the war against Troy, crossed the Bosporus into Europe and subdued all of Thrace, as far as the Adriatic coast, and marched south to the Peneus River.[13] [21] None of these armies, nor any other that has ever been sent on campaign, can compare with Xerxes' force.

What people of Asia did Xerxes not lead against Greece? What water source did they not drink dry, besides the great rivers? Some people

---

9. This Egyptian revolt is poorly known but seems to have occurred around 487 and taken several years of Persian campaigning to suppress.
10. Darius' campaign on the Black Sea steppes in 513. See Document 6.7; Herodotus, *Histories* 4.83–142.
11. Rather than an organized campaign of conquest, as Herodotus imagined it, steppe peoples took advantage of the power vacuum left by the collapse of the Assyrian Empire to raid and plunder the hinterlands of Mesopotamia.
12. The legendary Trojan War.
13. The campaign of the Mysians and Teucrians (two peoples of Anatolia) cannot be securely connected with any actual historical event and may have been a legend invented to explain a more complicated history of migration and settlement on both sides of the Aegean.

furnished ships. Some mustered infantry while others were ordered to serve as cavalry. Some provided transport ships for the horses while also themselves serving in the army. Some supplied ships for the construction of the great bridges, others both food and ships.

[22] Furthermore, since the previous attempt to sail around Athos[14] had ended in shipwreck, special preparations had been underway there for three years. Triremes were anchored at Elaeus in the Chersonese. Commanded from there, all sorts of soldiers were forced to dig a canal,[15] working in relays under the whip.[16] Those who lived around Athos dug as well. Two Persians, Bubares, son of Megabyzus, and Artachaees, son of Artaeus, were in charge of the work.

Athos is a large and famous mountain, well inhabited, which comes right down to the sea. On the side toward the mainland, it forms a peninsula which is about twelve *stadia* wide.[17] There is a region of plains and low hills here from the Acanthian sea on one coast to the sea toward Torone on the other.[18] On the isthmus that connects Mount Athos to the mainland is a Greek town, Sane.[19] Between Sane and Mount Athos are a number of other towns—Dion, Olophyxus, Acrothoum, Thyssus, and Cleonae—which Xerxes intended to cut off from the mainland. [23] These are the towns spread around the Athos peninsula.

The barbarians measured out the digging work and assigned a portion to each ethnic group among the workers. They measured a straight line

---

14. Athos: a mountain at the end of one of the three peninsulas of the Chalcidice. The extreme difference in elevation between the mountain peak and the sea below often creates strong winds that make sailing in the nearby waters treacherous. A previous Persian attempt to attack Greece, in 492, failed when the ships transporting the soldiers were wrecked off the coast of Athos.
15. The remains of this canal can still be seen, even though the channel silted up after it was no longer in use and is now dry land. See B. S. J. Isserlin et al., "The Canal of Xerxes: Summary of Investigations 1991–2001," *Annual of the British School at Athens* 98 (2003): 381–82.
16. The image of Persian workers suffering under the whip is a Greek fantasy with little basis in reality.
17. The *stadion* (plural *stadia*) was a unit of length. There was no consistent standard for the length of a *stadion*, which could vary from around 160 to around 190 meters. Herodotus' measure of twelve *stadia* comes to around two kilometers, which matches modern measurements of the narrowest part of the peninsula.
18. Acanthus is a town on the northern side of the Athos peninsula. Torone is a town on the Sithonian peninsula to the south of Athos.
19. Much of this region was inhabited by Macedonians, Thracians, and other local peoples, but there were also a number of Greek settlements, particularly on the coast.

starting near Sane, and when they had dug the canal to a certain depth, while those at the bottom continued to dig, others passed the dirt up by stages, passing from hand to hand until it reached the surface where it was carried away and dumped. All but the Phoenicians doubled their work because the sides of the trench kept falling in as they dug, as was sure to happen since they made the top of the trench the same width as the bottom. The Phoenicians showed their usual wisdom here. They took their allotted section in hand and began by digging the top of the trench twice the width that was required. They made their trench narrower as they dug down, so that by the time they reached the bottom it was the same width as all the other trenches.

There is a meadow nearby where they made an open market, and a great deal of ground grain was regularly brought in from Asia.

[24] As far as I can tell, it seems that Xerxes ordered the digging of this canal out of sheer pride, wishing to show off his power and leave a memorial. They could have dragged their ships over the isthmus with very little effort, yet he ordered the construction of a canal from sea to sea wide enough for two triremes to row abreast.

The same men who dug the canal were also commanded to build a bridge over the Strymon River. [25] Xerxes did all this, and he ordered the Phoenicians and Egyptians to prepare cables for the bridges out of papyrus and esparto.[20]

He also ordered them to stockpile provisions so that neither the soldiers nor the pack animals would go hungry on their march into Greece. When he had made careful inquiries about the terrain, he ordered them to establish these stockpiles in the most suitable places, with food delivered by cargo ship and transport from all over Asia. The largest stockpile was placed at the headland called the White Point in Thrace, with others assigned to Perinthian Tyrodiza, Doriscus, Eion on the Strymon, and Macedonia.

(...)

[36] They built the bridge [over the Hellespont] in this way. Fifty-oared ships and triremes were positioned side by side, 360 carrying the bridge that ran nearer to the Black Sea, 314 for the other one. These were positioned at right angles to the Black Sea and in line with the current of the Hellespont so as to lighten the strain on the cables. Once the ships were in position, they dropped enormous anchors to secure them. On

---

20. esparto: a grass-like plant native to Spain and North Africa used for its tough fibers.

the Black Sea side, these anchors held the ships against the winds coming from that direction; those toward the west and the Aegean against the western and southern winds. They left a narrow opening between the ships so that those who wished could get into or out of the Black Sea by small craft.

Once this was done, they stretched the cables across, tightening them up with wooden windlasses. They did not keep the cables separate as they had done before but assigned two cables of esparto and four of papyrus to each bridge. These cables were of the same thickness and fineness, but the esparto cables were heavier, weighing a talent to the cubit.[21]

Once the channel was bridged, they sawed tree trunks to a length matching the width of the boats and laid them one beside another along the cables. These were fastened down to the boats. They piled brushwood on top of the logs and then covered them with earth stamped down flat. Then they built fences along either side so that the horses and pack animals would not be spooked by the sight of the sea.

10.4: List of Greeks who gave earth and water to Xerxes

Herodotus, *Histories* 7.131–132

Most of the peoples along the route of the Persian army's march surrendered rather than fight such a large force. The peoples Herodotus lists represent most of the inhabitants of eastern mainland Greece north of Attica.

[131] The heralds who had been sent to Greece to demand earth now returned, some bringing earth and water, some not. [132] Those who gave earth and water included the Thessalians, the Dolopians, the Ainianes, the Locrians, the Magnesians, the Malians, the Achaeans of

---

21. talent: a unit of weight whose exact value varied from place to place. Herodotus probably meant the Attic talent, which weighed approximately twenty-six kilograms; cubit: a unit of length whose exact value could also vary. The typical Greek cubit measured approximately half a meter.

Phthiotis, and the Thebans along with the rest of the Boeotians except for the Thespians and the Plataeans.

10.5: The story of the Persian and Spartan heralds

Herodotus, *Histories* 7.133–134, 136–137

Xerxes did not make diplomatic overtures to Athens or Sparta, which had made their opposition to Persia clear by the murder of Persian heralds sent to them earlier. The murder of heralds was a serious affront to the norms of international relations. Heralds played an important role in the ancient world, making diplomacy possible by carrying messages between states, including hostile ones. To ensure that heralds could safely carry out their duties, many peoples, including the Greeks and Persians, promised safety to heralds, even in hostile territory, a practice somewhat akin to the modern principle of diplomatic immunity. The story of the murder of the Persian heralds and how the Spartans tried to atone for it reminds us of how interconnected the Greek world already was with the Persian Empire.

[133] Xerxes did not send heralds to Athens or Sparta to demand earth and water, because of what happened when Darius had sent heralds to these cities. The heralds sent to Athens were tossed into a cleft in the rock and told to get the king's earth and water from there. Those sent to Sparta were thrown down a well and told the same. So, Xerxes did not send them heralds again.

I cannot say what the Athenians suffered in retribution for what they did to the heralds, apart from seeing their land and city ravaged (though there is a better reason for that[22]), [134] but the wrath of Talthybius, Agamemnon's herald,[23] fell upon the Spartans. You see, there is a temple to Talthybius in Sparta, and his descendants, called the Talthybiads, hold the exclusive privilege of acting as Sparta's heralds. After the murder of

---

22. Herodotus most likely means the Athenians' participation in the burning of Sardis and its temples (see Document 8.1, section 102).
23. See Homer, *Iliad* 1.320.

the heralds, the Spartans could not get favorable omens from their sacrifices, and this went on for some time.

The Spartans were troubled and grieved, and they held frequent assemblies in which they called for some Spartan to voluntarily lay down his life for their city. Sperthias, son of Aneristus, and Boulis, son of Nicolaus, two Spartiates[24] of good family and surpassing wealth, offered themselves to go to Xerxes and suffer the punishment for the murder of Darius' heralds. The Spartans sent these two to Persia to be killed.

(...)

[136] When they arrived at Susa and came before the king, the guards at first ordered them—and even tried to force them—to bow and prostrate themselves before the king. They replied that they would never do this, not even if pushed down headfirst, for it was not their way to bow to any person, nor was that the reason for their coming.

After refusing to bow, they said what they had come to say: "King of the Persians, the Spartans have sent us here to pay the price for the murder of your heralds in Sparta."

Xerxes answered them considerately that he would not behave like a Spartan, for the Spartans had made a mockery of the laws recognized by all humanity in killing the heralds. He himself would not commit against them the same crime he condemned them for, nor would he release the Spartans from the consequences of their own offense by slaying their emissaries.

[137] The wrath of Talthybius against the Spartans was alleviated for a little while by this act, even though Sperthias and Boulis came home to Sparta alive.

10.6: The battle of Thermopylae

Herodotus, *Histories* 7.210–225

The first clash between Xerxes' army and the allied Greeks of the Hellenic League in 480 came at Thermopylae, a narrow coastal pass mostly blocked by the remains of an old wall, where a force made up of soldiers from several Greek cities was led by the

---

24. Spartiates: full citizens of Sparta, who were a small elite minority among the people under Spartan authority.

Spartan king Leonidas. Herodotus' account of the battle, written about fifty years later, shows how much the Greek memory of this event had already become tangled up with heroic legends and postwar politics.

Beneath the morality play Herodotus imagines between steadfast Leonidas and temperamental Xerxes, there are the traces of a more realistic account of the tactical situation at Thermopylae. The Greeks could not expect their defensive position to hold out indefinitely. At the same time, the Persians, experienced at fighting in mountainous terrain, would hardly have been at a loss for what to do about a pass occupied by opposing forces. Both sides must have recognized that the fighting at Thermopylae was only a holding action: The Greeks were trying to delay the Persian advance and strain their supply lines. Meanwhile the Persians kept the main Greek forces engaged at Thermopylae while searching for a land or sea route by which they could encircle the defenders.

Herodotus' narrative picks up after the Persian army has arrived and found the pass defended.

[210] Xerxes waited four days, hoping that the Greeks would flee. On the fifth day, it seemed to him that the Greeks were still making a show of their impudence and foolishness, so he angrily sent the Medes and Cissians against them with orders to capture them and bring them to him. Many of the Medes fell in the fighting. Wave after wave of troops attacked the Greeks, but they could not drive them back, despite the intensity of the fighting. It was made clear to everyone, not least the king himself, that among many people, few are men. The clash lasted all day.

[211] After this rough handling, the Medes fell back and the Persians took their turn. These were the ones the king calls his Immortals, who were led by Hydarnes. They were expected to easily accomplish the task. When they engaged with the Greeks, however, they did no better than the Medes, since they were using shorter spears and fighting in a narrow pass where they could not take advantage of their greater numbers. The Spartans fought admirably and showed that they were experienced warriors among novices when they turned their backs and pretended to flee in disorder. When the barbarians saw this, they rushed to chase after them, but when they caught up, the Spartans turned back and struck them down in uncountable numbers while losing few of their own. When the Persians had no success in assaulting the pass, neither in organized

formations nor in any other way, they fell back. [212] The king was watching from a throne and it is said that during this battle, he jumped up three times in alarm. So they fought on that day.

The next day went no better for the barbarians. They had hoped that the Greeks, being so few, would be debilitated by their wounds and unable to raise a hand against them, but the Greeks were well organized in squadrons according to their places of origin, and each took its turn in the fight with the exception of the Phocians, who were stationed in the mountains to guard the upper path. Finding that they made no more headway than the previous day, the Persians fell back. [213] The king declared himself at a loss as to what to do. Then a Malian, Ephialtes, son of Eurydemus, in hopes of a rich reward, came and offered to show him a path through the mountains to Thermopylae by which he might surround and destroy the Greeks.

Later, to escape revenge by the Spartans, this Ephialtes fled into Thessaly, and the Pylagori, meeting in the Amphictyony at Pylae,[25] offered a reward for his capture. Still later he returned to Anticyra and was killed by Athenedes, a Trachinian. Athenedes killed him for an entirely different reason, which I will explain later, but the Spartans honored Athenedes for the deed no less. That is how Ephialtes was later killed.

[214] Some people say that it was Onetes, son of Phanagoras, a Carystian, and Corydallus, an Anticyran, who spoke to the king and showed the Persians the route through the mountains, but I don't believe a word of it. Keep in mind that the Pylagori did not issue the reward for Onetes and Corydallus but for Ephialtes the Trachinian,[26] and they no doubt knew the truth of the matter. We know that Ephialtes was banished on these grounds. Onetes might have known about that path, even though he was not a Malian, if he had had much business in that region, but it was Ephialtes who led the Persians to the path through the mountains, and so that is what I have written.

[215] Xerxes was elated at what Ephialtes promised to do and sent Hydarnes off with his troops at once. They set out from the camp soon after dusk. This path had been discovered by the local Malians, who used it to guide the Thessalians into Phocis when the Phocians had closed off

---

25. Pylagori: delegates to the Delphic Amphictyony, an association that coordinated religious and political activity among several cities and rural peoples of northern Greece.
26. Ephialtes was from the city of Trachis in the region of Malis, thus Herodotus sometimes calls him a Trachinian and sometimes a Malian.

the coastal pass with a wall to protect themselves from invasion. So long ago the Malians had shown that the path could be dangerous.

[216] The path runs like this: it starts from the Asopus River where it flows through a ravine. The path is called Anopaea, the same name as the mountain it climbs. The Anopaea path stretches along the back side of the mountain. It ends at the village of Alpenos, which is the part of Locris nearest to Malis, and at its narrowest point it passes the stone called the Black Rump or the Seat of the Cercopes.[27]

[217] The Persians marched along this path all night, crossing the Asopus and keeping the Oetaean Mountains on their right and the Trachinian Mountains on their left. As dawn approached, they were nearing the highest point of the mountain path. A thousand Phocian hoplites, as I mentioned above, were stationed on this part of the mountain, guarding the entry to their own land and keeping watch on the path. The coastal pass was guarded by those I noted earlier, but the Phocians had volunteered for this duty and promised Leonidas to guard the approach through the mountains.

[218] The Persian troops had made it up the ascent unnoticed because the mountain was covered in trees. The night was a still one, though, so the Phocians realized that the Persians were coming up the path when they heard the sound of dead leaves being stirred by many feet. They rushed to take up arms just as the barbarians were upon them. When the Persians saw men readying for battle in front of them, they were startled, for they had hoped to encounter no opposition. Hydarnes, fearing that these men might be Spartans, asked Ephialtes where this army came from. When he learned that they were Phocians, he ordered the Persians to form up and attack.

When a hail of arrows fell upon the Phocians, they believed that they were the target of the Persians' assault, so they fled to the mountain peak and prepared to fight to the death. That is what they thought, but the Persians with Hydarnes and Ephialtes had no interest in them and hurried on down the mountain.

[219] The seer Megistias, who was divining for the Greeks at Thermopylae, was the first to foretell, from inspecting the sacrifices, that their death would come at dawn. Then deserters from the Persian camp came

---

27. Cercopes: troublemakers of Greek myth. When the hero Heracles caught them and tied them upside down on a pole over his shoulder, they made jokes about his darkly suntanned bottom until he finally let them go.

during the night and reported the encircling move. The third report came from the lookouts at sunrise running down from the heights. The Greeks held a discussion and opinions were divided: some were against abandoning their position, but others wanted to retreat. Afterward, the force broke up. Some were released to return to their own cities, while others remained under Leonidas and prepared for battle.

[220] Some say that Leonidas sent most of the troops away to save their lives, but that he thought it would be wrong for himself or the Spartiates[28] who were with him to abandon the ground that they had come to defend. It seems more likely to me that when Leonidas realized that the allies were dispirited and unwilling to face the coming danger, he sent them away, but he felt that it would not be right for him to leave his post. By staying he earned great glory for himself and saved Sparta from obliteration, for when the Spartans had consulted the Delphic oracle at the beginning of the war, the Pythia[29] had proclaimed that either Sparta would be wiped off the map or a king of Sparta would die. She spoke in these verses:

> To you, O Spartans of uncrowded ways,
> I say: your famous city must be sacked
> by Perseids,[30] or else you must lament
> a fallen king, a scion of Heracles.[31]
> The strength of bulls or lions cannot stop
> the man empowered with the might of Zeus.
> Your town or king must fall to turn him back.

Having this in mind, and wishing to win glory for the Spartans alone, Leonidas thought it was better to dismiss the allies than to have them break up in disorder over a difference of opinion. [221] There is proof for this view, I think, in the fact that Leonidas publicly dismissed the

---

28. Spartiates: full citizens of Sparta, who were a small elite minority among the people under Spartan authority.
29. Pythia: the title of the chief priestess of Apollo at Delphi, who induced an altered state of consciousness during which the Greeks believed that Apollo spoke directly to humans through her.
30. Perseids: descendants of the mythic hero Perseus. Based on the coincidental similarity of names, the Greeks believed that the Persians were among Perseus' progeny. See Document 7.4.
31. The Spartan kings claimed to be descended from Heracles.

seer who accompanied the army, Megistias the Acarnanian, the one who foretold the doom of the Greeks and who was said to be a descendant of Melampus,[32] so that he would not perish along with the Spartans. Megistias did not depart when ordered to, but he did send away his only son, who was with him on the campaign.

[222] The allies obeyed Leonidas and retreated, except for the Thespians and Thebans, who stayed with the Spartans. The Thebans did not want to stay, but Leonidas forced them to and treated them as hostages.[33] The Thespians stayed gladly, saying that they would not leave Leonidas and his companions but would rather stand and die alongside them. Their general was Demophilus, son of Diadromes.

[223] As the sun was rising, Xerxes made an offering of wine to the gods. He held his troops back until mid-morning, as Ephialtes had advised him, since the descent from the mountain is much shorter than the ascent and the path around. Then the barbarians with Xerxes began to advance. The Greeks with Leonidas, who knew that they were going to their deaths, came much farther out onto the plain than before. In previous days they had fought close to the wall in the narrow part of the pass. Now they gave battle outside the narrow pass and many of the barbarians fell. The Persian commanders lashed their troops with whips from the rear to drive them forward. Many of them were driven into the sea and perished there; many more were trampled alive in the heedless throng.[34]

Knowing that they would be killed by the force that had come through the mountains to surround them, the Greeks now fought with all their strength against the barbarians in reckless disregard for their own lives. [224] By now, most of their spears had been shattered, but they fought on against the Persians with their swords.[35] Leonidas died in that struggle, proving himself a man among men, and many other worthy Spartans with him, whose names I have learned, as indeed I have learned the

---

32. Melampus: a famous seer from the legends of the Trojan War.
33. It is unlikely that Leonidas kept Theban troops against their will. Herodotus here reflects the anti-Theban prejudices that were common in Athens after the war because Thebes had surrendered after Persian forces pushed through Thermopylae.
34. The image of disorganized Persian troops driven on by the lash is pure Greek fantasy with no basis in the reality of the Persian army.
35. The primary weapon of a Greek hoplite was the spear. Swords were only used as a backup when the spear was broken or lost.

names of all three hundred.[36] Many famous Persians fell in that battle, too, including two sons of Darius, Abrocomes and Hyperanthes, who were born to Darius by Phratagune, the daughter of Artanes. Artanes was a brother of Darius, the son of Hystaspes, son of Arsames. When Artanes gave his daughter in marriage to Darius, he gave his whole estate as dowry, since she was his only child. [225] These two brothers of Xerxes fell in the fighting.[37]

A great struggle unfolded between the Greeks and Persians over the body of Leonidas, during which the Greeks, by their courage, four times pushed the enemy back and dragged the body away.[38] This contest went on until the forces with Ephialtes arrived. When the Greeks saw them coming, the battle shifted. All but the Thebans fell back into the narrowest part of the pass, abandoning the wall, and took a stand on a hill. This hill is at the mouth of the pass, where there is now a stone lion dedicated to Leonidas. There they defended themselves with knives, if they had them, or with their hands and teeth. The barbarians pelted them with missiles, some attacking from the front and demolishing the wall, others surrounding them on all sides.

10.7: The battle of Cape Artemisium

Herodotus, *Histories* 8.6–21

While the allied Greek forces blocked the pass at Thermopylae, the Hellenic League fleet was stationed at Cape Artemisium at the northern end of Euboea to prevent the Persian fleet from coming to Xerxes' aid and ferrying Persian forces around Thermopylae for an attack from the rear. The engagements between Greek and Persian naval forces were not decisive for either side, but the Greeks nevertheless kept the Persian fleet from reaching Thermopylae to assist the land forces there. Once the Persians overcame the resistance at Thermopylae, the Greek fleet withdrew from

---

36. The Spartan contingent at Thermopylae was only the three hundred picked troops who served as the king's personal guard.
37. The family tree of Xerxes and Darius is difficult to reconstruct. The information given here is not necessarily reliable.
38. In ancient warfare, capturing the dead body and armor of an enemy leader could provide a valuable boost to morale and strike a psychological blow against the opposing side.

Euboea, since it no longer served any strategic purpose there. Herodotus' account is, as usual, long on Greek heroics and short on reliable military detail.

[6] The barbarians arrived at Aphetae in the early afternoon, already informed that a few Greek ships were at anchor around Artemisium. Once they caught sight of the Greek ships, they were eager to sail out against them in hopes of capturing them. They figured it would not do to try to attack them directly, though, since the Greeks would see them coming and could escape into the gathering dusk. They were sure the Greeks would make a run for it and they wanted to destroy the Greek fleet down to the last man.

[7] Given the circumstances, they came up with this plan: two hundred ships were detached from the fleet with orders to sail around the far side of Sciathus, out of sight of the enemy, and circle Euboea, rounding Caphereus and Geraestus, and passing through the Euripus strait. By this maneuver, they would surround the Greek ships, their main fleet chasing the Greeks from the front while the detachment blocked their escape in the rear.[39] Once these plans had been made, the selected ships were sent on their way. The rest of the fleet had no intention of attacking the Greeks that day, or indeed at all until they got the signal to let them know that the detachment had arrived at its appointed position. They sent the two hundred ships on their way and took a count of those that remained.

[8] Now, they had with them Scyllias of Scione, the world's greatest diver at that time. He had salvaged a great deal of property for the

---

39. Sciathus was a small island off the coast from the Persian fleet's anchorage. Passing around the island to seaward, the detachment would in theory be hidden from the Greek fleet's view. Caphereus and Geraestus are headlands at the southern end of Euboea. Euripus is the strait between Euboea and the mainland at its narrowest point. Many naval experts have regarded this whole maneuver as unrealistic, and some historians speculate that Herodotus simply invented both the detachment of 200 ships and its subsequent destruction (see section 13 in this document) in order to account for a discrepancy in his figures for the Persian fleet between when it set out and when it fought at Salamis. Other historians defend the plausibility of the maneuver. W. W. Tarn, "The Fleet of Xerxes," *Journal of Hellenic Studies* 28 (1908): 204; Charles Hignett, *Xerxes' Invasion of Greece* (Oxford: Clarendon Press, 1963), 87–90; Anthony Bowen, "The Place That Beached A Thousand Ships," *Classical Quarterly* 48, no. 2 (1989): 361–63; George Cawkwell, *The Greek Wars: The Failure of Persia* (Oxford: Oxford University Press, 2005), 264–65; H. T. Wallinga, *Xerxes' Greek Adventure: The Naval Perspective* (Leiden: Brill, 2005), 4.

Persians from their ships that had been wrecked off Mount Pelion,[40] and gotten a lot for himself besides. Scyllias, you see, had been planning for some time to defect to the Greeks, but he had not had an opportunity to do it until now while they were counting the ships. I cannot say exactly how he managed to get over to the Greeks, but if the story is true it is an amazing one: they say he dove under the water at Aphetae and did not come up until he reached Artemisium, some eighty *stadia*[41] away, having swum all the way under water. A lot of stories are told about this man, some of which are true and some of which sound like fish tales. As for this one, I bet he actually got to Artemisium by boat.

As soon as he arrived, he told the commanders about the effects of the storm on the Persian fleet and about the detachment that had been sent around Euboea. [9] Once they heard this report, the Greeks held a council and there was much debate. The prevailing opinion was that they should stay where they were and make camp for that day, then, after midnight, put to sea and meet the ships that were sailing around Euboea. By the late afternoon, though, when no attack came against them, they decided to put to sea and make a foray against the barbarians, to see what the Persian fleet was made of and how they attacked a squadron in line.

[10] When Xerxes' commanders and soldiers saw the Greeks coming at them with such a small fleet, they thought the Greeks had completely lost their minds, so they took to their own ships, hoping to win an easy victory—as well they might, since they could see that the Greeks had only a few ships, while their own ships were not only more numerous but more seaworthy. Feeling such disdain, they encircled the Greek ships.

Now, those Ionians who were sympathetic to the Greek cause and were in Xerxes' fleet against their will thought it was a terrible misfortune to have to watch the ships being encircled. The Greek fleet looked so weak that it seemed certain no one in the Greek crews would ever see home again. Those who were there gladly, though, were vying with each other to be the first to capture an Athenian ship and win the king's favor, since it was the Athenians who were the most talked about in the fleet.

---

40. Part of the Persian fleet had been sunk in a storm off the coast north of Aphetae. See Herodotus, *Histories* 7.188.
41. The *stadion* (plural *stadia*) was a Greek unit of length. There was no consistent standard for the length of a *stadion*, which could vary from around 160 to around 190 meters. Eighty *stadia* would be around fifteen kilometers.

[11] At a signal, the Greek ships drew together into a circle with their sterns inward and their prows pointed out toward the barbarians. At a second signal, they engaged the enemy, even though they were confined in a small space and were facing the enemy ships prow to prow. They took thirty enemy ships and captured Philaon, son of Chersis, the brother of King Gorgus of Salamis in Cyprus, a man of some repute in the fleet. The first Greek to take an enemy ship was Lycomedes, son of Aeschraeus, from Athens, who also won the prize for bravery.[42]

Neither side had claimed a clear victory by the time the nightfall brought the battle to a close. The Greeks sailed back to Artemisium, the Persians to Aphetae. The battle had not gone the way either side had expected.

In this battle, only one of the Greeks who was fighting on the Persian side, Antidorus of Lemnos, defected and joined the Greeks. For this act, the Athenians gave him land on the island of Salamis.

[12] That night, even though it was in the middle of summer, a storm blew in from the direction of Mount Pelion, bringing heavy rain and crashing thunder all through the night. Dead bodies and pieces of flotsam were driven against Aphetae, where they got tangled up on the prows of the ships and fouled the blades of the oars. The sailors there were weighed down with fear and the expectation of disaster. They were in a wretched state, having hardly had time to catch their breath after the shipwreck and storm they had endured off Pelion before being thrust into a tough sea battle, followed by a ferocious rainstorm, torrents of water flowing toward the sea, and harsh thunder. [13] That was how they fared that night.

The same night was crueler to those who had been sent to sail around Euboea, since it fell on them while they were out at sea and brought them a terrible end. The storm caught them off the Hollows of Euboea.[43] Without knowing where they were, they were hurled against the rocks by the winds. All of this was accomplished by the gods to ensure that the Persian fleet should be about equal in size to the Greek, rather than much bigger. [14] These men died off the Hollows of Euboea.

---

42. Greeks often awarded an *aristeion*, an award for exceptional bravery or effectiveness in battle, after the end of a conflict. The form of the award could vary, including such possibilities as a crown of leaves, a public celebration, or a choice piece of plunder from the enemy camp. Borimir Jordan, "The Honors for Themistocles after Salamis," *American Journal of Philology* 109, no. 4 (Winter 1988).

43. Hollows of Euboea: a treacherous region of rocky bays on the coast of Euboea.

At Aphetae, the coming of dawn was very welcome. The Persian crews there were content to leave their ships alone and do nothing, given the awful state they found themselves in. At the same time, fifty-three Athenian ships joined the Greek contingent and raised their spirits both by their arrival and by the news they brought of the destruction of the Persian detachment that had been sent around Euboea. The Greeks stood on guard until the same time of day, then sailed out and seized some Cilician ships, which they destroyed before sailing back to Artemisium at nightfall.

[15] On the third day, the Persian admirals, finding it intolerable that their ships should be so abused by such a small Greek force, and also fearing Xerxes' displeasure, decided not to wait for the Greeks to begin the battle but made preparations and put their ships to sea at midday. So it happened that these sea battles were fought on the same days as the land battle at Thermopylae. The whole task of the fleet was to hold the Euripus strait, just as Leonidas' forces were guarding the pass. While the Greeks were fighting to allow the barbarians no passage into Greece, the Persians were trying to destroy the Greek forces and conquer the passages.

[16] While Xerxes' ships were sailing out, the Greek fleet remained steadfast at Artemisium. The barbarians arrayed their fleet in a crescent shape, aiming to encircle the Greeks. At this point, the Greeks put to sea and joined battle. In this battle, their forces were a match for one another. Xerxes' fleet was hampered by its size as the ships were pushed together and fouled on one another. All the same, they held fast and did not turn tail, since they thought it would be a disgraceful thing to flee in the face of a smaller fleet. Many Greek ships were lost there and many Greeks perished, yet the Persian losses were even greater. So the fighting went until the two fleets withdrew from one another.

[17] Among Xerxes' fleet, it was the Egyptians who acquitted themselves the best in that fight. Besides their other worthy deeds, they captured five Greek ships along with their crews. Of the Greeks, it was the Athenians who stood out on that day, and among the Athenians, Clinias, son of Alcibiades, who commanded a ship and two hundred men all paid for at his own expense.

[18] So the fleets parted and each returned to its own anchorage. The Greeks were glad to get back to the shore and recover the wreckage and the bodies from the battle, but they had been roughly handled, not least

the Athenians, half of whose ships were disabled. The common opinion was that they should withdraw back into Greece.

[19] It occurred to Themistocles that, if the Ionian and Carian contingents could be broken off from the Persian force, the Greeks might be able to overcome the rest. He gathered the admirals and told them that he had thought of a cunning plan by which he hoped to split off the best of the king's allies.[44] That was all he would reveal for the moment. For now, all he said was to advise them to kill as many of the Euboean animals as they wished (it was the Euboeans' custom to drive their flocks down to the shore where they were), since it was better they should have them than the enemy. Further, he instructed each of them to lay a fire, while he would take care to time their departure so that they should all get safely back to Greece. They agreed and began laying fires and going after the flocks.

[20] The Euboeans had disregarded the oracle of Bacis[45] and thought it carried no weight, so they had neither taken their possessions away nor brought in supplies in preparation for the war that was coming. The oracle of Bacis about this event goes:

> When a foreign man casts a yoke
> of papyrus into the salty sea,[46]
> keep the bleating goats far from Euboea.

The Euboeans put no stock in this pronouncement, but in the troubles of that day and those yet to come, they suffered terribly.

[21] While the Greeks were busy with these tasks, the lookout from Trachis arrived. There was a lookout placed at Artemisium, one Polyas, from Anticyra, with a boat ready to hand, whose job it was to alert the army at Thermopylae if the fleet was overwhelmed. Similarly, Abronichus, son of Lysicles, an Athenian, was stationed with Leonidas and provided with a thirty-oared boat to get word to Artemisium if the army was defeated. Abronichus now arrived and informed the fleet about what had happened to Leonidas and his troops. Once the fleet got the news,

---

44. Themistocles' plan was to leave messages to the Ionians carved into the rocks at the shore urging them to desert, or at least deliberately fight badly. This plan had little success. See Document 10.9, section 85.
45. Bacis: the name of several legendary seers to whom a number of oracular predictions were attributed.
46. Presumably referring to the bridging of the Hellespont. See Document 10.3.

they delayed their retreat no longer but set off in their appointed order, the Corinthians leading the way and the Athenians bringing up the rear.

10.8: A message to Xerxes

Herodotus, *Histories* 8.75–76

While the Greek and Persian fleets were preparing for battle in the straits between Athens and the island of Salamis, a message was apparently sent to the Persians informing them that the Greeks were planning to retreat under cover of darkness. Herodotus and Aeschylus both mention this message (see Document 10.10, lines 355–60), as well as the result that the Persians divided their forces to try to block any escape. Herodotus presents this message as a ploy by Themistocles to force his unwilling allies to fight rather than flee, although it may also have been a stratagem agreed on by all the Greek allies to lure the Persians into a fight in the narrow straits, or, indeed, a private act by Themistocles, getting into Xerxes' good graces in case the battle went against the Greeks (see Document 12.1, section 137).

[75] Since Themistocles found that he could not win over the Peloponnesians, he quietly left the meeting and sent Sicinnus, a slave of his household who attended to his children, to go to the Persian camp by boat with a message. For this service, Themistocles later made Sicinnus a Thespian, when the Thespians were accepting new citizens, and made him rich, too.

When Sicinnus reached the barbarian generals by boat, his message for them was: "I have been sent, in secret, by one of the Greek generals, because he favors your king and would rather see him victorious than the Greeks. I am to inform you that the Greeks are terrified and are planning to flee. You now have the chance to accomplish a great feat if you can prevent them from escaping. They cannot agree with each other or put up a united front against you. Instead, you will see them fighting among themselves, those who support your side against those who do not." [76] Once he had delivered this message, he sailed away again.

Section 10: Xerxes' Aegean campaign, 480–479 BCE   147

The Persians believed this message and acted accordingly. First they landed a large number of troops on Psyttaleia, a small island between Salamis and the mainland. In the middle of the night, they brought the western wing of the fleet in a circle toward Salamis. They also brought up the squadrons from Ceos and Cynosura to occupy the whole channel as far as Munychia.[47] They drew up their ships in this way so that the Greeks would have no way to escape. Thus they would be certain of getting revenge for their defeat off Artemisium. They landed troops on Psyttaleia because it lay in the path of the upcoming battle, so most of the wrecked ships and sailors would wash up there, where the Persians could save their own comrades and kill the enemy survivors.

They made these preparations in silence, to keep the enemy from knowing what they were doing. That night, the Persians got no sleep.

10.9: The battle of Salamis

Herodotus, *Histories* 8.83–97

The battle of Salamis is the low point of Herodotus' battle narration. He was clearly even less familiar with (or interested in) the practicalities of naval warfare than those of land warfare, and his narrative quickly devolves into a mass of disjointed anecdotes. Generations of historians have tried to salvage some tactically plausible sequence of events from this tangle, but consensus remains elusive. Some historians see Salamis as an intricately arranged trap intended to lure the Persians into a battle in narrow, treacherous waters where local knowledge of shoals, tides, and currents would count for more than the superior sailing skill of Persia's mostly Egyptian and Phoenician navy. Others see it as a desperate gamble whose main architect, Themistocles, was hedging his bets by currying favor with the enemy leader.

[83] At dawn, the marines[48] held an assembly and Themistocles gave the best of all the speeches. His words contrasted the best and the worst

---
47. Munychia: a place on the southern coast of Piraeus, the port of Athens.
48. marines: soldiers who fought on board ship, as distinct from the rowers. At this period of Greek history, naval battles were largely fought by the marines who attempted

of human nature and conditions. He wrapped up his speech by exhorting them to choose the better of these, and then gave the order to board the ships. As they were embarking, the trireme which had been sent to Aegina to retrieve the images of the Aeacids[49] arrived.

[84] All the Greek ships advanced, and the barbarians at once closed with them. While all the other Greek ships began to retreat and made to put back into shore, Ameinias of Pallene, an Athenian, charged ahead and rammed an enemy ship. The two ships became tangled on one another and could not pull apart, so the rest of the Greek fleet came to Ameinias' aid and joined battle. This, the Athenians say, is how the battle began, but the Aeginetans say that it was the ship which had been sent to Aegina after the Aeacids which first entered combat. It is also said that the image of a woman appeared who cried out commands and reproaches in a voice loud enough for the whole Greek fleet to hear. "You madmen," she began, "how much further will you go astern?"

[85] The Phoenicians were arrayed on the western wing of the Persian fleet, toward Eleusis, facing off against the Athenians, while the Ionians were on the eastern wing, toward Piraeus, facing the Spartans. Few of the Ionians took Themistocles' instructions to play the coward;[50] most of them, in fact, did not. I could list the names of many Ionian captains who captured Greek ships, but I will mention just two, both of them Samians: Theomestor, son of Androdamas, and Phylacus, son of Histiaeus. I mention these two in particular because Theomestor was made tyrant of Samos for his accomplishments and Phylacus was recorded among the benefactors of the king (those whom the Persians call *orosangai*) and granted a large amount of land. [86] That was how these men fared.

Most of the Persian ships at Salamis were devastated in the battle. The Athenians destroyed some, the Aeginetans others. The battle was bound to go this way, since the Greeks fought in good order and according to a plan, whereas the barbarians had no organization and gave no thought to tactics. Yet the Persians did fight more bravely on that day than they had

---

to disable or board and capture enemy ships. Ships could ram one another, but it was not the primary tactic.
49. Aeacids: descendants of the mythic hero Aeacus, including the Trojan War heroes Achilles and Greater Ajax. The ship brought sacred images of these heroes from their shrine in Aegina. For the dispatch of this ship, see Herodotus, *Histories* 8.64.
50. See Document 10.7, section 19.

at Euboea,[51] spurred on by fear of Xerxes and the knowledge that the king was watching them.

[87] I cannot say exactly how any other ship, whether Greek or barbarian, did in that battle, but this is what happened to Artemisia[52] and won her even greater respect in the eyes of the king. The Persian fleet was in chaos and an Athenian ship was bearing down on Artemisia's. There was nowhere for her to flee to since her ship was hemmed in by friendly ships and close to the enemy lines, so she made a decision which turned out very well for her. Pursued by the Athenian, she rammed a friendly ship at full speed. This ship was crewed by the Calyndians and carried not only many Calyndian men but also their king, Damasythimus. I cannot say whether there had been some quarrel between Artemisia and Damasythimus when they were stationed at the Hellespont, or if she had planned to attack him, or if it was just by chance that the Calyndian ship was nearby. In any case, when Artemisia rammed and sank that ship it turned out well for her in two ways. In the first place, when the Athenian captain saw her ship sink one of the barbarians, he thought she was either on the Greek side or was coming over to their side, so he broke off and turned his attention elsewhere, [88] and so she got away. In the second place, even though she was doing harm to his own fleet, she won high praise from Xerxes.

They say that as the king was watching the battle and saw her ship ram the other one, someone by his side said: "My lord, do you see what a good fight Artemisia is putting up and how she has sunk one of the enemy's ships?"

The king asked it if was really Artemisia and the bystander confirmed it, since he knew the markings of her ship well and assumed that the ship she destroyed must be an enemy. As I said, all this turned out to her benefit, since no one from the Calyndian ship survived to accuse her.

In response to this observation, it is reported that Xerxes remarked: "My men have become women, and my women have become men!"

[89] The Persian commander Ariabignes, son of Darius and brother of Xerxes, died in the fighting. So did many other famous men of the Persians, the Medes, and their other allies, but few Greeks, since they knew how to swim. Those whose ships were destroyed and did not fall

---

51. See Document 10.7.
52. Artemisia: queen of Halicarnassus, who commanded a contingent of ships in the Persian fleet and served as an adviser to Xerxes in his Greek campaign.

in the hand-to-hand fighting swam to shore on Salamis, but many of the barbarians perished at sea because they could not swim.

Most of the ships were destroyed when those in the front line turned to flee, since those stationed in the rear were urging their way into the front trying to accomplish some worthy deed in the sight of the king and ran afoul of their own comrades who were in flight. [90] In the midst of this confusion, some Phoenicians, whose ships had been destroyed, came to the king and accused the Ionians of treason, saying that it was the Ionians' fault that their ships had been lost. But it so happened that it was not the Ionian commanders but the Phoenicians accusing them who paid the price. While the Phoenicians were still speaking, a Samothracian[53] ship rammed an Athenian ship and sank it. An Aeginetan ship then rammed and sank the Samothracian, but the Samothracian javelin-throwers swept the Aeginetan marines off the attacking ship and captured the very ship that had sunk their own. This act saved the Ionians, for when he saw what the Samothracians had accomplished, Xerxes, furious and casting blame everywhere, turned on the Phoenicians and ordered them beheaded for being worthless and daring to accuse better men.

Whenever Xerxes, seated on the mountain opposite Salamis that is called Aegaleus, saw someone among his forces accomplish some noteworthy deed, he inquired who it was and had his scribes record the captain's name together with his father's name and what city he came from. The fact that Ariaramnes, a Persian who was friendly to the Ionians, was with the king made things all the worse for the Phoenicians. The king's attendants dealt with the Phoenicians.[54]

[91] Those barbarians who were put to flight and tried to reach Phalerum were ambushed by the Aeginetan ships stationed in the strait, who accomplished deeds worthy of note. The Athenians destroyed those ships who put up a fight or tried to flee from the main battle while the Aeginetans took those sailing out of the strait. Those who escaped the Athenians were caught up by the Aeginetans.

[92] The ship under Themistocles' command, which was pursuing an enemy ship, happened upon the ship commanded by the Aeginetan

---

53. The Samothracians were among the Ionian contingents in the Persian fleet.
54. On the Phoenicians at Salamis: Josette Elayi, "The Role of the Phoenician Kings at the Battle of Salamis (480 B.C.E.)," *Journal of the American Oriental Society* 126, no. 3 (July–September 2006).

Polycritus, son of Crius, which had rammed a Sidonian[55] ship. This Sidonian ship was the one which had captured the Aeginetan ship stationed to keep watch off Sciathus. This same ship was the one on which the Persians kept Pytheas, son of Ischenous, whose bravery they had all marveled at when he was so badly hacked up in the fighting. This Sidonian ship was now captured and so Pytheas made it safely back to Aegina.[56]

When he saw the Athenian ship, Polycritus recognized the commander's markings, so, after ramming an enemy ship, he shouted out to Themistocles and taunted him over the old accusations about the Aeginetans siding with the Persians.[57]

The barbarians whose ships were still intact fled to Phalerum and the protection of the army.

[93] The Aeginetans are held to have been the best fighters in this battle, followed by the Athenians. Among individuals, the Aeginetan Polycritus was considered best, along with the Athenians Eumenes of Anagyrus and Ameinias of Pallene, the one who pursued Artemisia. If he had known that Artemisia was in command of that ship, he would not have broken off his pursuit until he either captured her or was captured himself. The Athenians were so outraged that a woman should make war upon them that they had specifically ordered their captains to hunt her down and promised a prize of ten thousand drachmas[58] for anyone who took her alive. But, as I said before, she escaped along with the others whose ships made it to Phalerum.

[94] The Athenians say that the Corinthian admiral Adeimantus, out of his wits with terror, hoisted sail and fled the battle as soon as the first ships entered the fray, and the rest of the Corinthians, seeing their commander in flight, did likewise. When, in their retreat, they passed the shrine of Athena Sciras on Salamis, a small boat approached them, sent by the gods. No person seems to have sent it, and the Corinthians knew nothing about what was happening with the fleet when it came near, and so they suppose that the gods were behind it.

When they came near the Corinthian ships, those on the boat said: "Adeimantus, you have betrayed the Greeks by turning tail, but now their prayers are coming true and they are triumphing over the enemy."

---

55. Sidon: one of the major Phoenician cities.
56. For the story of Pytheas, see Herodotus, *Histories* 7.181.
57. See Document 9.1.
58. drachma: a silver coin worth roughly a day's wage for a skilled laborer.

Adeimantus did not believe what they were saying, but they offered to come aboard his ship as hostages and pay with their lives if the Greeks were not clearly victorious. Adeimantus turned his contingent around and headed back to the fleet where they found the victory already accomplished.

This is the rumor the Athenians spread about the Corinthians, but the Corinthians themselves disagree. They hold that they were among the foremost fighters in the battle, and the rest of the Greeks back them up as witnesses.

[95] Aristides, son of Lysimachus, an Athenian whom I mentioned a little earlier as a man of first-rate quality,[59] did this deed in the midst of the commotion at Salamis: he gathered many of the Athenian hoplites who had been stationed on the shores of Salamis and led them to Psyttaleia where they slew all the Persians on the island.[60]

[96] Once the battle had broken up, the Greeks hauled whatever shipwrecks were still in the nearby waters to Salamis and prepared themselves for another battle, expecting that the king would make use of his remaining fleet.

Many of the wrecks were blown by the west wind onto the cape in Attica known as Colias. Thus all the oracles about this sea battle were fulfilled, not only those of Bacis and Musaeus, but also the one about the wrecks given many years earlier by Lysistratus, an Athenian diviner, which no other Greek had caught onto:

> The women of Colias will cook with oars.

This would come true after the king had retreated.

[97] When Xerxes learned the scope of the calamity, he was afraid that some Ionian would suggest that the Greeks sail to the Hellespont and break the bridges there. If that happened, he would be stranded in Europe and risk annihilation, so he decided to retreat.

---

59. Aristides: an Athenian aristocrat in exile, rival of Themistocles. See Herodotus, *Histories* 8.79.
60. See Document 10.8.

10.10: An eyewitness account of Salamis

Aeschylus, *The Persians* 353–471

The Athenian playwright Aeschylus boasted of having fought at the battle of Marathon and almost certainly fought at Salamis as well. In The Persians, Aeschylus gives us the closest we have to an eyewitness account of the battle. The play is set at the Persian court, where Xerxes' mother, Atossa, anxiously waits for news of her son's campaign in Greece. This account of the battle is put into the mouth of a messenger, who relates the events from a Persian perspective.

Messenger:
My queen, our doom began
when some evil or vengeful spirit appeared.
A man came from the Athenian fleet   355
and told your son, Xerxes,
that with the coming of night
the Greeks would not stay put
but leap to the oars and flee
hither and thither to save their lives by stealth.   360
But your son was not wary of Greek wiles
or the gods' spite. At once he gave the order
to all his admirals: as soon as the sun
ceased to shine upon the earth
and night claimed its place in the sky,   365
they should draw up their ships, some in triple line
to guard the channels and routes of escape,
others to ring the island of Ajax.[61]
If any Greeks should escape their dire fate
and find some way to safety for their ships,   370
then all his captains would pay with their lives.
He gave these orders in high spirits,
not knowing what the gods had planned.
In good order and with obedient hearts,
our sailors took their evening meal,   375

---
61. Ajax: a mythic Greek hero from Salamis.

and each one readied his oar firmly in place.
When the sun's light faded
and night had come, every masterful oarsman
and every soldier boarded the long ships,
line after line, cheering one another on. 380
Through the night they kept their stations,
arrayed across the straits
as the captains kept their ships in line.
The night passed, and yet the Greek fleet
made no move to slip away. 385
When dawn's white coursers
gleamed over all the land,
a roar rang out from the Greeks,
echoed at once like a hopeful hymn
by the rocky islands. 390
Terror fell upon all the barbarians
as their wits deserted them, for the Greeks
did not cry out like men fleeing,
but sang their battle anthem with eager hearts.
A trumpet rang out and set them aflame, 395
then at once, upon command, the steady stroke
of their oars churned the salty deep
and they came swiftly into our view.
First their right wing advanced
in fine formation, then their whole fleet 400
fell upon us, and in that moment we heard
a mighty voice cry: "Sons of Greece, onward!
Free your homeland, free your children,
your wives, the temples of your ancient gods
and your ancestors' tombs. Everything is now at stake!" 405
We let loose a clamor of Persian tongues
and the moment of battle was upon us.
At once the bronze prows clashed,
ship against ship. A Greek ship
began the fight and sliced a Phoenician's sternpost 410
right off, while spears flew on every side.
At first, the Persian fleet held firm,
but when the mass of our ships was hemmed in
by the narrow strait, no one could come to another's aid.

Our ships smashed their bronze beaks together   415
and sheared their own oar-banks off.
The Greeks saw their chance and surrounded us.
Our ships capsized,
and the sea was hidden
by the wreckage and the bodies of the dead.   420
The shores and shoals were covered with corpses,
and every ship of the barbarian fleet
turned to flee in a reckless rout.
The Greeks kept hacking at us with broken
spears and oars, like fishermen   425
after a run of tuna. Groans and wailing
filled the salty air
until night descended.
The full weight of the calamity is more than
I can tell you, not even if I had ten days to tell it.   430
But of this be sure: such a great number
never before died on a single day.

Queen:
Alas! What a wave of woe has crested upon
the Persians and all the barbarians!

Messenger:
Nor is that even the half of our suffering,   435
for then came a further calamity
to outweigh even this twice over.

Queen:
What fate could be more hateful than this?
Speak! Tell me what worse disaster
dragged down the scales of our army's doom?   440

Messenger:
The Persians who were in their prime,
the noblest souls, the best-born,
foremost in fidelity to the king,
died a most disgraceful death.

Queen:
Oh, what misery has come of this, my dear ones! 445
Tell me, by what fate did they fall?

Messenger:
An island stands off the shore of Salamis,[62]
small, a poor anchorage, frequented by
light-footed Pan, no more than a watery shoal.
Xerxes sent his favored troops here 450
to make quick work of any Greeks
who survived the wreck of their fleet
and to rescue their comrades from the sea's currents.
An ill-considered plan! For once the gods
had given the Greeks glory in the clash at sea, 455
the Greeks, girt in bronze,
leapt from ships to shore
and encircled the whole island, leaving our soldiers
nowhere to turn. Many fell
wounded by hurled stones or 460
arrows from the bowstring.
At last, like one crashing wave, the Greeks rose up
and butchered our wretched men
until not one was left alive.
Xerxes wailed to see the depths of our disaster, 465
for he could behold the whole force from his seat
high on a headland above the salty sea.
Tearing his robes and shrieking aloud
he gave his orders to the army
and sent them into headlong flight. This, too, is to be mourned, 470
beyond the calamity that came before.

---

62. Psyttaleia.

10.11: Diplomatic outreach to Athens

Herodotus, *Histories* 8.136, 140–144

The outcome of Salamis led to a change in Persian strategy. Mardonius, left in command of the Persian forces in the region, saw that his best strategic move would be to break up the Greek alliance, in particular to detach the Athenians and their fleet from the Spartan land forces. His use of the Macedonian king as part of this diplomatic effort reflects the complex interrelations that bound the Greek world to the Persian Empire.

[136] Mardonius sent Alexander,[63] son of Amyntas, a Macedonian, as an ambassador to Athens. Alexander was connected to the Persians through his sister Gygaea, daughter of Amyntas, who was married to a Persian, Bubares.[64] Gygaea's son, named after his grandfather and known as Amyntas of Asia, dwelt in Alabanda, a great city in Phrygia given to him by the Persian king. Another reason why Mardonius chose Alexander as his emissary is because he had learned that Alexander was a friend and benefactor of the Athenians.[65] He thought this would be the best way to gain the favor of the Athenians, whom he knew by report to be a large city of brave people, and who were responsible for most of the trouble the Persians had encountered at sea. He believed that by gaining their friendship he would have mastery over the sea, and indeed he would have had. Since he already commanded superior land forces, he reckoned that this move would give him a decisive advantage over the Greeks.

(...)

[140A] When Alexander came to Athens at Mardonius' order, he said: "Athenians, Mardonius sends me with this message from the king:

"'I forgive the Athenians for their offenses against me. Now, Mardonius, I order you to do as follows. Restore the land taken from the Athenians, and give them more besides, wherever they would like. Let them

---

63. Alexander: Alexander I, king of Macedonia, great-great-great-grandfather of Alexander the Great.
64. Possibly the same Bubares who oversaw construction of the Athos canal. See Document 10.3, section 22.
65. Alexander had been named a proxenos of Athens, an official friend of the city among a foreign people.

have their own laws. Rebuild all of their temples that I burned. Do all this, if they will come to terms with me.'

"'These are my orders,' says Mardonius, 'and I will carry them out, so long as you give me no reason not to. For my part, I say: Why are you so insane as to make war against the king? You cannot defeat him, nor can you resist him forever. You have seen how great an army he commands and what they can do. You know the force that I now have at my disposal. Even if you defeat us—which, if you are in your right minds, you know you have no hope of—another, even larger force will follow. Therefore do not seek to contend with the king and thus lose your lands and be forever in danger. Let this quarrel go. Since the king himself wants peace, it is no shame for you to seek the same. This is not a trick or a trap. Be free and stand together with us.'

[140B] "This, Athenians, is what Mardonius directed me to say to you. I will say nothing of my good will for you, since you need no reminder of it, but I urge you to heed Mardonius' words. I can see for myself that you cannot hold out against the king forever. If I thought you could, I would never come to you with such a message, but the king's power is more than human and his reach is long. If you do not make terms with him now, when the terms he offers are so generous, I fear for your fate. Of all the allies, you are most at risk of destruction, for your land has been chosen as the battlefield. Do make peace. It is quite right that you should, since the king offers his forgiveness and friendship to you alone of all the Greeks." [141] That is what Alexander had to say.

When the Spartans learned that Alexander had gone to Athens to persuade the Athenians to make peace with the barbarians, they at once sent emissaries of their own to make sure that no such deal was struck. They remembered the oracle's words that they and the other Dorians would be driven out of the Peloponnese by the joint forces of Athens and Persia.

It came about that both these envoys presented their cases to the Athenians at the same time, since the Athenians delayed the discussions, knowing full well that the Spartans would hear that Alexander was coming to offer them a deal and that they would send their own messengers as soon as they could. They held off on hearing Alexander, therefore, so that the Spartans would hear their response as well.

[142] Once Alexander had finished, the Athenians called on the Spartan emissaries to speak. This is what they said:

"The Spartans have sent us to make sure that you do not change your minds about the defense of Greece or take any offers from the barbarians. That would not be just or fitting for any Greek to do, but especially not for you, for many reasons. In the first place, you were the ones who started this war.[66] We wanted no part of it, but this fight that you started now affects all of Greece. Furthermore, it is intolerable that you Athenians should be responsible for the enslavement of other Greeks when you have long been famous as champions of human freedom.

"However, we do feel compassion for your suffering. You have lost two harvests and have borne the ravaging of your homes for a long time. In recognition of these facts, the Spartans and their allies will provide food for your women and noncombatants for as long as the war goes on. Do not be taken in by Alexander the Macedonian and his praise of Mardonius' polished words. This is his business, for, as a tyrant himself, of course he takes the tyrant's side. But you should have nothing to do with him. If your minds are clear, you will see that there is nothing trustworthy or true in these barbarians." That was the Spartan message.

[143] The Athenians answered Alexander with these words:

"We know perfectly well that the Persian army is much bigger than ours, so do not rub that in our faces. We love our freedom so much that we will defend ourselves with whatever strength we have. Do not try to talk us into making terms with the barbarian. We will not be persuaded. Now, go back and tell Mardonius that the Athenians say: 'So long as the sun keeps to its course, we will never make terms with Xerxes. Rather we will resist him with all our strength, trusting in the gods and heroes whom he despises and whose shrines and sacred ornaments he burned.'

"As for you, Alexander, do not show your face in Athens if you bring this sort of message and do not pretend to be doing us a service by suggesting something so despicable. We would not want anything unpleasant to happen to a friend of the city." [144] That was their answer to Alexander.

To the Spartan envoys, they said: "It was perfectly human of the Spartans to be afraid of us making terms with the barbarian, but if you knew the Athenians' character, you would be ashamed to be so fearful. Nowhere on earth is there enough gold or a land of such beauty and fineness that receiving it would make us side with the Persians and enslave Greece.

---

66. The Spartans blame the Athenians' involvement in the Ionian Revolt for causing the larger conflicts between Persia and the European Greeks.

Even if we wanted to, there are many weighty reasons why we would not. First and foremost, the burning and destruction of the temples and treasures of the gods, which we are duty-bound to avenge rather than come to terms with the perpetrator. Besides this there is the common ancestry and language we share with all Greeks, the shrines and common sacrifices to the gods, and our shared way of life. To betray all of this would be no credit to the Athenians. Know this if you did not know it before: while even one Athenian still lives, we will never make terms with Xerxes.

"However, we appreciate your thoughtful offer to provide food for our households, since our own fields have been ravaged. You have been nothing but generous to us, but we will make do on our own as best we can, so as not to be a burden on you.

"As things stand, send out your army as soon as you can, for we can guess that the king will attack us again before long—indeed, as soon as he hears that we will not do as he demands."

10.12: Maneuvers and skirmishing at Plataea

Herodotus, *Histories* 9.19–25, 38–40

The last battle between Greeks and Persians in mainland Greece came at Plataea in western Boeotia in 479. Both sides delayed engaging in battle, the Greeks evidently waiting for more reinforcements, the Persians hoping that the Greek alliance would break down. A long period of skirmishing, harassment, and maneuvering led up to the outbreak of fighting, during which tensions among the Greeks rose and weaknesses emerged in their positioning and supply lines. The Persian forces were led by Mardonius, and the allied Greeks were led by the Spartan Pausanias, nephew of Leonidas, who served as regent for Leonidas' underage son Pleistarchus.

[19] The Spartans made camp in the Isthmus once they arrived. The rest of the Peloponnesians who had joined the cause saw the Spartans marching out and decided that they should not lag behind. Once they had received good omens from the sacrifices, they all marched out together from there to Eleusis. The Athenians joined them there after crossing over from Salamis. When the sacrifices produced favorable omens again,

they marched on to Erythrae in Boeotia. There they learned that the barbarians were encamped near the Asopus River, so they made their camp on the upper slopes of Mount Cithaeron.

[20] Since the Greeks refused to come down and fight on the plain, Mardonius sent the cavalry commanded by Masistius to attack them. Masistius (whom the Greeks called Macistius) was a man much honored among the Persians and he rode a Nisaean horse[67] beautifully decked out with a golden bit. The cavalry charged the Greek lines, one squadron after another, causing them serious harm and calling them women.

[21] The Megarians were stationed in the most vulnerable part of the field where they were most exposed to cavalry attack. Because they were suffering so badly from the Persian assault, they sent a herald to the Greek generals with this message: "We Megarians, your allies, cannot withstand the attack by the Persian cavalry in the place where we were originally stationed, even though we have fought with determination and honor thus far. If you do not send forces to relieve us, we will abandon the position."

The herald relayed this message, and Pausanias asked if any contingent of the Greeks would volunteer to take over the position from the Megarians. No one else was willing, but three hundred chosen men of Athens under the command of Olympidorus, son of Lampon, undertook the mission. [22] The volunteers took up their position at Erythrae, ahead of the other Greeks who were then present, accompanied by the archers. After a long fight, things ended as follows.

The Persian cavalry attacked, squadron after squadron, and when Masistius' horse was struck in the flank by an arrow, it reared up in pain and threw him off. When he fell, the Athenians closed in on him at once. They captured his horse, and, though Masistius defended himself at first, they killed him in the end. He was armored with a shirt of gilded scales, over which he wore a purple tunic. The scales protected him from their blows, until someone noticed what was happening and killed him with a stab to the eye.

The rest of the Persian cavalry did not know what had happened, since none of them had seen Masistius thrown from his horse or killed as they were turning and riding back to their lines. Once they had stopped,

---

67. Nisaean horse: a special breed of horse from Central Asia with exceptional strength and endurance.

however, they realized that their commander was not with them, so they urged one another onward to go back and recover his corpse.

[23] When the Athenians saw the cavalry come at them again, not in squadrons but as a whole force, they called out for help from the rest of the Greek army. While the rest of the infantry was coming up to their aid, an intense struggle arose over the body of Masistius.[68] As long as the three hundred Athenians were fighting alone, they were nearly overwhelmed and were ready to abandon the corpse, but once most of the rest of the army came to their aid, the Persian cavalry could no longer hold their ground or make any move to recover the body. Many of them fell alongside their commander. The surviving Persians fell back two *stadia*[69] and considered what to do. Since they no longer had a leader, they retreated to Mardonius.

[24] When the cavalry reported back to their camp, Mardonius and the rest of the army went into deep mourning for Masistius. They cut their own hair and the hair of their horses and pack animals. The sound of their wailing filled all of Boeotia, for the man who had died was second only to Mardonius in the estimation of the king and all Persia.

[25] While the barbarians were mourning the death of Masistius according to their customs, the Greeks, buoyed by their success in withstanding the Persians' cavalry assault, had the dead body paraded on a cart for every division of the army to see. Masistius was quite a sight to see, tall and handsome, so Greeks would leave their ranks and come running to look at his body.

After this, the Greeks decided to march down to Plataea, since the ground there seemed more suitable for setting up camp than at Erythrae and the water sources were better. They decided to encamp in their divisions there and by the spring at Gargaphia. They took up their arms and marched along the lower slopes of Mount Cithaeron to the territory of Plataea, by way of Hysiae, where they formed up in divisions by their cities of origin in the low hills and flat land near the Gargaphian spring and the sacred ground of the hero Androcrates.[70]

---

68. In ancient warfare, capturing the dead body and armor of an enemy officer could provide a valuable boost to morale and strike a psychological blow against the opposing side.
69. The *stadion* (plural *stadia*) was a Greek unit of length. There was no consistent standard for the length of a *stadion*, which could vary from around 160 to around 190 meters.
70. The locations of both the Gargaphian spring and the shrine of Androcrates are uncertain, which makes reconstructing the exact disposition of the Greek army difficult.

(…)
(Further maneuvering follows as the Greek allies argue over who will take the places of prestige in their formation.)
(…)
[38] The Persians could get no favorable omens from their sacrifices, and neither could the Greeks who were on their side (who had their own diviner, Hippomachus of Leucas). Meanwhile, the allied Greek army kept growing as more soldiers flowed in to join them.

It was then that a Theban, Timagenides, son of Herpys, advised Mardonius to block the Cithaeron pass, saying that by doing so he would cut off the Greek reinforcements that were coming in every day. [39] The armies had been staring each other down across the field for eight days when he gave this advice.

Mardonius saw that this was good advice, so, when night had fallen, he sent his cavalry to the pass over Cithaeron where it comes out near Plataea, the passage the Thebans call the Three-Headed and the Athenians call Oak-Head. This attack was not in vain, since they captured there five hundred transport animals and their drivers who were bringing food supplies to the Peloponnesians. The Persians fell upon their victims without mercy, killing people and animals alike. When they had had their fill of killing, they drove the survivors back to Mardonius' camp.

[40] After this, they delayed for another two days, as neither side wanted to commit to a battle. The barbarians came as far as the Asopus to see what the Greeks would do, but neither army crossed the river. In the meantime, Mardonius' cavalry kept up their constant harassment of the Greeks.

10.13: The battle of Plataea

Herodotus, *Histories* 9.49–63

The battle of Plataea arose out of the same disorder and confusion that had characterized the standoff before (Document 10.12). Although the Persians do not come off very well in this account themselves, even Herodotus struggles to make a heroic story out of the internal dissension, poor communication, and bungled maneuvers on the Greek side. While some of the most egregious details probably come from postwar Athenian propaganda that sought to diminish the contribution of non-Athenian forces to the victory, it is hard to escape the sense the battle did not play out as either side intended.

[49] Mardonius was delighted with this appearance of victory, so he sent his cavalry to attack the Greeks. The cavalry caused casualties throughout the Greek army with its arrows and javelins, because the Greeks found the Persians' mounted archers hard to come to grips with. They also ruined and blocked up the Gargaphian spring, from which the whole Greek army was drawing its water. (The way the army was drawn up, the Spartans were the only ones stationed near the spring while the rest of the Greeks were far away from it and closer to the Asopus, but they came to the spring to get their water because the Persian cavalry and archers kept them from getting close to the Asopus.)

[50] Given the situation, as they were cut off from their water supply and harried by the enemy cavalry, the Greek generals gathered with Pausanias at his position on the right wing of the army to discuss these and other matters. They had even more serious problems to consider, for they were out of food, and the servants they had sent back to the Peloponnese for supplies could not reach the camp because of the Persian cavalry. [51] So they resolved that, if the Persians did not engage them in battle that day, they would move the army to the "island," a region close to Plataea and a distance of ten *stadia*[71] from the Gargaphian spring and the Asopus River. This place is like an island on the land, since the river flowing down from Cithaeron splits into two streams which flow three *stadia* apart before joining together again. This river is called the Oeroe, and the locals call it the daughter of Asopus. The generals decided to make this move so that they could be sure to have plenty of water and to keep the Persian cavalry from getting close and doing them any more harm, and to move under cover of night so that the Persians would not see them and send their cavalry out to follow and harass them. They further decided that, once they had reached the ground encircled by the Oeroe where it flows down off Cithaeron, they would send half the army that very night out of the camp and up the slopes of Cithaeron to rescue their servants who had gone for food and who were now cut off from them in the pass.

---

71. The *stadion* (plural *stadia*) was a Greek unit of length. There was no consistent standard for the length of a *stadion*, which could vary from around 160 to around 190 meters. Ten *stadia* would be somewhat less than two kilometers.

[52] Once this decision was made, they endured the constant cavalry attacks for the rest of the day. Once the day was over, though, and the Persian cavalry broke off their harassment, they left their positions at the agreed-upon time of the night, but not all of them went to their assigned places. Instead, many of them, once they got moving, were so glad to be free of the cavalry assault that they made a run for Plataea and arrived at the nearby temple of Hera, which is twenty *stadia* from the Gargaphian spring. When they arrived, they threw down their arms in front of the temple [53] and made camp there.

When Pausanias saw these troops moving, he ordered the Spartans to take up arms and follow them, thinking that they were heading for their appointed places. While all the other Spartans were obeying this command, Amompharetus, son of Poliades, the commander of the Pitanate battalion,[72] refused to fall back, saying that it would be a disgrace to Sparta. He was astounded to see what the rest of the army was doing, since he had not been part of the council's discussions. Pausanias and Euryanax were outraged at Amompharetus' disobedience, but they thought it would be more outrageous yet to abandon the Pitanate battalion, for they feared that if they marched off with the other Greeks, Amompharetus and his soldiers would be wiped out by the Persians. With this in mind, they kept the Spartan army in place and tried to convince Amompharetus that he was in the wrong. [54] So they tried to reason with Amompharetus, who was the only one out of the Spartans and Tegeans who refused the order to move.

The Athenians, meanwhile, were staying in their original position, too, knowing that what the Spartans said and what the Spartans did were not always the same thing. When the rest of the army got moving, they sent a rider to see whether the Spartans were preparing to move as well or if they intended to stay put, and to ask Pausanias what the Athenians should do.

[55] When the messenger reached the Spartans, he found them in their original positions and their officers embroiled in a dispute. Pausanias and Euryanax were urging Amompharetus not to endanger himself and his troops by remaining behind, alone out of all the Spartans, but he would not be moved and when the Athenian messenger arrived,

---

72. Amompharetus and the Pitanate battalion are not known from any other sources, and Herodotus' contemporary Thucydides states that no such battalion existed. See Thucydides, *History* 1.20.

things were getting heated. In the midst of this argument, Amompharetus seized a stone in both hands and placed it at Pausanias' feet, saying: "This is my vote against fleeing from the foreigners!"[73] At this, Pausanias called him a madman and out of his wits.

It was at this point that the Athenian put his question to Pausanias. Pausanias told him to report back to the Athenians on what was going on in his camp, and to implore them to stay close to the Spartans and fall back when they did. [56] The messenger returned to the Athenians with this answer.

Dawn came and found the argument still going on. Pausanias had kept his forces in position, but at this point, feeling sure that Amompharetus would not stay behind when all the other Spartans fell back, he gave the order to depart and led the rest of his forces into the hills. The Tegeans followed him, and so, in the end, did Amompharetus. The Athenians likewise organized themselves for the march, taking a different route than the Spartans, for the Spartans went up into the foothills of Cithaeron out of fear of the Persian cavalry, while the Athenians marched through the plain.

[57] At first Amompharetus was certain that Pausanias would never dare to leave them behind, so he insisted that his soldiers stand firm, but when Pausanias had gone on some way ahead, he became convinced that the general was quite serious in his intention, so he ordered his battalion to take up arms and march off after them. They found the rest of the army waiting for them some ten *stadia* away by the Moloïs River, at a place called Argiopium where there is a shrine to Demeter of Eleusis. They had stopped here so that they would be close enough to come to Amompharetus' aid if he insisted on keeping his battalion in position.

No sooner had Amompharetus' force rejoined the Spartan army than the barbarian cavalry attacked them. The cavalry had come out to harass the Greeks as usual, but when they found the Greeks' earlier positions empty, they had advanced farther and attacked the Greeks as soon as they caught up with them.

[58] When Mardonius learned that the Greeks had retreated under cover of night and saw the ground empty, he summoned Thorax of Larissa and his brothers, Eurypylus and Thrasydeias. He said to them:"What do you have to say now, children of Aleuas, when you see the empty land?

---

73. This detail betrays the Athenian origins of the story: while colored pebbles were used in Athenian voting, Spartans voted by voice.

You kept telling me that your Spartan neighbors are the foremost of warriors and they never run from a fight, but you just saw them changing their positions and now all of us can see that they have run away during the night.[74] When they measured themselves against those who really know how to fight, they plainly showed that neither they nor any of the rest of the Greeks amount to anything. Well, you are strangers to the Persians and I can forgive you for speaking highly of those you know well. I am much more astonished at Artabazus for being so terrified of these Spartans and like a coward proposing that we shut ourselves up in Thebes to be besieged.[75] The king will hear from me about Artabazus, but that is a matter for another time. Now we must not let our enemies get away but hunt them down until they have paid the full price for opposing the Persians."

[59] With that, he led the Persians across the Asopus in pursuit of the Greeks, thinking that they were running away. His target was only the Spartans and the Tegeans, since he could not see the Athenians who were marching on the plain behind the hills. Seeing the Persians setting off in pursuit of the Greeks, the rest of the barbarians also hoisted their standards and went after them as fast as they could with no regard to order or formation. [60] The whole throng simply ran off whooping, thinking they were about to plunder the Greeks.

When Pausanias' forces were attacked by the cavalry, he sent a rider to the Athenians with this message: "Athenians, you and we Spartans have both been betrayed in this great struggle for the freedom of Greece by our allies who ran away in the night. Now this is what we must do: we must defend one another by fighting our best. If the cavalry had come against you first, it would have fallen to us and to the Tegeans who are with us and have not betrayed Greece to come to your defense, but since they have come against us, it is your duty to relieve that part of the army that is most sorely pressed. If something has happened that prevents you from coming to our aid, be good enough to send us your archers. We know that our plea to you who have been the most committed to this war will not fall on deaf ears."

---

74. Herodotus mentions Thorax as an ally of the Persians, but does not report his opinions on the Spartans. See Herodotus, *Histories* 9.1.

75. Artabazus, an officer of Mardonius' force, had recommended keeping the army safe in Thebes while using diplomacy and bribery to splinter the Greek alliance. See Herodotus, *Histories* 9.41.

[61] When this message reached the Athenians, they began to move toward the Spartans to help protect them, but once they had started to march off, they were set upon by the Greeks who had joined the Persian ranks and been stationed opposing them. Since they were being wounded by nearby foes, they could not go off to aid the Spartans. So the Spartans and Tegeans were left to face the Persians alone. There were, in addition to the lightly armed troops, fifty thousand Spartans and three thousand Tegeans, who were never separated from the Spartans. They offered sacrifices, hoping for good fortune against Mardonius and his army, but they could not get favorable omens. While they waited for good signs, many were killed and many more wounded, for the Persians had made a wall of their wicker shields and their archers rained arrows down on them from behind its cover.

When the Spartans were so hard-pressed and the sacrifices still did not produce favorable signs, Pausanias turned his eyes to the temple of Hera near Plataea and called upon the goddess to give them good omens and not dash their hopes. [62] While he was still in the act of praying, the Tegeans took the initiative and charged against the barbarians. As soon as they did, the Spartans' sacrifices immediately yielded positive omens. The Spartans swiftly joined the Tegeans in their charge, and the Persians dropped their bows to fight them hand to hand. First they fought at the Persian shield wall, and when that had fallen there was a fierce battle around the temple of Demeter which went on for a long time and ended up in a shoving match, for the barbarians grabbed the Greeks' spears and snapped off their points. The Persians were not weaker or less brave than their opponents, but they had lost their shields and were not as well trained, so they rushed out to attack the Spartans individually or by tens, or in larger or smaller groups, and so they fell and were slaughtered.[76]

[63] The Persians fought the hardest around Mardonius, who rode a white horse and was surrounded by a thousand elite troops. As long as Mardonius was alive, these soldiers stood their ground and felled many Spartans, but once Mardonius had been killed and those around him, who were the best of the army, had fallen, the rest of the force gave way and fled before the Spartans. What hurt them most was their lack of armor, for they fought against armed men as if they were naked.

---

76. On the details of this final engagement, see Michael B. Charles, "Herodotus, Body Armor, and Achaemenid Infantry," *Historia* Bd. 61, H. 3 (2012): 257–69.

SECTION 11
The Persian response to the wars in Greece

11.1: A Persian version of the wars in the Aegean

The outcome of Xerxes' invasion of mainland Greece was certainly not what the king intended, but neither was the campaign an outright failure. Xerxes had induced several major Greek cities, most notably Thebes and Argos, to come over to his side, had slain a king of Sparta in battle, and had burned Athens, thus dealing a serious blow to the two major opponents of Persia in Greece. Even without conquest of new territory, these accomplishments could be presented as a victory.

Herodotus credits this idea to Artemisia, queen of Halicarnassus, in her advice to Xerxes after the battle of Salamis, when Mardonius was offering to stay behind and continue the war in Xerxes' absence. Dio Chrysostom records a version of the wars in Greece as told from a Persian perspective, which seems to follow the same line.

Herodotus, *Histories* 8.102

When consulted on the question of what to do, Artemisia said: "Sire, it is hard to give good advice in such a case, but what seems best to me is for you to march home and leave Mardonius and whatever troops wish to remain with him here, if he is willing to undertake this task. If Mardonius is successful and accomplishes what he says he can, the credit for it will belong to you, since he is your servant. If he is wrong and things go against him, it will be no great disaster for you and your house. As long as you and your line endure, the Greeks will often face great struggles, and no one will much care if anything happens to Mardonius, nor will defeating your servant count as a great victory for the Greeks. You, however, will depart having accomplished what you set out to do, which was to burn Athens."

Dio Chrysostom, *Discourses* 11.148–149

[148] I heard a Mede say that the Persians do not agree at all with the Greeks' version of events. Instead, he said that Darius sent Datis and Artaphernes against Naxos and Eretria, and that after capturing these cities they returned to the king. A few of their ships—not more than twenty—were blown off course to Attica and the crews had some kind of scuffle with the locals. [149] Later on, Xerxes made war on the Spartans. He defeated them at Thermopylae and slew their king Leonidas. Then he captured the city of Athens, razed it, and enslaved those who did not flee. When this was done, he made the Greeks pay him tribute and returned to Asia.

11.2: Greek booty distributed in Persia

As part of demonstrating their successes in Greece, the Persian kings distributed booty captured from Greece to various cities around the empire for public display. The first document records a specific statue taken from Athens and put on display in Sardis; the second speaks more generally of treasures taken from Greece by the Persians and returned after the conquest of Persia by Alexander the Great.

Plutarch, *Parallel Lives*, "Themistocles" 31.1

When Themistocles[1] came to Sardis and was occupying his time viewing the temple buildings and the many offerings there, he saw the bronze statue known as the Water-Carrying Maiden in the temple of the Great Mother. This statue was two cubits[2] tall, and he had paid for its creation himself out of the fines paid by people convicted of illegally

---

1. This anecdote comes from after the war when Themistocles joined the Persian court. See Document 12.1.
2. cubit: a unit of measure based on the length of a man's forearm from elbow to fingertip. The exact length varied in different cultures and times, but most were around half a meter.

tapping the public water supply when he was the overseer of water in Athens. Perhaps feeling affronted at the despoiling of this sacred offering, or perhaps out of a desire to show the Athenians the honor and power he enjoyed in the king's service, he sent word to the satrap of Lydia requesting that the Maiden be returned to Athens.

Arrian, *Anabasis* 7.19.2

Alexander allowed the emissaries to take back to Greece the statues of men and gods and other such sacred offerings that Xerxes had taken from Greece to Babylon, Susa, or anywhere else in Asia.

11.3: Reorganization in Anatolia

Part of the Persian response to the end of Xerxes' campaign was a reorganization of local administration on the Aegean frontier. Herodotus provides a colorful tale set during the Persian retreat after Salamis. Xenophon offers a more straightforward report from many years later in 399 BCE. Both these accounts indicate a move toward entrusting Persian interests in the Aegean to Greeks with proven loyalty to the Persian king.

Herodotus, *Histories* 9.107

As they were making their way along the road, Masistes, son of Darius, who had been present for the Persian defeat [at Salamis], began heaping abuse on the admiral, Artayntes. He taunted him for being worse than a woman as a commander and said he deserved every possible punishment for having made the king's estate worse off. Among the Persians, to call a man worse than a woman is the greatest insult.

After putting up with a great deal of this abuse, Artayntes drew his sword and went at Masistes, aiming to kill. Xenagoras, son of Praxilaus, a Halicarnassian, was standing behind Artayntes and saw him draw his sword, so he grabbed him around the waist and wrestled him to the ground, which gave Masistes' bodyguards a chance to intervene.

With this deed, Xenagoras gained the favor of both Masistes himself and Xerxes as well. The king made Xenagoras ruler of all Cilicia as a reward for saving his brother.

Xenophon, *Hellenica* 3.1.6

Eurysthenes and Procles, descendants Demaratus the Spartan,[3] ruled Teuthrania and Halisarna.[4] These lands had been a gift to Demaratus from the king for his aid in war. (...) The cities of Myrina, Gryneium, Gambrium, and Palaegambrium[5] were a gift from the king to Gongylus, who fled Eretria where he was the Persians' only supporter.

---

3. Demaratus: an exiled Spartan king who accompanied Xerxes on his Greek campaign as an adviser. See Document 7.3.
4. Teuthrania and Halisarna: two cities in northwestern Anatolia.
5. Myrina, Gryneium, Gambrium, and Palaegambrium: four cities in western Anatolia.

SECTION 12
A troublesome frontier, 478–451 BCE

12.1: Greek leaders collaborating with Persia

Political and diplomatic relationships between Greeks and Persians were always unstable. Even those Greeks who had fought hardest to prevent a Persian conquest of Greece could also look to Persia as a source of patronage and support as their fortunes changed. In the aftermath of invasion, Persians found that personal relationships with Greek leaders could be used to serve the empire's aims.

Themistocles and Pausanias, the leaders behind the Greek victories at Salamis and Plataea, respectively, were both accused of conspiring with Persia in the years after the war. It is not clear in either case how much substance there was to the charges and how much was just political muckraking, but their stories fit a pattern already well established by figures like Hippias and Demaratus (see Documents 7.2, 7.3).

Thucydides, *History* 1.128–129, 135–138

[128] Pausanias the Spartan was recalled from his command in the Hellespont for the first time to be put on trial. He was acquitted, but he was not sent out again on official business. On his own and without any commission from Sparta, however, he took a ship from Hermione[1] and sailed to the Hellespont. He claimed that he was going to aid in the war for Greece, but in reality he was conspiring with the Persian king and aimed at seizing power over Greece.

He first made himself useful to the king and so laid the foundation for his scheme in this way: When he had captured Byzantium, after

---
1. Hermione: a port town south of Argos.

returning from Cyprus, he had also captured some relatives and familiars of the king. He now let them go, without the knowledge of the Greek allies. When they were discovered missing, he claimed that they had escaped. He accomplished this with the help of Gongylus,[2] an Eretrian, whom he had left in charge of Byzantium and the prisoners. He also used Gongylus to send a letter to the king. The letter's contents were later discovered. It said:

"Pausanias, general of Sparta, sends you these prisoners of war and this message. I propose, if it pleases you, to marry one of your daughters and to make Sparta and all of Greece subject to you. If this is agreeable to you, send someone trustworthy to the Aegean through whom we may continue our discussions."

[129] That was all the letter said, but it pleased Xerxes, so he sent Artabazus, son of Pharnaces, to take over the satrapy of Dascylium[3] from Megabates, the previous satrap, and sent with him a letter to Pausanias. His orders were to deliver the letter to Pausanias at Byzantium as soon as possible, to show him the royal seal, and to carry out any instructions Pausanias had for him as well and faithfully as he could. Artabazus did all this when he arrived in the region, including delivering the letter, which said:

"From King Xerxes to Pausanias: You will have favor in my house forever for those whom you rescued for me from Byzantium beyond the sea. I approve of your proposals. Lose not a moment in carrying out what you have undertaken on my behalf. Gold, silver, and troops are at your disposal wherever they may be needed. Together with Artabazus, the reliable man whom I sent to you, boldly do whatever will best serve our common interests."

(...)

(Pausanias' activities are uncovered and he returns to Sparta, but dies before he can be brought to trial.)

(...)

[135] The Spartans sent envoys to Athens to report that their inquiry into Pausanias' treason had implicated Themistocles as well and to demand that he be punished. The Athenians were convinced, but as it

---

2. Gongylus: see Document 11.3.

3. Dascylium: a city in northwestern Anatolia, the capital of the satrapy of Hellespontine Phrygia, a region on the south coast of the Hellespont and Propontis.

happened, Themistocles had been ostracized[4] and was at that time residing in Argos and making frequent visits to the rest of the Peloponnese. The Spartans were prepared to go in pursuit of him, so the Athenians sent some men along with them with orders to get ahold of Themistocles wherever he might be.

[136] Themistocles got wind of the pursuit and fled to Corcyra, where he was in good graces, but the Corcyraeans said they were afraid of provoking the Athenians and Spartans by sheltering him, so they conveyed him across to the mainland.

(...)

(Themistocles narrowly escapes his pursuers and makes his way to Persian territory on the coast of Anatolia.)

[137] (...) As he was making his way inland along with some Persian person, Themistocles sent a letter to Artaxerxes, who had just succeeded his father Xerxes as king. The letter said:

"I, Themistocles, am coming to you, I who of all the Greeks did the most harm to your house in the days of your father when his invasion forced me to fight in defense of my people. I did much more to his benefit, however, during his retreat, when he was in danger and I was not. You are in my debt for my favors in the past." (Here he mentioned the message he sent to the king at Salamis advising him to retreat and assuring him that the bridges had not been broken, for which he also falsely took credit.[5]) "And now I am in your land and intend to do great things for your benefit, but the Greeks are pursuing me because of my friendship for you. Still, I wish to hold off for a year before declaring my intentions to you in person."

[138] The king, they say, was astonished at the intention he expressed and told him in reply to do as he had written. Themistocles used the year to learn as much as he could of the Persians' language and customs. A year later, when he was received at court, the king accorded him a greater station than any Greek had achieved before. This esteem came partly from his past good services and partly in the hope that he might help bring Greece under Persian rule, but mostly for the keen intellect he displayed in his actions.

---

4. ostracism: a procedure by which an individual could be exiled from Athens for a period of ten years. Originally intended as a check against the rise of a tyrant, it could also be exploited by political factions against their rivals.
5. See Herodotus, *Histories* 8.110.

Plutarch, *Parallel Lives*, "Themistocles" 21.5

When Themistocles was accused of working with the Persians, Timocreon[6] wrote this poem against him:

> Timocreon was not the only one who took oaths with Medes.[7]
> There are other schemers. I am not the only short-tail—
> there are other foxes, too.

12.2: The formation of the Delian League

Thucydides, *History* 1.96

After the defeat of Xerxes' army, the Hellenic League developed into a new alliance with an initial aim of keeping Persian influence out of the Aegean. In time, this new alliance, known to historians as the Delian League, became an Athenian-dominated empire extracting tribute from cities around the Aegean and maintained by force, but Thucydides records its beginnings and original intent.

The Athenians took over leadership of the alliance, as offered to them by the allies out of their hatred for Pausanias. In that role, the Athenians determined which cities should contribute money and which ones should contribute ships for the war against the barbarians. As justification, they declared their intention of taking revenge for what they had suffered by ravaging the king's lands.

The Athenians then first instituted the "Treasurers of Greece." These treasurers collected the tribute, as the contributions in money were called, which was initially fixed at 360 talents.[8] The treasury was kept at Delos, where the common meetings of the alliance were also held in the temple.

---

6. Timocreon: a poet from Rhodes who was known to have sided with the Persians.
7. Greeks often referred to Persians as Medes, even those who were aware that they were two different ethnicities. See Christopher Tuplin, "Intolerable Clothes and a Terrifying Name: The Characteristics of an Achaemenid Invasion Force," *Bulletin of the Institute of Classical Studies*, suppl. no. 124 (2013): 225–28.
8. talent: a measure of weight, which in Athens was set at about 26 kilograms. Also a unit of monetary value based on the value of a talent's weight of silver, conventionally equivalent to 6,000 drachmas. A drachma was roughly a day's wage for a skilled laborer.

12.3: Greek victory at Eurymedon

Diodorus of Sicily, *Library of History* 11.60–61

In 466, Athenian-led forces of the Delian League won a decisive victory over a Persian army encamped at the mouth of the Eurymedon River in southern Anatolia, and also captured or destroyed most of the Persians' accompanying fleet. The historian Diodorus, writing several centuries later, provides the fullest account of the battle. Not all Diodorus' details are necessarily reliable,[9] but the result of this battle was a definite shift in Persian strategy away from direct military engagement in the Aegean region.

[60] The Athenians chose Cimon, son of Miltiades, as general. They assigned him a sizable force and tasked him to go to the coast of Asia to assist their allies there and to free the cities still held by Persian garrisons.

Cimon also took the fleet stationed at Byzantium and sailed to Eion, which he captured from the Persians. Next he laid siege to Skyros, which was inhabited by Pelasgians and Dolopians. Here he established a colony by appointing an Athenian as founder and portioning out the land for settlers.

Once these things were accomplished, he had a mind to embark on even greater enterprises, so he returned to Piraeus where he assembled more ships and gathered supplies on a grand scale. He set sail again with 200 ships, but later, when he had called on the Ionians and others for reinforcements, the fleet totaled 300. With this fleet, he sailed to Caria,[10] where the coastal cities, which had been settled by Greeks, willingly abandoned the Persians and joined him. The other cities, the ones where two languages are spoken and had Persian garrisons, had to be besieged and won by force. When he had taken the cities of Caria, he persuaded the Lycians to join him as well. He increased the size of his fleet further by taking ships from the cities that kept signing on with him.

The Persians fielded an army of their own people, but for the fleet they pressed the Phoenicians, Cypriots, and Cilicians into service. The commander was Tithraustes, an illegitimate son of Xerxes.

---

9. Plutarch gives a much briefer and less detailed account of a pitched battle on the shore rather than Diodorus' stealthy nighttime raid. See Plutarch, *Parallel Lives*, "Life of Cimon" 13.
10. Caria: a region in southwestern Anatolia.

When Cimon learned that the Persian fleet was stationed at Cyprus, he sailed there and engaged the barbarians in a sea battle, fighting his 250 ships against their 340. The battle was hard fought on both sides, but in the end the Athenians triumphed, destroying many enemy ships and capturing more than a hundred along with their crews. The rest of the ships fled to shore where their crews escaped onto land, and these abandoned ships likewise fell into Cimon's hands.

[61] Cimon was not content with such a magnificent victory, so he turned his entire fleet at once to attack the Persian land army, which was encamped at the Eurymedon River. Wishing to overcome the barbarians by a clever ruse, he outfitted his own best troops with headdresses and other Persian garb and embarked them on the captured ships. When these ships approached the Persian camp, the barbarians were taken in by the deception and thought these were their own ships, so they welcomed the Athenians as friends.

Once night had fallen, Cimon landed his troops and attacked the camp of the Persians who had greeted him as a friend. As the Persians were thrown into total confusion, Cimon and his followers cut down everyone who crossed their path. They seized Pherendates, the barbarians' other general and a nephew of the king, and slew him in his tent. The rest of the Persians were either killed or wounded and the survivors were driven into flight by the chaos.

The Persians were taken completely by surprise and most of them had no idea who was attacking them, since they did not know the Greeks had an army at all. They thought the Pisidians, hostile natives of the area, had come against them in force. Since they thought the attack was coming from the hills, they fled to the ships, which they believed to be in friendly hands. Because it was a dark and moonless night, their confusion was all the greater and no one knew what was really happening. In the chaos, many barbarians were slain.

Cimon then had a torch lit near the ships, a signal he had prearranged to gather his troops out of fear that his plans might go awry if the soldiers spread out to loot the camp. The soldiers all stopped their plundering and assembled around the torch, then boarded the ships. The next day they set up a trophy[11] and sailed back to Cyprus with two great victories to their credit, one at sea and the other on land.

---

11. trophy: a rough wooden model adorned with armor captured from the defeated forces set up by the victor on the battlefield.

12.4: Revolt in Egypt

The assassination of Xerxes in 465 and the resulting turmoil in the Persian court while his son Artaxerxes I secured his hold on power created an opening for revolt in Egypt. Between the late 460s and the mid 450s, a delta aristocrat named Inarus led the Egyptian revolt and secured Athenian assistance to bolster his ranks.

Thucydides, *History* 1.104, 109–110

[104] Inarus, son of Psammetichus, a Libyan and king of the Libyans on the Egyptian border, led most of Egypt in revolt against Artaxerxes. He based himself at Marea, a town inland from Pharos,[12] and he sought support from Athens.

The Athenians and their allies were engaged in a campaign on Cyprus with two hundred ships, but they abandoned this project and sailed to Egypt. There, making their way inland from the sea, they took control of the Nile River and two thirds of Memphis. They then pressed the attack on the remaining third of the city where the Persians and Medes, along with those Egyptians who were not part of the rebellion, had taken refuge in the White Fortress.[13]

(...)

[109] At first the Athenians were successful in Egypt, so the king sent Megabazus, a Persian, to Sparta with money to try to induce the Peloponnesians to invade Attica and draw the Athenians off from Egypt.[14] But Megabazus made no progress and the money was just being wasted, so the king recalled him with the unspent funds and instead sent Megabyzus, son of Zopyrus, a Persian, to Egypt with a large army.

Megabyzus marched into Egypt, defeated the Egyptians and their allies, and drove the Greeks out of Memphis. He bottled the Greeks up on the island of Prosopitis and besieged them there for a year and a half.

---

12. Pharos: an island off the coast from the westernmost mouth of the Nile. In later centuries, it was the site of the great lighthouse that guided ships to Alexandria.
13. The White Fortress or White Wall was an ancient fortress in Memphis possibly dating back to the earliest years of the Old Kingdom. Egyptian kings and foreign occupiers alike had used the fortress as a base for exerting control over the Nile valley.
14. By this date, relations between Athens and Sparta, who had been allied during Xerxes' invasion, had deteriorated. The two states were not yet openly at war, but tensions were building between them.

At last, by diverting the water through another channel, he stranded the Greek ships and joined most of the island to the mainland. He then took it by force with his infantry. [110] So after six years of war, this Greek expedition came to ruin. Of the many who had set out very few returned, making their way through Libya to Cyrene. Most of them perished.

Egypt returned to the Persian king's control, except for Amyrtaeus, who was king in the marshlands.[15] The Persians were unable to bring him to heel because of the vastness of the marshes and because the marsh-dwellers are the toughest fighters in Egypt. Inarus, the Libyan king who had been behind the revolt, was betrayed to the Persians and crucified.

Fifty ships sent as reinforcements by the Athenians arrived at the Mendesian mouth[16] of the Nile knowing nothing of what had happened. The Persians attacked this force on land and sent the Phoenicians against them by sea. Most of the ships were destroyed, while a few survived by fleeing. So ended the great Athenian adventure in Egypt.

12.5: An Athenian expedition in Cyprus

Thucydides, *History* 1.112

Even after the defeat of their forces in the Egyptian revolt, Athens continued to use its naval power to interfere in the western Persian frontier. This expedition took place in the late 450s; the exact date is unclear.

The Athenians launched an expedition to Cyprus under the command of Cimon with 200 ships of their own and drawn from their allies. When Amyrtaeus, the king in the marshland, requested aid, sixty of the ships were dispatched to Egypt. The rest blockaded Citium.

When Cimon died and a famine struck Citium, the fleet departed. They cruised off Salamis[17] where they fought Phoenicians, Cilicians, and Cypriots. After scoring victories both at sea and on land, they returned home. The detachment sent to Egypt returned with them.

---

15. marshlands: the Nile delta.
16. Mendesian mouth: one of the northeastern mouths of the Nile.
17. Salamis: a city on Cyprus, not the island near Athens.

SECTION 13
Diplomacy and stability, 450–387 BCE

13.1: The "Peace of Callias"

Diodorus of Sicily, *Library of History* 12.4

Diodorus of Sicily records a peace treaty made between Athens and Persia around 450 BCE, but historians are divided over whether to trust his account or not.[1] Diodorus wrote centuries later, and the sources he used for his Athenian history are lost to us now, so it is hard to judge the reliability of his information.

Nevertheless, whether there was a formal agreement or not, there was a clear shift in relations between Athens and Persia around this time. Both had suffered losses and needed time to regroup. They entered a period of détente during which they largely avoided direct military confrontations.

When King Artaxerxes learned how poorly things were going on Cyprus,[2] he consulted with his advisers and decided that the best course of action would be to make peace with the Greeks. He therefore wrote to the generals and satraps on Cyprus setting out the terms on which they were to negotiate with the Greeks. Artabazus and Megabyzus accordingly dispatched emissaries to Athens for discussions about reaching an agreement.

The Athenians were receptive to these efforts, so they sent ambassadors of their own with full authority, led by Callias, son of Hipponicus. The Athenians and their allies concluded a peace treaty with the Persians whose principal terms were as follows:

---

1. Loren J. Samons, "Kimon, Kallias, and Peace with Persia," *Historia* Bd. 47, H. 2 (2nd quarter 1998).
2. See Document 12.5.

- All the Greek cities in Asia will be under their own laws.
- The Persian satraps will not come within three days' march of the sea.
- No Persian warship will sail between Phaselis and the Cyanaean Rocks.[3]
- As long as the king and his generals abide by these provisions, the Athenians will not make war on any land ruled by the king.

Once these terms had been agreed upon, the Athenians pulled their forces out of Cyprus, with a great victory and noteworthy peace treaty to their credit.

13.2: Pericles honors the peace with Persia

Plutarch, *Parallel Lives,* "Pericles" 20.2

Pericles, one of the leading politicians in Athens in the later fifth century, evidently used his influence to stifle ambitions for new campaigns against Persia and maintain the peace established around 450 (see Document 13.1).

[Pericles] did not support the impulses of the citizens who got carried away with their strength and good fortune and proposed expeditions to Egypt or against the king's coastal territories.

13.3: Athens at war with Samos

Plutarch, *Parallel Lives,* "Pericles" 25

Despite the suspension of direct hostilities between Athens and Persia (see Document 13.1), Athenians continued to interfere with the Persian Empire's clients and allies in the Aegean, such as the city of Samos. Samos had long had close ties to Persia but

---

3. Phaselis is a city on the southwestern coast of Anatolia; the Cyanaean Rocks are islands and shoals at the Black Sea entrance to the Bosporus. The territory marked out by these landmarks would leave the entire Aegean free of Persian ships.

was also a rival of Athens for naval power in the Aegean. When Athens attacked Samos in 440, the satrap of Lydia, Pissouthnes, used his financial resources to support Samos without exerting direct military force.

[Samos and Miletus] were fighting over control of Priene and the Samians were coming out on top, so the Athenians ordered them to halt the fighting and refer the question to them for arbitration. The Samians and Milesians refused to do so. So Pericles sailed to Samos, dissolved the oligarchic government there, and took fifty of the leading men along with fifty of their children as hostages to Lemnos. In fact, they say that each of these hostages offered a talent[4] for his freedom, and those who did not want to have a democracy in the city offered many more besides. Even Pissouthnes, the Persian, who had friendly relations with the Samians, sent him ten thousand gold pieces to intercede for the city. But Pericles accepted none of this money. Instead he established a democracy in Samos, just as he had intended, then sailed back to Athens.

The Samians revolted at once, since Pissouthnes had secretly gotten the hostages back from Lemnos and in other respects prepared them for war. Pericles sailed out against them once more, since they would not give up or be cowed into submission but were eager to fight for control of the sea. In a fierce naval battle near the island of Tragia, Pericles won a stunning victory, defeating seventy ships, twenty of them transports, with his fleet of forty-four.

13.4: Unproductive negotiations

Thucydides, *History* 4.50

Tensions between the Athenian-led Delian League and the Spartan-led Peloponnesian League broke out into open war in 431, known to modern historians as the Peloponnesian War. By the end of 425, both sides had suffered unexpected losses without scoring a decisive victory over the other. That winter, it emerged

---

4. talent: a measure of weight, which in Athens was set at about 26 kilograms. Also a unit of monetary value based on the value of a talent's weight of silver, conventionally equivalent to 6,000 drachmas. A drachma was roughly a day's wage for a skilled laborer.

that the Spartans had been attempting to enter into negotiations
of some kind with the Persian king Artaxerxes I. The Athenians
attempted to do the same, but all these diplomatic efforts came
to nothing. These events show not only how uncertain diplomatic
endeavors could be, but also the Persians' flexibility when it came
to potential allies in the Aegean.

The following winter [425–424], Aristides, son of Archippus, was sent out [from Athens] to collect back tribute owed by the allies. At Eion on the Strymon River he apprehended Artaphernes, a Persian who was on his way to Sparta on the king's business. He was sent to Athens, where the Athenians had the letters he carried translated from Assyrian.[5] Among other matters, their main point was this: the king did not know what the Spartans wanted, because however many ambassadors they sent, no two ever told the same story. If they wanted to speak plainly, therefore, they should send someone back with Artaphernes.

Later on, the Athenians sent this Artaphernes to Ephesus by trireme along with some ambassadors of their own. When they arrived, though, they learned of the death of Artaxerxes, son of Xerxes, which had just recently happened, so they returned home.

13.5: A treaty between Persia and Sparta

As the Peloponnesian War dragged on longer than either side
had expected, both sides continued to make overtures toward
the Persians, whose financial and military resources could make
them valuable allies in an ongoing war in the Aegean. The Spartans were the first to conclude an alliance. Thucydides records
its terms.

A fragmentary inscription from the Lycian city of Xanthos in
southwestern Anatolia refers to an occasion on which the local
king acted as arbiter for negotiations between Persians and Spartans who were jointly at war with Athens. Given the mention of
Tissaphernes as the Persians' representative in both cases, it seems

---

5. Possibly meaning Aramaic, which was widely used as a language for trade and official business in the empire.

likely that this inscription refers to the same treaty described by Thucydides.

Thucydides, *History* 8.17–18

[17] When Miletus rebelled, the Spartans made their first alliance with the king. Arrangements were made through Tissaphernes and Chalcideus to the following effect:

[18] "On these terms the Spartans and their allies make an alliance with the king and Tissaphernes:

- The king will have control over any cities or lands he currently possesses or which his ancestors previously possessed.
- Whatever tribute the Athenians were collecting from these lands, the king and the Spartans together with their allies will prevent them from collecting it.
- The king and the Spartans with their allies will carry on the war against Athens and they will not make peace except by joint action.
- Any rebels against the king will also be enemies of the Spartans and their allies, and any rebels against Sparta will also be enemies of the king."

TAM I, 44, b64–c9[6]

The Spartans [. . .] to Tissaphernes, son of Hystaspes, and the Persians in Caunus[7] when they and the Spartans were at war with Athens. I arbitrated for them. They undertook a joint offering. They will set up a stela[8] in honor of Maliya[9] in Hytenna[10] in the place where [. . .] the

---

6. Due to the fragmentary nature of the text and the difficulties of interpreting the Lycian language, which is not well preserved, the translation offered here is a somewhat loose one. For a discussion of the text and its problems, see H. Craig Melchert, "A New Interpretation of Lines C 3–9 of the Xanthos Stele," in *Akten des II. Internationalen Lykien-Symposions*, ed. Jürgen Bochhardt and Gerhard Dobesch (Vienna: Verlag der Österreichischen Akademie der Wissenschaften, 1993).
7. Caunus: a city in Lycia.
8. stela: a stone monument carved with the text of the agreement. Negotiating parties would jointly set up monuments stating their mutual promises in sanctuaries or other public places as a way of ensuring that the details of the agreement were publicly accessible and preserved for the future.
9. Maliya: a Lycian goddess. In later periods, she was equated with the Greek Athena.
10. Hytenna: a city in Lycia.

fighters [...] and also in Caunus, both for the local sanctuary, in honor of Maliya and Artemis, and for the King of Caunus.[11]

13.6: Cyrus the Younger's revolt

Xenophon, *Anabasis* 1.1.3–11

The alliance between Persia and Sparta crumbled in 401, as soon as the war with Athens was over, because of Spartan support for the Persian prince Cyrus the Younger's failed bid to seize the throne from his older brother Artaxerxes II after the death of their father, Darius II. Cyrus' ability to draw on support from Greece and the consequences for Persian-Spartan relations show how the complicated politics on either side of the Aegean frontier could spill over to the other.

[3] When Darius died and Artaxerxes assumed the throne, Tissaphernes came to him with an accusation that Cyrus was plotting against him. Artaxerxes had Cyrus arrested and intended to put him to death, but their mother interceded for him and Cyrus was sent back to his satrapy. [4] When Cyrus returned, having been threatened and humiliated, he began to make plans to ensure that he would never be in his brother's power again. Indeed, if at all possible, he hoped to take his brother's place as king. Their mother Parysatis supported Cyrus in this plan, since she loved him even better than she loved his brother Artaxerxes.

[5] Anyone who came to Cyrus from the king's court was treated so well that they went away feeling more loyalty to him than to Artaxerxes. Cyrus made sure that the people of his province were both fit for war and on his side. [6] He also gathered a force of Greeks in as much secrecy as he could, so that he could take the king by surprise.

This is how he assembled his troops. He sent word to the garrison commanders in all his cities to recruit Peloponnesian soldiers—as many as they could get of the best quality—on the grounds that Tissaphernes had designs on his cities. The Ionian cities had originally been given to Tissaphernes by the king, but all except Miletus had gone over to Cyrus.

---

11. King of Caunus: title of a Carian god (not a human ruler).

[7] When Tissaphernes got wind that the Milesians intended to do the same, he intervened by killing some of their leaders and exiling others. Cyrus took in the exiles and assembled an army to lay siege to Miletus by land and sea in an attempt to restore them to their home, which provided him with another excuse for assembling an army.

[8] Cyrus sent word to the king to make the case that, as his brother, he should hold these cities in place of Tissaphernes, and his mother took his side in the matter. Artaxerxes therefore remained unaware of the plot against him but believed that it was the conflict with Tissaphernes leading Cyrus to spend so much money on his forces. He made no objection to their fighting, especially because Cyrus kept sending the king the tribute revenues that were due from the cities that had been allotted to Tissaphernes but were under his control.

[9] In the Chersonese opposite Abydus, yet another army was being gathered for him in this way. Clearchus the Spartan was an exile whom Cyrus had come to admire after meeting him, so he gave Clearchus ten thousand darics. With this money, Clearchus assembled an army and started fighting the Thracians who live above the Hellespont. The Greek cities of the Hellespont benefited from this campaign, so they voluntarily sent him additional money for the support of his troops. By these means, this army was also being secretly kept in readiness for Cyrus.

[10] Aristippus the Thessalian happened to be a friend of Cyrus. When he found himself hard pressed by his opponents at home, he came to Cyrus and requested pay for two thousand mercenaries for three months so that he could defeat his opponents. Cyrus gave him enough money to pay four thousand mercenaries for six months, and also asked him not to come to terms with his opponents without consulting him. In this way, another army was quietly being prepared for Cyrus in Thessaly.

[11] Cyrus ordered his friend Proxenos of Boeotia to come to his aid with as many men as he could gather, on the pretext of fighting the Pisidians, who he said were causing trouble in his province. He likewise ordered Sophaenetus the Stymphalian and Socrates the Achaean, other friends of his, to come to him with as many men as they could, on the grounds that he was fighting Tissaphernes on behalf of the Milesian exiles. They did as they were told.

13.7: Diplomatic complications

Xenophon, Hellenica 4.8.24

Diplomatic relations between the Greek cities and Persia continued to be fluid. By 391 BCE, Persia was allied with Athens and at war with Sparta. In that year, the bewildering complexities of frontier diplomacy were made plain in the interactions of the Spartan admiral Teleutias, the Athenian commander Philocrates, and the Cypriot king Euagoras, who was in revolt against Persia.

[Teleutias] sailed to Rhodes with twenty-seven ships. On his way, he came across Philocrates, son of Ephialtes, who was sailing from Athens to Cyprus to the aid of Euagoras. Teleutias captured all these ships.

Both these forces were acting against their own interests: the Athenians, who were allied with the Persian king, were sending aid to Euagoras, who was at war with him, whereas Teleutias destroyed a force that was sailing to the aid of the king's enemies, even though the Spartans were at war with Persia.

13.8: A Persian arbitration between Greek cities

SIG 13 no. 134[12]

Persian satraps continued to supervise the Ionian cities. This inscription, partially damaged, records a case sometime between 391 and 388 when the satrap of Ionia stepped in to arbitrate a boundary dispute between the cities of Miletus and Myous. The way this case was resolved suggests that the Greek cities of Ionia largely managed their own affairs, but that the Persian satrap could be looked to as a final arbiter.

[. . .] sending, the king and the satrap of Ionia, Strouses.[13] They were in dispute over the land in the plain of the Maeander River, and

---

12. Due to damage to the inscription, this translation is somewhat speculative, but the overall point that the Persian satrap served as final arbiter in the dispute is clear.
13. "Strouses" can be identified with Struthas, satrap of Ionia from the late 390s to the early 380s. See Xenophon, *Hellenica* 4.8.17.

there were many conflicts between them. Now they have turned to the king and presented the matter to his satrap, Strouses, so that the Ionian judges, coming together [...]

(...)

(The inscription here lists the Ionians from Erythrae, Chios, Clazomenae, Lebedus, and Ephesus who had served as judges in the dispute.)

(...)

After the Milesians and Myesians had presented their cases and an examination of the boundaries had been carried out, the judges were about to give their verdict when the Myesians withdrew their case. The judges wrote this down and presented it as evidence to the cities that were hearing the case. When Strouses, satrap of Ionia, heard from the Ionian judges that the Myesians had withdrawn their case, he made a final judgment that the land belonged to the Milesians.

13.9: The King's Peace

Xenophon, *Hellenica* 5.1.25, 29–31

In 387 BCE, the major powers of mainland Greece—Athens, Sparta, Corinth, Thebes, and Argos—had exhausted themselves in a struggle for dominance known as the Corinthian War. Artaxerxes II took this opportunity to impose new diplomatic arrangements on Persia's northwestern frontier. The terms of this agreement were negotiated between the king and the Spartan Antalcidas, so the resulting treaty is known as either the King's Peace or the Peace of Antalcidas.

[25] Antalcidas returned from Persia along with Tiribazus after making an agreement that the king would take the side of the Spartans if the Athenians and their allies did not accept the peace that he had negotiated.

(...)

[29] The Athenians could see that their enemies had many ships. They were afraid of being completely overwhelmed, as they had been before, now that the king had made common cause with the Spartans. They were also suffering from raiding by the Aeginetans. For all these reasons, they were eager to make peace.

The Spartans, for their part, were maintaining a battalion at Leuchaeum and another at Orchomenos, keeping watch over their allies—over those they trusted, to keep them safe from attack, and over those they did not, to keep them from revolting—and they were constantly getting dragged into trouble around Corinth. With all of that, they had little appetite to go on fighting.

The Argives, hard-pressed by Sparta and knowing that the plea of sacred months[14] would not help them, were also eager for peace.

[30] And so, when Tiribazus sent out word to summon all those who wished to hear the king's peace terms, they all gathered without delay. When the emissaries from these cities had assembled, Tiribazus showed them the king's seal and read out the document. It ran as follows:

[31] "King Artaxerxes thinks these terms are just:

- All the Greek cities in Asia will belong to the king, as well as the islands of Clazomenae and Cyprus.
- All the other Greek cities, large or small, will be separate and independent, except for Lemnos, Imbros, and Skyros, which will belong to Athens as they did in times gone by.

"I, together with those who accept this agreement, will make war on land and by sea, with ships and with money, against anyone who breaks it."

---

14. Many Greek cities recognized certain months of the year as sacred when it was forbidden to go to war. (See Document 9.2, section 106.) Since each city maintained its own calendar, these sacred months were sometimes manipulated when negotiating with other cities to avoid fighting on unfavorable terms.

SELECT BIBLIOGRAPHY

Asmonti, Luca. *Conon the Athenian: Warfare and Politics in the Aegean, 414–386 B.C.* Stuttgart: Franz Steiner Verlag, 2015.
Balcer, Jack Martin. "The Greeks and the Persians: The Processes of Acculturation." *Historia* Bd. 32, H. 3 (3rd quarter 1983): 257–67.
———. "The Persian Wars Against Greece: A Reassessment." *Historia* Bd. 38, H. 2 (2nd quarter 1989): 127–43.
Barkworth, Peter R. "The Organization of Xerxes' Army." *Iranica Antiqua* 27 (1993): 149–67.
Billows, Richard A. *Marathon: How One Battle Changed Western Civilization.* New York: Overlook Duckworth, 2010.
Bowen, Anthony. "The Place That Beached A Thousand Ships." *Classical Quarterly* 48, no. 2 (1989): 345–64.
Briant, Pierre. *From Cyrus to Alexander: A History of the Persian Empire.* Translated by Peter T. Daniels. Winona Lake, IN: Eisenbrauns, 2002.
———. "History and Ideology: The Greeks and 'Persian Decadence.'" Translated by Antonia Nevill, in Harrison (2002), 193–210.
———. "Histoire et archéologie d'un texte. La Lettre de Darius à Gadatas entre Perses, Grecs et Romains." In *Licia e Lidia prima dell' ellenizzazione*, edited by Mauro Giorgeri et al., 107–44. Rome: Consiglio nazionale delle ricerche, 2003.
Briant, Pierre, Wouter F. M. Henkelman, and Matthew Stolper, eds. *L'archive des fortifications de Persépolis. État des questions et perspectives de recherches* Paris: De Boccard, 2008.
Bridges, Emma, Edith Hall, and P. J. Rhodes, eds. *Cultural Responses to the Persian Wars: Antiquity to the Third Millennium.* Oxford: Oxford University Press, 2007.
Brosius, Maria. *Women in Ancient Persia, 559–331 BC.* Oxford: Clarendon, 1996.
———. *The Persian Empire from Cyrus II to Artaxerxes I.* London: London Association of Classical Teachers, 2006.
———. *The Persians.* London: Routledge, 2006.
———. "Persian Diplomacy between 'Pax Persica' and 'Zero Tolerance.'" In *Maintaining Peace and Interstate Stability in Archaic and Classical Greece*, edited by Julia Wilker, 15–164. Mainz: Verlag-Antike, 2012.

Cameron, George G. "Darius' Daughter and the Persepolis Inscriptions." *Journal of Near Eastern Studies* 1, no. 2 (April 1942): 214–18.

———. *Persepolis Treasury Tablets*. Chicago: University of Chicago Press, 1948.

Cawkwell, George. *The Greek Wars: The Failure of Persia*. Oxford: Oxford University Press, 2005.

Charles, Michael B. "Immortals and Apple Bearers: Towards a Better Understanding of Achaemenid Infantry Units." *Classical Quarterly*, new series 61, no. 1 (May 2001): 114–33.

———. "Herodotus, Body Armor, and Achaemenid Infantry." *Historia* Bd. 61, H. 3 (2012): 257–69.

———. "The Persian Καρδακες." *Journal of Hellenic Studies* 132 (2012): 7–21.

Colburn, Henry P. "Connectivity and Communication in the Achaemenid Empire." *Journal of the Economic and Social History of the Orient* 56, no. 1 (2013): 29–52.

Conklin, Beth A. "'Thus Are Our Bodies, Thus Was Our Custom': Mortuary Cannibalism in an Amazonian Society." *American Ethnologist* 22, no. 1 (February, 1995): 75–101.

Dalley, Stephanie. *Esther's Revenge at Susa: From Sennacherib to Ahasuerus*. Oxford: Oxford University Press, 2007.

Dandamayev, M. A. "Achaemenid Imperial Policies and Provincial Governments." *Iranica Antiqua* 34 (1999): 269–82.

De Backer, Fabrice. "Some Basic Tactics of Neo-Assyrian Warfare." *Ugarit-Forschungen* 39 (2007): 69–116.

———. "Some Basic Tactics of Neo-Assyrian Warfare 2: Siege Battles." *State Archives of Assyria Bulletin* 18 (2009): 265–68.

Dodds, Eric R. "Supernormal Phenomena in Classical Antiquity." In *The Ancient Concept of Progress and Other Essays on Greek Literature and Belief*, edited by Eric R. Dodds, 156–210. Oxford: Clarendon, 1973.

Doenges, Norman A. "The Campaign and Battle of Marathon." *Historia* Bd. 47, H. 1 (1st quarter 1998): 1–17.

Dusinberre, Elspeth R. M. *Empire, Authority, and Autonomy in Achaemenid Anatolia*. Cambridge: Cambridge University Press, 2013.

Elayi, Josette. "The Role of the Phoenician Kings at the Battle of Salamis (480 B.C.E.)." *Journal of the American Oriental Society* 126, no. 3 (July–September 2006): 411–18.

Evans, J. A. S. "Notes on Thermopylae and Artemisium." *Historia* Bd. 18, H. 4 (August 1969): 389–406.

Fagan, Garret G. "'I Fell upon Him Like a Furious Arrow': Toward a Reconstruction of the Assyrian Tactical System." In Fagan and Trundle (2010), 81–100.

Fagan, Garret G., and Matthew Trundle, eds. *New Perspectives on Ancient Warfare*. Leiden: Brill, 2010.

Forsdyke, Sara. "Athenian Democratic Ideology and Herodotus' 'Histories.'" *American Journal of Philology* 122, no. 3 (Autumn 2001): 329–58.

Fromherz, Peter. "The Battlefield of Marathon: The Tropaion, Herodotos, and E. Curtis." *Historia* Bd. 60, H. 4 (2011): 383–412.

Gehrke, Hans-Joachim. "From Athenian Identity to European Ethnicity—the Cultural Biography of the Myth of Marathon." In *Ethnic Constructs in Antiquity: The Role of Power and Tradition*, edited by Ton Derks and Nico Roymans, 85–99. Amsterdam: Amsterdam University Press, 2009.

Georges, Pericles B. "Persian Ionia under Darius: The Revolt Reconsidered." *Historia* Bd. 49, H. 1 (1st quarter 2000): 1–39.

Hallock, Richard T. *Persepolis Fortification Tablets*. Chicago: University of Chicago Press, 1969.

Hammond, N. G. L. "The Battle of Salamis." *Journal of Hellenic Studies* 76 (1956): 32–54.

Hanson, Victor Davis. *The Western Way of War: Infantry Battle in Classical Greece*. Berkeley: University of California Press, 2009.

Harrison, Thomas, ed. *Greeks and Barbarians*. New York: Routledge, 2002.

———. *Writing Ancient Persia*. London: Bristol Classical Press, 2011.

Henkelman, Wouter. "The Other Gods Who Are: Studies in Elamite-Iranian Acculturation Based on the Persepolis Fortification Texts." PhD diss., University of Leiden, 2008.

Hignett, Charles. *Xerxes' Invasion of Greece*. Oxford: Clarendon Press, 1963.

Hodkinson, Stephen. "Sparta: An Exceptional Domination of State over Society?" In Powell (2017), 29–55.

Hyland, John O. "Contesting Marathon: Billows, Krentz, and the Persian Problem." *Classical Philology* 106, no. 3 (July 2011): 265–77.

———. *Persian Interventions: The Achaemenid Empire, Athens, and Sparta, 450–386 BCE*. Baltimore, MD: Johns Hopkins University Press, 2018.

———. "The Achaemenid Messenger Service and the Ionian Revolt: New Evidence from the Persepolis Fortification Archive." *Historia* Bd. 68, H. 2 (2019): 150–69.

Isserlin, B. S. J., R. E. Jones, V. Karastathis, S. P. Papmarinopoulos, G. E. Syrides, and J. Uren. "The Canal of Xerxes: Summary of Investigations 1991–2001." *Annual of the British School at Athens* 98 (2003): 369–85.

Jacoby, Felix. *Fragmente der griechischen Historiker*. Weidmann: Berlin, et al., 1923–.

Jordan, Borimir. "The Honors for Themistocles after Salamis." *American Journal of Philology* 109, no. 4 (Winter 1988): 547–71.

Kallet, Lisa. "The Origins of the Athenian Economic Arche." *Journal of Hellenic Studies* 133 (2013): 43–60.

Katchoudorian, Lori. *Imperial Matter: Ancient Persia and the Archaeology of Empires*. Oakland: University of California Press, 2016.

Kennel, Nigel M. *Spartans: A New History*. Chichester: Wiley-Blackwell, 2011.

King, L. W., and R. C. Thompson. *The Sculptures and Inscription of Darius the Great on the Rock of Behistûn in Persia*. London: British Museum, 1907.

Konijnendijk, Roel. "'Neither the Less Valorous nor the Weaker': Persian Military Might and the Battle of Plataia." *Historia* Bd. 61, H. 1 (2012): 1–17.

———. *Classical Greek Tactics: A Cultural History*. Leiden: Brill, 2018.

Krentz, Peter. *The Battle of Marathon*. New Haven: Yale University Press, 2010.

———. "Hoplite Hell: How Hoplites Fought." In *Men of Bronze: Hoplite Warfare in Ancient Greece*, edited by Donald Kagan and Gregory Viggiano, 134–56. Princeton: Princeton University Press, 2013.

Kuhrt, Amélie. *The Persian Empire*. London: Routledge, 2007.

Lanfranchi, Giovanni B., Michael Roaf, and Robert Rollinger, eds. *Continuity of Empire(?): Assyria, Media, Persia*. Padua: S.A.r.g.o.n., 2003.

Lang, Mabel. "Herodotus and the Ionian Revolt." *Historia* Bd. 17, H. 1 (January 1968): 24–36.

Larsen, Stephanie L. *Tales of Epic Ancestry: Boiotian Collective Identity in the Late Archaic and Early Classical Periods*. Stuttgart: Steiner, 2007.

Lateiner, Donald. *The Historical Method of Herodotus*. Toronto: University of Toronto Press, 1989.

Lee, John W. I. *A Greek Army on the March: Soldiers and Survival in Xenophon's "Anabasis."* Cambridge: Cambridge University Press, 2008.

Lewis, David. "Persian Gold in Greek International Relations." *Revue des Études Anciennes* T. 1, no. 1–2 (1989): 227–34.

———. "Near Eastern Slaves in Classical Attica and the Slave Trade with Persian Territories." *Classical Quarterly* 61, no. 1 (2011): 91–113.

Lichtheim, Miriam. *Ancient Egyptian Literature*. Vol. 3, *The Late Period*. Berkeley: University of California Press, 1980.

Lincoln, Bruce. *"Happiness for Mankind": Achaemenian Religion and the Imperial Project*. Paris: Leuven, 2012.

Littman, Robert J. "The Religious Policy of Xerxes and the Book of Esther." *Jewish Quarterly Review*, new series 65, no. 3 (January 1975): 145–55.

Liverani, Mario. "The Rise and Fall of Media." In Lanfranchi, Roaf, and Rollinger (2003), 1–12.

Llewellyn-Jones, Lloyd. *King and Court in Ancient Persia 559–331 BCE*. Edinburgh: Edinburgh University Press, 2013.

Llewellyn-Jones, Lloyd, and James C. Robson. *Ctesias' History of Persia: Tales of the Orient*. London: Routledge, 2010.

Maeir, Aren M., Brent Davis, and Louise A. Hitchcock. "Philistine Names and Terms Once Again." *Journal of Eastern Mediterranean Archaeology and Heritage Studies* 4, no. 4 (2016): 321–40.

Maurice, F. "The Size of the Army of Xerxes in the Invasion of Greece in 480 B.C." *Journal of Hellenic Studies* 50, no 2 (1930): 210–35.

Melchert, H. Craig. "A New Interpretation of Lines C 3–9 of the Xanthos Stele." In *Akten des II. Internationalen Lykien-Symposions*, edited by Jürgen Bochhardt and Gerhard Dobesch, 31–4. Vienna: Verlag der Österreichischen Akademie der Wissenschaften, 1993.

Melville, Sarah C. *The Campaigns of Sargon II, King of Assyria 721–705 BC*. Norman: University of Oklahoma, 2016.

Miller, Margaret C. *Athens and Persia in the 5th Century BC: A Study in Cultural Receptivity*. Cambridge: Cambridge University Press, 1997.

Missiou, Anna. "Δοῦλος τοῦ βασιλέως: The Politics of Translation." *Classical Quarterly* 43, no. 2 (1993): 377–91.

Mitchell, Lynnette G. *Greeks Bearing Gifts: The Public Use of Private Relationships in the Greek World 435–323 BC*. Cambridge: Cambridge University Press, 1997.

Morgan, Janett. *Greek Perspectives on the Achaemenid Empire: Persia through the Looking Glass*. Edinburgh: Edinburgh University Press, 2016.

Munson, Rosaria Vignolo. "Who Are Herodotus' Persians?" *The Classical World* 102, no. 4 (Summer 2009): 457–70.

Neville, J. "Was There an Ionian Revolt?" *Classical Quarterly* 29, no. 2 (1979): 268–75.

Ober, Josiah. "Inequality in Late-Classical Democratic Athens: Evidence and Models." In *Democracy and an Open-Economy World Order*, edited by George Bitros and Nicholas C. Kyraizis, 125–46. Cham: Springer, 2017.

Oppen, Simone. "Comparative Perspectives on Persian Interactions with Greek Sanctuaries during the Greco-Persian Wars." PhD diss., Columbia University, New York, 2019.

Parker, Holt N. "The Linguistic Case for the Aiolian Migration Reconsidered." *Hesperia* 77, no. 3 (July–September 2008): 431–64.

Parker, Victor. "Τύραννος The Semantics of a Political Concept from Archilochus to Aristotle." *Hermes* Bd. 126, H. 2 (1998): 145–72.

Powell, Anton, ed. *A Companion to Sparta*. Hoboken, NJ: Wiley-Blackwell, 2017.

Pritchett, W. Kendrick "Toward a Restudy of the Battle of Salamis." *American Journal of Archaeology* 63, no. 3 (July 1959): 251–62.

Pugliese Carratelli, Giovanni. "Greek Inscriptions of the Middle East." *East and West* 16, no. 1 (March–June 1966): 31–36.

Romm, James S., and John Herrington. *Herodotus*. New Haven: Yale University Press, 1998.

Rood, Tim. "Xenophon's Parasangs." *Journal of Hellenic Studies* 130 (2010): 51–66.

Rop, Jeffery. *Greek Military Service in the Ancient Near East 401–330 BCE*. Cambridge: Cambridge University Press, 2019.

Rung, Edward. "War, Peace, and Diplomacy in Graeco-Persian Relations from the Fourth to the Sixth Century BC." In *War and Peace in Ancient and Medieval History*, edited by Philip de Souza and John France, 28–50. Cambridge: Cambridge University Press, 2008.

Ryder, Timothy T. B. *Koine Eirene: General Peace and Local Independence in Ancient Greece*. London: Oxford University Press, 1965.

Samons, Loren J., "Kimon, Kallias, and Peace with Persia." *Historia* Bd. 47, H. 2 (2nd quarter 1998): 129–40.

Schmidt, Rüdiger. "Achaemenid Throne-Names." *Annali dell'Instituto Orientale di Napoli* 42 (1982): 83–95.

Shrimpton, Gordon, "The Persian Cavalry at Marathon." *Phoenix* 34, no. 1 (Spring 1980): 20–37.

Stolper, Matthew W. *Entrepreneurs and Empire: The Murashu Archive, the Murashu Firm, and Persian Rule in Babylonia*. Leiden: NINO, 1985.

Stoneman, Richard. *Xerxes: A Persian Life*. New Haven: Yale University Press, 2015.

Tarn, W. W. "The Fleet of Xerxes." *Journal of Hellenic Studies* 28 (1908): 202–33.

Thomas, Rosalind. *Herodotus in Context: Ethnography, Science, and the Art of Persuasion*. Cambridge: Cambridge University Press, 2000.

Tiribilli, Elena. "New Documents of the Renep-Priest of the Delta Horemheb, Son of Ankhpakhered." *Egitto e Vicina Oriente* 41 (2018): 140–42.

Trundle, Matthew. *Greek Mercenaries: From the Late Archaic Period to Alexander*. London: Routledge, 2004.

Trundle, Matthew, and Christopher Matthew. *Beyond the Gates of Fire: New Perspectives on the Battle of Thermopylae*. Barnsley: Pen and Sword Military, 2013.

Tuplin, Christopher. "Xenophon and the Garrisons of the Achaemenid Empire." *Archäologische Mitteilungen aus Iran* 20 (1987): 167–245.

———. "The Gadatas Letter." In *Greek History and Epigraphy: Essays in Honour of P. J. Rhodes*, edited by Lynette Mitchell and Lene Rubinstein, 155–84. Swansea: Classical Press of Wales, 2009.

———. "All the King's Horse: In Search of Achaemenid Persian Cavalry." In Fagan and Trundle (2010), 101–82.

———. "Intolerable Clothes and a Terrifying Name: The Characteristics of an Achaemenid Invasion Force." *Bulletin of the Institute of Classical Studies*, supplement no. 124 (2013): 223–39.

Van Wees, Hans. *Greek Warfare: Myths and Realities*. London: Duckworth, 2004.

Vasunia, Phiroze. *The Gift of the Nile: Hellenizing Egypt from Aeschylus to Alexander*. Berkeley: University of California Press, 2001.

Wallace, Paul W. "The Final Battle at Plataia." *Hesperia Supplements* 19 (1982): 183–92.

Wallinga, H. T. *Xerxes' Greek Adventure: The Naval Perspective*. Leiden: Brill, 2005.

Waters, K. H. "Herodotus and the Ionian Revolt." *Historia* Bd. 19, H. 4 (November 1970): 504–8.

Waters, Matt. *Ancient Persia: A Concise History of the Achaemenid Empire, 550–330 BCE*. Cambridge: Cambridge University Press, 2014.

Whatley, N. "On the Possibility of Reconstructing Marathon and Other Ancient Battles." *Journal of Hellenic Studies* 84 (1964): 119–39.

Wieshöfer, Joseph. "From Achaemenid Imperial Order to Sasanian Diplomacy: War, Peace, and Reconciliation in Pre-Islamic Iran." In *War and Peace in the Ancient World*, edited by Kurt Raaflaub, 121–40. Malden, MA: Blackwell, 2007.

Wrightson, Graham. *Combined Arms Warfare in Ancient Greece: From Homer to Alexander the Great and his Successors*. London: Routledge, 2018.

Young, Cuyler T. "480–479 BC: A Persian Perspective." *Iranica Antiqua* 15 (1980): 213–39.

INDEX

Abetteya, 97
Abiradu, 91
Abrocomes, 140
Abronichus, 145
Abu Simbel, 75
Abydus, 107, 187
Acanthus (town), 130
Acarnanians, 139
Achaeans, 132, 187
Achaemenes, 17, 89
Achaemenids, 17, 29, 45–46, 55, 56, 84, 88–89
Achilles, 148
Acina, 90
acropolis, Athenian, 26, 121
Across-the-Euphrates, 62
Acrothoum, 130
Adeimantus, 151–52
Adriatic Sea, 129
Aeacids, 148
Aeacus, 148
Aegaleus, 150
Aegean Sea, 6, 10, 14–16, 18–24, 28–33, 112, 116–18, 130–31, 182–83
Aegilia, 122
Aegina, Aeginetans, 20, 24, 75, 115, 148, 150–51, 189
Aeolians, 75, 108–9, 118
Aeschines, 119
Aeschraeus, 143
Aeschylus, 36–37, 153
Agamemnon, 133
Agesilaus II, 98–99
Ahasuerus, 63–64
Ahura Mazda, 6, 45–46, 53–57, 84, 87–90, 92, 127

Ainianes, 132
Ajax (Greater), 148n49, 153
Akaufaka, 55
Akkad, 66–70
Akkadian language, 35, 41, 87
Alabanda, 157
Alchimachus, 119
Alcibiades (father of Clinias), 144
Alcmaeonids, 25, 126
Aleian plain, 117
Aleuas, 166
Alexander I, 157–59
Alexander the Great, 32, 39, 83, 170–71
Alpenos, 137
Alyattes, 71
Amasis (Egyptian general), 75
Amasis (Egyptian king), 47, 74, 76–77, 81n13, 83
Amathus, Amathusians, 103–7
Ameinias, 148, 151
Amoibichus, 75
Amompharetus, 165–66
Amorges, 108
Ampe, 112
Amun, 60
Amun-Re, 61
Amurru, 69
Amyntas I (king of Macedonia), 23, 157
Amyntas of Asia (grandson of Alexander I), 157
Amyrgian Scythians. *See* Scythians
Amyrtaeus, 31, 180
Amytis, 128
Anagyrus, 151

Anatolia, 10, 12, 16, 19, 29, 32, 40, 46, 70, 75, 101n5, 108, 109n22, 129n13, 171–72, 177, 184
Anaxandridas, 122
Andousius, 48
Androcrates, 162
Androdamas, 148
Andromeda, 95
Aneristus, 134
animals, 59, 98, 132, 145, 163
Ankarakkan, 57
Anopaea, Mount, 137
Anopaea path, 137
Anshan, 5, 68–69
Ansukka, 49
Antalcidas, 189
Anthylla, 51
Anticyra, Anticyrans, 136, 145
Antidorus, 143
Aphetae, 141–44
Aphidnae, 123
Apis, 80–82
Apollo, 13, 20, 62, 71, 75, 112n27, 118n9, 121n20, 138n29. See also Helios
Arabia, 45–46, 55
Arachosia, 55, 91
Arakadri, 87
Arakha, 90
Aramaic, 34–35, 47n6, 184n5
arashshara, 9, 49–50
archers, 21, 26, 125, 161, 164, 167, 168
Archippus, 184
Archon (personal name), 75
archons (magistrates), 110
Argiopium, 166
Argos, Argives, 14, 25, 28, 32, 36, 95–96, 106, 111–12, 169, 175, 190
Aria, 45, 47
Ariabignes, 149

Ariaramnes (ancestor of Darius), 88–89
Ariaramnes (companion of Xerxes), 150
Aristagoras, 100–104, 109, 111
aristeion, 143
Aristides (early fifth century), 152
Aristides (later fifth century), 184
Aristippus, 187
Aristocyprus, 106
Aristogeiton, 123
Armenia, Armenians, 45–46, 55, 85, 90
Arrian, 39
Arsames, 89, 140
Artabazus, 167, 174, 181
Artachaees, 130
Artaeus, 130
Artanes, 140
Artaphernes, 114, 184. See also Artaphrenes
Artaphrenes (Persian commander at Marathon), 20, 117. See also Artaphernes
Artaphrenes (Persian satrap of Ionia), 93, 94, 102, 109, 113. See also Artaphernes
Artaxerxes I, 30–31, 96, 118, 175, 179, 181, 184
Artaxerxes II, 32, 38, 39, 62, 64, 186–87, 189–90
Artayntes, 171
Artemis, 71n20, 118n9, 186
Artemisia, 149, 151, 169
Artemisium: Cape, 25, 140; battle of, 26, 140–46, 147
Artozostre, 113
Artybius, 105–6
Artystone, 48–49
Aryans, 45, 55
Ashbashtiya, 57
Ashbashuptis, 97

Ashshur, 69
Asopus River, 123, 137, 161, 163, 164, 167
Assurbanipal, 70
Assyria, Assyrians, 4, 45–46, 55, 91
Assyrian Empire, 4–6, 11, 40, 58, 73, 129n11; army, 4, 6
Astyanax (father of Eucles), 111
Athamaita, 92
Athena, 26, 110; Sciras, 151
Athenedes, 136
Athens, Athenians, 1, 2, 14–16, 18–22, 24–32, 36–38, 64, 93–94, 96, 98, 100–104, 110, 115–17, 119–26, 128, 133, 142–46, 148–53, 157–68, 170–71, 174–86, 188–90
Athos, Mount *and* peninsula, 20, 23, 117, 130–31, 157n64
Atossa, 153
Atreus, 129
Attica. *See* Athens
Atum, 77

Babylon, Babylonians, 5–7, 23, 45–46, 55, 57–60, 66–70, 86–87, 90, 91, 127–28, 171. *See also* Neo-Babylonian Empire
Babylonia. *See* Babylon
Babylonian Captivity, 58
Babylonian kings, 58, 66; religion, 57, 59
Bacchylides, 37, 71
Bacis, 145, 152
Bactria, Bactrians, 45, 47, 55, 86, 91
Balaṭu, 86
Bardiya, 17, 85–88, 90, 113n31
Barziya. *See* Bardiya
beer, 49, 76, 109
bees, 107
Behistun Rock. *See* Bisitun Rock

Bel, 69. *See also* Bel-Marduk
Bel-Marduk, 128n4
Bel-nadin-apli, 86
Belitanas, 128
Beluris, 64
Bigthana, 63
Bisitun Rock, 17, 34–35, 87, 89, 91
Black Rump, 137
Black Sea, 18, 131–32
Boeotia, Boeotians, 21, 27, 122–23, 133, 160–62, 187
Boeotian League, 122n22
Bosporus, 129, 182n3
Boulis, 134
Branchidae. *See* Didyma
bread, 24, 76
brick, 57, 70, 91
bridges, 23, 128–32, 152, 175
Bubares, 130, 157
bulls, 76, 80–81, 138. *See also* Apis, cattle
Byzantium, 103, 173–74, 177

Cadusia, 85
Callias, 30, 96, 181
Callimachus, 123–25
Calyndians, 149
Cambyses I, 5, 57, 69–70
Cambyses II, 5n3, 11–12, 16–17, 22–23, 40, 47, 48n9, 59, 76–88
canals, 9, 23, 129–31, 157n64
cannibalism, 65
Canopic branch (Nile), 75
Caphereus, 141
Cappadocia, 45–46, 55
Caria, Carians, 45, 48, 55, 73–75, 91, 103, 106–8, 112, 145, 177, 186n11
Carmania, Carmanians, 86, 91
Carneia, 121n20

carnelian, 91
Carystus, Carystians, 119, 136
Caspian Sea, 18
cattle, 65, 76, 80–83
Caunus, 103, 185–86
cavalry, 21–22, 24, 71n4, 101, 119–20, 125, 130, 161–67
Cayster River, 102
Ceos, 103, 147
Cepheus, 95
Cercopes, 137
Chalcedon, Chalcedonians, 128
Chalcideus, 185
Chalcidice, 130n14
Chalcis, Chalcidians, 102, 119
Chaldeans. *See* Neo-Babylonian Empire
chariots, 106, 120
Charopinus, 102
Chersis, 103, 106, 143
Chersonese, 120–21, 130, 187
childbirth, 49–51, 97
Chios, Chians, 75, 101–2, 189
Choereae, 119
Chorasmia, Chorasmians, 45, 47, 55, 86, 91
Cilicia, Cilicians, 48, 105, 107, 113, 117, 144, 171, 177, 180
Cimmerians, 129
Cimon (Athenian general), 177–78, 180
Cimon (father of Miltiades), 120
Cineas, 119
Cissians, 135
Cithaeron, Mount, 161–64, 166
Citium, 180
Cius, 108
Clazomenae, 75, 109, 189, 190
Clearchus, 187
Cleisthenes, 93
Cleomenes I, 93, 100–101, 122
Cleonae, 130

Clinias, 144
clothing, 51–52, 64, 76, 82, 105, 111, 125, 161, 178
Cnidus, 75
Colias, 152
colonies, 74, 103n11, 177
Corcyra, Corcyraeans, 175
Corinth, Corinthians, 26, 28, 32, 123, 146, 151–52, 189–90
Corinthian War, 189
Corydallus, 136
Cos, 117n6
Crius, 151
Croesus, 70–72
crowns, 64
Ctesias, 38, 86, 128
cuneiform, 34–35
Curium, Curians, 106
Cyanaean Rocks, 182
Cyaxares, 90
Cybele, 102
Cyme, 109
Cynegirus, 125
Cynosarges, 126
Cynosura, 147
Cyprus, Cypriots, 15, 19, 29, 30, 48, 103–7, 143, 174, 177–82, 188, 190
Cyrene, 180
Cyrus I, 5
Cyrus II, 5–8, 10–11, 16–18, 24, 37, 48, 57–60, 66–71, 85–88, 90
Cyrus Cylinder, 67–70
Cyrus the Younger, 31, 37, 52n12, 186–87

Dahae, 55
daivas, 54–55
Damasythimus, 149
Danae, 95
Danube River, 128n3
Dardanus, 107

Index

Darius I, 1–2, 9, 13, 16–18, 20, 22–23, 28, 34–36, 45–49, 53–56, 60–62, 65, 76, 79, 81, 84, 85, 87–92, 94–95, 100–101, 103–5, 107, 109–110, 112, 115, 117–19, 127–29, 133–34, 140, 149, 170, 171
Darius II, 52n13, 186
Dascylium, 174
Datis, 20, 109–111, 117–18, 128, 170
Daurises, 107–8
Delian League, 25, 29–31, 37, 176, 177, 183
Delos, Delians, 118
Delphi, 13
Delphic Amphictyony, 136; oracle, 94, 111, 138
Demaratus, 25, 94–95, 172, 173
Demeter of Eleusis, 166, 168
democracy, 14–15, 19, 101, 113, 183
Demophilus, 139
Der, 69
Diadromes, 139
Didyma, 112
Dio Chrysostom, 39
Diodorus of Sicily, 38
Dion, 130
diplomacy, 15, 20, 23, 30–33, 100–101, 113–14, 181–86, 188–90
disease, 64, 109
Dolopians, 132, 177
Dorians, 75, 158
Doriscus, 102, 131
Drangiana, 45, 47, 55
dreams, 110, 121–22
dukshish, 48n9

earth and water (sign of submission), 20, 93, 115, 117, 132, 133

earthquakes, 118
Ecbatana, 7, 60, 88, 128
Egypt, Egyptians, 2–5, 8, 11–13, 15, 16, 22–24, 30–32, 34–36, 39–41, 45–47, 51, 55, 60, 73–87, 91, 129, 131, 144, 179–180, 182; Lower, 11, 30, 73, 180; Upper, 11, 75
Egyptian kings, 11–13, 23, 41, 60, 75, 77, 84; navy, 24, 77, 144, 147; religion, 75–76, 80–83
Eion, 131, 177, 184
Elaeus, 130
Elam, Elamites, 5–6, 45–46, 55, 79, 90–92
Elamite language, 34–35, 41; religion 56–57
Elephantine, 8, 35, 75
Eleusis, 148, 160
Elis, 94–95
Enlil-of-the-gods, 68
Epaphus. *See* Apis
Ephesus, Ephesians, 102–3, 184, 189
Ephialtes (father of Philocrates), 188
Ephialtes (guide for Xerxes), 136–37, 139–40
Eretria, Eretrians, 2, 18–20, 102–3, 110, 112, 116–22, 125, 128n3, 170, 172, 174
Erythrae (Boeotia), 161–62
Erythrae (Ionia), 189
Esagil, 57, 66–67
Eshnunna, 69
esparto, 131–32
Esther, 63
Ethiopia, Ethiopians, 45, 55, 91
Euagoras (Cypriot king), 188
Euagoras (Spartan horse racer), 120
Eualcides, 103
Euboea, Euboeans, 25, 119, 140–45, 149

Eucles, 111
Euelthon, 103
Eumenes, 151
Euphorbus, 119
Euphorion, 125
Euphrates River, 4
Euripus strait, 141, 144
Euryanax, 165
Eurybiades, 25
Eurydemus, 136
Eurymedon River, 29; battle of, 29, 177–78
Eurypylus, 166
Eurysthenes, 172
exiles, 16, 25, 94, 120, 152n59, 172n3, 175n4, 187
Ezida, 57

forgery, 89
fowl. See poultry
Frada, 90
frankincense, 118
Friends of the King, 7, 8, 12, 64
frontiers, 1–3, 7–10, 16, 18–19, 29–30, 33, 46, 85, 92, 98, 186, 188

Gadatas, 61–62
Gambrium, 172
Gandara, 45, 47, 55, 91
Gargaphia, 162, 164–65
Gaumata, 87–88, 90
Geraestus, 141
Gergithae, 108
gifts, 62, 64–65, 74
goats, 145
Gobryas, 92, 113
gold, 9, 59–60, 62, 45, 73, 80, 88, 91, 102, 128, 159, 161, 174, 183
Gongylus, 172, 174
Gorgus, 103, 107, 143
grain, 9, 12, 24, 49–52, 83, 97, 131

Greece, Greeks, 1–3, 10, 12–16, 18–33, 65, 74–75, 95–96, 97–99, 115, 132–33, 167, 169–70, 173, 186–87, 189–90. *See also* Hellenic League, Ionia
Greek language, 96–97; religion, 61–62, 74–75, 118
Gryneium, 172
Gubaru, 67
guest-friendship. See *xenia*
Gutium, 66
Guzanu, 86
Gygaea, 157
Gyges (father of Myrsus), 108

hair, 112, 162
Halicarnassus, Halicarnassians, 37, 75, 149n52, 169, 171
Halisarna, 172
Halys River, 103
Haman, 63–64
Harmodius, 123
Harriena, 49
Hatrabanush, 57
Hecataeus, 114
Helios, 111. *See also* Apollo
Hellenic League, 25–28, 95–96, 134, 140, 157–60, 163, 176
Hellenion, 74–75
Hellespont, 23, 103, 107–8, 109n22, 113, 117, 120n17, 131, 145n46, 149, 152, 173–74, 187
helots, 14, 21
Hemag, 76, 80
Hera, 75, 165, 168
Heracles, 122, 126, 137n27, 138
Heraclides, 108
heralds, 95, 105, 115, 118, 124, 132–34, 161
Hermione (town), 173
Hermophantus, 102

Hermus River, 102
Herodotus, 1, 19n35, 28, 37–38, 81, 92, 100, 128, 135, 147, 163
Herpys, 163
Hibis, 60–61
Hipparchus, 120n15, 123n25
Hippias, 15, 19, 20, 22, 25, 94, 100n2, 120–23, 173
Hippocrates (father of Peisistratus), 120
Hippomachus, 163
Hipponicus, 96, 181
Histiaeus (father of Phylacus), 148
Histiaeus (tyrant of Miletus), 100, 104–5
Hollows of Euboea, 143
hoplites, 21, 116, 125n29, 137, 139n35, 52
horses, 24, 64, 71, 89, 99, 106, 109, 115, 117, 119–20, 128n7, 130, 132, 161–62, 168
Horus, 61, 77, 81, 84
hostages, 119, 139, 152, 183
House of Life, 79
Humban, 56–57
Huputish River, 57
Hydarnes, 135–37
Hymaees, 107
Hyperanthes, 140
Hysiae, 123, 162
Hystaspes (father of Darius), 45–46, 56, 84, 93, 118, 140
Hystaspes (father of Tissaphernes), 185
Hytenna, 185

Ibanilus, 108
Icarian Sea, 117
Icaros (island), 117n6
Idaeus, 99
Idria, 107
Ilium, 108, 129

Imanish, 90
Imbros, 121, 190
Imet, 79
Imgur-Enlil, 70
Immortals, 23–24, 26, 135
Inarus, 30, 179–80
incense, 20, 76. *See also* frankincense
India, Indians, 18, 65, 91
Ionia, Ionians, 10, 12, 16, 18–20, 24–25, 28, 31–32, 45–47, 55, 74–75, 91, 97–98, 100–107, 109, 111–14, 142, 145, 148, 177, 182, 186–87, 188–90
Ionian Revolt, 18–20, 28, 100–114, 116–17, 159n66
Irdabama, 50
Irishtimanka, 52
Irkezza, 51
Irshena, 50, 52
Irtuppiya, 52
Ischenous, 151
Israel, 59
Isthmus (of Corinth), 26, 160
ivory, 91

Jeremiah, 59
Jerusalem, 6, 40, 58–60
Jews, 6, 8, 35, 40, 58–59, 63–64
Judah. *See* Judea
Judaism, 59–60
Judea, 6, 13

Kallatiai, 65
Kerkis, 75
Keys of Cyprus, 105
Kharga Oasis, 60
Khonsu, 60
Khshathrita, 90
King of Caunus, 186
King's Peace, 32, 189–90
Kuntukka, 50
Kurra, 52

labor, 9–10, 49–52, 91, 130–32
Labraunda, 108
Lade, battle of, 111
Lampon, 161
Lampsacus, 107
language, 65, 75, 87, 177
Lanunu, 50–51
lapis lazuli, 91
Larissa, 166
laws, 47, 55–56, 83, 113, 123–24, 133–34, 158, 182
Lebanon, Mount, 91
Lebedus, 189
Le'ea, 87
Lemnos, 143, 183, 190
Leonidas, 25, 135, 137–40, 144–45, 160, 170
Lesbos, Lesbians, 102
Leto, 71
Letopolis, 84
Leucas, 163
Leuchaeum, 190
Levant, 4, 11, 35
Levites, 59
Libya, Libyans, 13, 45, 55, 74, 179–80
Liduma, 50
Lie, the (Persian religion), 53, 87
Lindos, Lindians, 110–111
linen, 80, 83
lions, 138, 140
Locris, Locrians, 132, 137
Lycia, Lycians, 40, 52, 177, 184–85
Lycian language, 185
Lycomedes, 143
Lydia, Lydians, 10, 12, 16, 18, 37, 52, 70–72, 102–3, 171, 183. *See also* Sardis
Lysicles, 145
Lysimachus (father of Aristides), 152
Lysistratus (Athenian diviner), 152

Macedonia, Macedonians, 12, 18, 23, 25, 32, 39, 45, 83, 101n5, 130n19, 131, 157
Macistus. *See* Masistius
Maeander River, 107–8, 188
magi, 17, 56–57, 87–88, 90
Magnesians, 132
Maka, 45, 47, 55
Malis, Malians, 132, 136–37
Maliya, 185–86
Manzaturrush, 51
Marathon, 20, 120; battle of, 20–22, 25, 28, 33, 116, 120–26, 153
Mardonius, 27, 113, 117, 128, 157–69
Marduk, 59, 66n3, 67–70. *See also* Bel-Marduk
Marduk-shumu-iddin, 66
Marea, 179
Margiana, Margians, 90
Marsyas River, 107–8
Martiya, 90
Masistes, 171
Masistius, 161–62
Mausolus (father of Pixodarus), 107
Mazara, 49
Media, Medes, 5–6, 45–46, 55, 56, 60, 68, 85, 87–88, 90–91, 117, 129, 135, 149, 170, 176, 179
Median religion, 56, 87–88
medicine, 79
Megabates, 174
Megabazus, 179
Megabyzus (general of Darius), 101
Megabyzus (general of Xerxes), 128, 130, 179, 181
Megarians, 161
Megistias, 137, 139
Mehenet sanctuary, 77
Melampus, 139
Melanthius, 101

Memnon, 96
Memphis, 11, 30, 73–74, 80–84, 179
Mendesian branch (Nile), 180
Menekhib. *See* Psammetichus II
mercenaries, 1, 3, 8, 12, 15–16, 22, 35, 38, 52n12, 73–75, 187
merchants. *See* trade
Meska, 61
Mesopotamia, 4–6, 11, 19, 34–35, 46, 58, 68–69, 129n11
Messene, 14
Mesuti-Re. *See* Cambyses II
Meturnu, 69
Miletus, Milesians, 19–20, 75, 100–104, 108–9, 111–12, 114, 183, 185–89
Miltiades (Athenian general), 120–21, 123–24, 177
Miltiades (half-brother of Cimon), 120
Mishshabadda, 97
Miṣiraya, 86
Mithra, 62
Molois River, 166
Momemphis, 74
Montu, 84
moon, 121, 178
Mordecai, 63–64
Mukallim, 86
mules, 128
multiculturalism, 65
mummification, 80
Munychia, 147
Muranu, 86
Musaeus, 152
Mushezib-Marduk, 86
Mut, 60
Mycale, battle of, 28
Mylasas, 108
Myous, Myesians, 188–89
Myrina, 172

Myrsus, 108
Mysia, Mysians, 108, 129
Mytilene, 75

Nabonidus, 66–68, 70, 90
Nabonidus Chronicle, 66–67
Nabu, 69–70
Nabû-aḫê-iddin, 87
Nabû-dannu-ilāni, 86
Nabû-naʾid, 87
Nabû-shum-lishir, 87
Nabu-shum-uṣur, 86
Nabu-shumu-uṣur, 86
Nadin, 86
Naqsh-e Rustam, 53
Naucratis, 13, 74–75
Naxos, Naxians, 20, 117, 128n3, 170
Nebuchadnezzar (Babylonian pretenders), 90
Nebuchadnezzar II (Babylonian king), 58, 60
Neith, 77–78
Neo-Babylonian Empire, 40, 58
Nico (Greek stone-cutter), 96
Nicolaus, 134
Nidintu-Bel, 90
Nile River, 4, 9, 11, 13, 18, 74–75, 179–80
Nine Bows, 84
Nisaea, 88
Nisaean horses, 161
Nothon, 119
Nubia, Nubians, 13

Oak-Head pass, 163
Oeroe River, 164
Oetaean Mountains, 137
oil, 12, 128
ointment, 76
Old Persian. *See* Persian language
oligarchy, 14, 183
Olophyxus, 130

Olympic Games, 71, 103n10, 120
Olympidorus, 161
Omisus, 62
Onesilus, 103–7
Onetes, 136
Opis, 66
oracles, 73, 94, 107, 111–12, 118, 138, 145, 152, 158
Orchomenos, 190
Oropus, 119
Osiris, 76–78, 81
Osiris-Hemag, 76
Ostanes, 64–65
Otanes, 107, 109, 113
Oudamos, 75

Pactolus River, 45, 102
Paeonia, Paeonians, 101–2
Paesus, 107
Paishiyauvada, 87
palaces, 58, 60, 63, 69, 77, 84, 90–91, 96n5
Palaegambrium, 172
Pallene, 148, 151
Pan, 121, 156
papyrus, 8, 35, 47, 131, 145
Parapita, 99
Parius, 107
Parrukkizzish, 51
Parthenium, Mount, 121
Parthia, Parthians, 45, 47, 55, 86
Parysatis, 186
Pasargadae, 7, 87n12
Pausanias (Spartan general), 15, 27, 29, 160–61, 164–68, 173–74, 176
Peace of Antalcidas. See King's Peace
Peace of Callias, 30, 96, 181–82
Pedasa, 108
Peftuaneith, 77
Peisistratus, 94, 117, 120–121
Pelasgians, 177
Pelekos, 75

Pelion, Mount, 140, 143
Peloponnese, Peloponnesians, 26–27, 146, 158, 160, 163–64, 175, 179, 186
Peloponnesian League, 25, 30–31, 37, 183
Peloponnesian War, 31, 37–38, 183–84
Pelusiac branch (Nile), 74
Peneus River, 129
Perapis, 83
Percote, 107
Pericles, 16, 182–83
Perinthus, 131
Perseids, 138
Persepolis, 7–8, 35, 46, 96–97, 109, 127
Perses, 95
Perseus, 95
Persia, Persians, 1–10, 13–18, 34–36, 45–47, 54–56, 87–90, 97–99, 112–14, 133–35, 168–75, 179–80
Persian army, 6–8, 67–69, 92, 102–9, 124–25, 135–40, 157–58, 161–62, 167–68, 177–78; court, 7, 51–52, 63–65, 95, 104–5, 117, 153, 174–75; Empire, 1–10, 46–47; kings, 45–46, 53–56, 62–65, 77–79, 85–90, 99, 117, 127–28, 179–182, 184, 189–90; language, 35, 41, 87–89, 118, 175; religion, 6, 54–57, 87
Persian Gulf, 69n15, 112
phalanx, 21
Phalerum, 126, 150–51
Phanagoras, 136
Pharnabazus, 98–99
Pharnaces, 48–49, 174
Pharos, 179
Phaselis, 75, 182
Pheidippides. See Philippides

Pherendates, 178
Philagrus, 119
Philaon, 143
Philippides, 121
Philocrates, 188
Philocyprus, 106
Phocaea, 75
Phocis, Phocians, 136–37
Phoenicia, Phoenicians, 24, 73, 103n11, 105–6, 121, 131, 147–51, 154, 177, 180
Photius, 38, 86n3, 127–28
Phraortes (Median pretender), 90
Phratagune, 140
Phrygia, 101, 157; Hellespontine, 174n3
Phthiotis, 133
Phylacus, 148
Pindar, 65
Piraeus, 147–48, 177
Pisidians, 178, 187
Pissouthnes, 183
Pitanate battalion, 165
Pixodarus, 107
Plataea, Plataeans, 21, 24, 116, 122–25, 133; battle of, 27–29, 33, 160–68, 173
Plato, 38
Pleistarchus, 160
Plutarch, 39, 177n9
polemarch, 123–25
Poliades, 165
Polyas, 145
Polycritus, 151
pomegranates, 62
Potasimto, 75
poultry, 70, 76, 83
Praxilaus, 171
Priene, 183
Procles, 172
propaganda, 87–89, 116, 163–64, 166

Propontis, 108, 174n3
Prosopitis, 179
Proxenos (personal name), 187
Psammatichus (Greek mercenary), 75
Psammetichus (Libyan aristocrat), 179
Psammetichus I (Egyptian king), 5, 11, 73–74
Psammetichus II (Egyptian king), 75
Psammetichus III (Egyptian king), 11, 76–77
Psyttaleia, 147, 152, 156
Ptah, 80–81
Ptolemy I, 83
Puksha, 52
Pylae, 136
Pylagori, 136
Pytharchus (Greek stone-cutter), 96
Pytheas, 151
Pythia, 138

Qutî, 68–69

racing, 120
rain, 72, 110, 143
Rannakarra River, 57
Rashda, 50
Re, 60, 77, 79, 81, 84
Red Sea, 9
relocation, forced, 4, 6, 10, 19–20, 40, 58, 101, 112, 117n5
Resenet sanctuary, 77
Rhenaea, 118
Rhodes, Rhodians, 75, 110, 176n6, 188
roads, 9, 120

Sacae, 125
sacrifices (religious), 60, 107, 108, 121–22, 124, 134, 137, 160, 163, 168

Sagartia, 47, 90
Saggilaya, 87
Sais, 11, 73, 75–78
Saite Dynasty. *See* Twenty-Sixth Dynasty
Salamis, Salaminians (city), 103–7, 143, 180
Salamis (island), 27, 143, 146–47, 160, 175; battle of, 27–29, 33, 141n39, 147–57, 169, 171, 173
Samos, Samians, 15, 75, 102, 106, 117, 148, 182–83
Samothracians, 150
Sane, 130–31
Sardinia, 105
Sardis, Sardians, 1, 9, 19, 45–46, 48, 52, 55, 71, 91, 93–94, 102–9, 113, 119, 133n22, 117
satrapies, 8–9, 17, 85–86, 174, 186
satraps, 8, 15, 17, 19, 23, 28, 47–48, 85, 98, 171, 174, 181–83, 188–89
Sattagydia, 45
Sciathus, 141, 151
Scione, 141
Scyllias, 141
Scythia, Scythians, 45, 47, 55, 92, 100, 128–29
Seat of the Cercopes, 137
Shapik-zēri, 86
Sharukba, 50
Shedda, 97
sheep, 48–49
shields, 21, 66, 101, 106, 126, 168
ships, 20, 22, 24, 26–27, 29, 75, 77, 100–102, 105–7, 110, 115, 117–20, 125–26, 130–32, 141–46, 148–56, 176–80, 188–89. *See also* triremes
shipwrecks, 20, 117, 130, 142, 143, 147, 152, 155

Shiraz, 50
Shuanna. *See* Babylon
Shaushaunush River, 57
Shumu-libshi, 86
Sicinnus, 146
Sidon, Sidonians, 151
siege engines, 48
sieges, 4, 6, 20, 26, 30, 104, 107, 110–12, 119, 167, 177, 179, 187
Sikayahuvati, 88
silver, 9, 59–60, 83, 86, 91, 174
Simonides, 103
Sind. *See* India
Sippar, 66
Siromus, 103
Sisimaces, 108
Skudra. *See* Thrace
Skunkha, 92
Skyros, 177, 190
slavery, 4, 6, 9–10, 49, 62n20, 112, 119
Smerdis. *See* Bardiya
Socrates (Achaean mercenary commander), 187
Sogdiana, 45, 47, 55, 91
Soli, Solians, 105–7
Solon, 106
Sophaenetus, 187
Sparta, Spartans, 14–15, 19, 21, 24–33, 36, 40, 93–96, 100–101, 111n26, 115, 133–40, 148, 158–61, 165–70, 172–75, 179, 183–90
Spartiates, 134, 138
Sperthias, 134
Sphendadates. *See* Gaumata
Stesagoras (brother of Miltiades), 120
Stesagoras (grandfather of Miltiades), 120
Stesenor, 106
Stesilaus, 125

stone, 15, 39, 60–61, 84, 91, 96, 137, 140, 156, 166, 185n8
storms, 20, 27, 142–43
Strouses. *See* Struthas
Struthas, 188
Strymon River, 131, 184
Stymphalians, 187
Styrians, 122
Sumer, 68–70
Sunium, 125–26
Susa, 7, 9, 20, 35, 45–46, 56, 69, 84, 90–91, 96, 105, 112, 134, 171
Syennesis, 107

Talthybiads, 133
Talthybius, 133–34
Tanaoxares. *See* Bardiya
Tanyoxarkes. *See* Bardiya
Tegea, Tegeans, 121, 165–68
Teispes, 5, 69, 89
Teleutias, 188
Temenos (Euboea), 119
Tempe Gorge, 25
temples, 11–13, 26, 40, 47, 57–61, 66–67, 73–80, 82–83, 88, 102–3, 110–12, 118–19, 128n4, 133, 154, 158, 160, 165, 168, 170, 176
Tenos, 118
Teos, 75
Teresh, 63
Teucrians, 129
Teuthrania, 172
Thebes, Thebans, 14, 21, 25–26, 28, 32, 36, 122–23, 133, 139–40, 163, 167, 169, 189
Themistocles, 15, 25, 29, 145–48, 150–52, 170, 173–76
Theocles, 75
Theomestor, 148
Thermopylae, 25–26; battle of, 26, 28, 33, 134–40, 144–45, 170

Thespians, 26, 133, 139, 146
Thessaly, Thessalians, 25, 27, 132, 136, 187
Thorax, 166–67
Thrace, Thracians, 12, 18, 45, 55, 117, 129, 130–31, 187
Thrasydeias, 166
Thrasylaus, 125
Three-Headed pass, 163
Through the Hollow, 120
Thucydides, 37–38, 165n72, 185
Thyssus, 130
Tigris River, 4, 66, 69, 112
Tikrakkash, 51
Timagenides, 163
Timagoras, 64–65
Timocreon, 176
Tintir. *See* Babylon
Tiribazus, 189–90
Tissaphernes, 98, 184–87
Tithraustes, 177
Tmolus, Mount, 102
tolerance, 6–7, 54–57, 59–62, 65, 80–81
tombs, 116, 128, 154
Torone, 130
Trachinian Mountains, 137
Trachis, Trachinians, 136, 145
trade, 1, 9, 12, 14, 16, 18, 20, 22, 24, 35, 73–75
Tragia, 183
translation, 65, 118, 184
tribute, 8, 19, 45–46, 48, 54–55, 62, 69, 83, 86, 105, 107n17, 112–15, 170, 176, 184–85, 187
triremes, 26, 102, 117, 130–31, 148, 184
Tritantaechmes, 90
Troad, 109
Trojan War, 96n5, 109, 129, 139n32, 148n49
Troy, Trojans, 109n22, 129

Truth (Persian religion), 6, 55–56, 62n22, 119n11
Turkama, 57
turquoise, 91
Twenty-Sixth Dynasty (Egypt), 11–13, 73–76
tyranny, 10, 12, 14–15, 18–20, 25, 94, 100–101, 104–6, 113–14, 120–21, 123n25, 148, 159, 175n4
Tyrodiza, 131

Udjahorresne, 12, 76–79
Ugbaru, 66–67
Umadadda, 52
Umpuranush, 50
Ur, 67
Urshaya, 57
Uruk, 57

Vahyazdata, 90

Wadjet, 79
walls, 26, 46, 48, 58, 70, 107, 111, 119, 134, 137, 139–40
water, 62, 107, 110–11, 129, 162, 164, 170–71, 180. *See also* earth and water
Wenkhem, 83

White Fortress, 179
White Point, 131
White Stones, 107
White Wall. *See* White Fortress
wind, 75, 130n14, 132, 152
wine, 12, 48–51, 56–57, 97, 139
wood, 61, 83, 91

Xanthos, 184–85
Xenagoras, 171
xenia, 15, 97–99
Xenophon, 38, 85n1, 86n4
Xerxes I, 13, 15, 23–30, 37, 54–56, 94–96, 118, 127–36, 139–40, 142, 144, 146, 149–50, 152–53, 156–60, 169–72, 174–75, 178–79

Yahweh, 59
Yamaksheda, 48

Zacynthus, 95
Zamban, 69
Zeus, 71–72, 75, 104, 108n19, 110, 138
Zeus of the Armies, 108
Zopyrus (Persian exile), 16
Zopyrus (Persian general), 128, 179